JOANIE'S COUNTRY COOKBOOK VOLUME 2

JOANIE'S COUNTRY COOKBOOK
VOLUME 2

JOANIE SUTTON

ILLUSTRATED BY DALE MCNEVIN

THE ACORN PRESS
CHARLOTTETOWN
2003

Joanie's Country Cookbook, Volume 2
Text © 2003 by Joanie Sutton
Illustrations © 2003 by Dale McNevin
ISBN 1-894838-06-8

Cover photography: John Sylvester
Editing: Jane Ledwell
Design: Matthew MacKay
Printing: Transcontinental Prince Edward Island

National Library of Canada Cataloguing in Publication

Sutton, Joanie, 1948-
   Joanie's country cookbook, volume 2 / Joanie Sutton. — 1st ed.

ISBN 1-894838-06-8

   1. Cookery — Maritime Provinces. I. Title.

TX715.6.S876 2003   641.59715   C2003 902906 9

The Acorn Press
PO Box 22024
Charlottetown, Prince Edward Island
Canada C1A 9J2

www.acornpresscanada.com

TABLE of CONTENTS

INTRODUCTION

"The Dixon Valley is a special and beautiful part of Prince Edward Island to me. Natural beauty is abundant: the hardwood stands, red and gold in the fall, green in the summer, mixed with the darker greens of the spruce stands, spread into the hillsides of the plowed red fields. In the spring wildflowers spread throughout the woods and over the fields in the summer, attracting birds and bees. Fresh-water springs bubble up in the woods on the hills.

It's a good place to live. But what makes it even more special is the people living here. Both old-timers and newcomers share the feeling that this land is special and we should all try and live in harmony with the land.

People are growing their own food, raising livestock, planting trees, cultivating fruit, keeping bees, caring for and replanting the woods when they harvest them. As a result, the Dixon Valley grows more beautiful and abundant every year. It is a simple life where you work hard and eat well."

So began my first cookbook. Twenty years later it still rings true, for the most part. The Dixon Valley is still a beautiful and wonderful place to live. We are still committed to raising as much of our food as we can, and we still enjoy cooking, eating, and sharing our abundance. Our friends are still here as well, and we've grown closer over the years sharing food and fun. We are blessed indeed. As one newer friend always says: "It doesn't get any better than this." He's right.

Unfortunately, this is not true across Prince Edward Island. Agribusiness is creeping in with its dependence on chemicals and large machinery that combine to wreak havoc upon our fragile ecosystem. There have been too many fish kills across the Island, too many contaminated wells, too much wind and water erosion. The small family farms, once the backbone of Island life, are fighting to stay alive. Can these dangerous trends be reversed? I hope so.

First of all, there are many Island farmers who do respect their land. There is a growing awareness that excessive use of chemicals has adverse affects on the health of land and people. Many family farmers know land is their greatest asset and are trying to keep it healthy by practising good farming. Others are developing, rather than depleting, the natural resources, adding to our supplies of wild blueberries and maple syrup and other wonderful foods. More farmers are turning to organic farming practices, growing even potatoes with success. There is a growing awareness that bigger might not be better: "Small is beautiful!" E. F. Schumacher told us, and perhaps it is not too late to listen. Prince Edward Island is small; let's keep it small and it will stay beautiful.

Other things have changed for the better, I hope! My cooking has changed as we get older and more aware of health issues. We use less fat, and more of the better unsaturated fats such as olive and canola oil.

Our gardens have grown more abundant over the years. The soil, and resulting crops, show the huge benefits of organic farming practices. When we first started gardening, thirty years ago now, organic was a new idea, although it is really just a return to the days of old when you used what you had. Now it is becoming more popular, and even "gourmet," as more people realize the value of chemical-free, good food. We now grow and use more herbs and a greater variety of vegetables and are always willing to try something new.

What we can't raise ourselves, we "buy Island," including great milk products such as ADL Cheese, Montague Dairy Sour Cream, and Wiltshire Creamery Butter, and good milk from any Island dairy. We buy locally raised and butchered meat and wonderful, fresh seafood, "les fruits de mer," from the shores of Prince Edward Island. This cookbook reflects these changes with a much wider variety of recipes. I think of it as "Country Cuisine."

The farmers' markets that were just beginning a rebirth twenty years ago are now thriving. Full of food, people, and crafts, they are the place to go for fresh local produce, great meat, and yummy meals and snacks. They are also a great meeting place for old friends.

In this book I hope my love of cooking (and eating) comes through. It is important in this world of instant food and gratification to spend time preparing and sharing good food. Everyone sitting down together to share a good meal brings and keeps people together, whether it is your family's dinner, or a special dinner for guests. We are famous out here for our potluck dinners. Feasts! We always marvel at how lucky we are to have such good friends, and good food.

My thanks go to my Publisher, Laurie Brinklow, who publishes beautiful Island books. Laurie was at Ragweed when my first *Joanie's Country Cookbook* came out. We've both come a long way!

To my editor, Jane Ledwell, who is such a wonderful, meticulous, yet kind editor who loves to cook as well. To John Sylvester, who got me to smile just right and to hold the platter at the perfect angle, and got a great picture of one who does not enjoy getting her picture taken. And to Dale McNevin: your illustrations are perfect! And thanks to all my potluck buddies, for all the food, fun, and inspiration along the way.

I dedicate this book to two very special people: my sister, Connie Heatter, who gave me my first cooking lesson and started my lifelong adventure with food. And to my husband, Jerry, who is still there raising our wonderful food, and helping more and more with the cooking as well.

HINTS FOR SUCCESSFUL COOKING

In this age of fast food and instant meals, why bother spending hours in the kitchen? Because it is fun, because you and your family will be healthier, and for the best reason, because you get to eat it! I firmly believe that anyone who likes to eat can be a good cook. It is a great activity to do with your children, no matter their age. Encouraging your children (and partners) to become involved in good cooking and eating habits is valuable and an ongoing learning experience—for everyone. Cooking is a daily chore that is better when it is shared and enjoyed with others. Many hands make light work. And light work keeps the cook(s) happy.

You will have many successes, and some failures as well. Following are some hints I have learned, often the hard way, so your cooking adventures can be more fun and successful:

Know your oven and stove: Every stove is different. Get to know yours. Some ovens bake much quicker and drier. If your cookies are always a bit dark, try turning the temperature down 25°. Take mental notes and adjust your timing. On the stove top as well, get comfortable with how quick, or slow, your burners are. Over time this will be easier, and your cooking will be better.

Invest in good pots, pans, and cooking utensils: There is nothing like a good pot to make your cooking easier. Paderno pots, made on PEI, are great. A wise woman once suggested I spend the extra money to buy a large Paderno pot for my harvesting needs, instead of the less expensive one I was planning to buy. I followed her advice, and 20 years later my pot is good as new after years of making many successful large batches of tomato sauce, applesauce, salsa, etc., with minimum problems. Cooking utensils as well get daily use, so invest in better quality. Utensils also make great gifts.

Learn to cook to your taste and needs: Learn to substitute what you like and have handy. This cookbook has many suggestions and options to give you ideas. Keep in mind others' health needs: allergies, diets, etc. Use less salt when you cook! People can always add more if they prefer, but many people are on salt-restricted diets. If you start cutting down now, you may never need to eliminate salt from your diet. Also, you will find that when you use good fresh ingredients and herbs, you do not need excessive salt for flavour. It is there already.

Eat fresh: Eat fresh, organic, and natural foods as much as possible. They taste better, and are better for your health. It is worth the time and expense of getting fresh and wholesome foods: fresh fruits and vegetables, grown locally; whole grains; fresh fish; free-range chicken and eggs; good lean meat, from your nearest good butcher. Farmers' markets have it all, if you can't grow your own.

Use less fat, and the good fats: Pay the extra money for leaner cuts of meat, and eat less of it. You can't afford not to. Always trim your meat and chicken of as much excess fat as you can. If you have time to cool down casseroles, soups, etc., the fat will rise to the top and congeal. Remove and discard as much as you can. Extra Virgin Olive Oil tastes so good, I can't imagine using anything else in many recipes. Canola oil is good in baking. I substitute either olive oil or canola for butter in many recipes and cut down the overall amount. This theory holds good until you get to the desserts: if you must make your favourite rich dessert, make it when you can share it with lots of people (potlucks, dinner parties). Have your portion, and enjoy it totally!

Size of servings: You may find my servings on the large size. We all have good appetites, and I tend to make more than needed, just in case. You wouldn't want anyone to leave the table hungry! Most things are fine the next day (except green salads), and many things are even better. Pack these off in lunch kits for those in school or working. We have several sizes of insulated bags and ice packs handy so leftovers can be taken along safely.

Traveling: When we hit the road, we take along as much of our own food and water as possible, especially when driving. The highways of North America are lined with fast-food restaurants, and unless you have the time and money to find a better restaurant and stop to enjoy the meal, you are better off with your own food. Oven-Fried Chicken (for the first day) is a favourite as well as pasta salads, at least those without mayonnaise, packed in a good cooler, with ice and ice packs. Muffins, cookies, fresh fruit, etc., can round out your meals. There are many roadside parks along the way where you can stop and have a lovely picnic while saving time and money.

Potlucks: We have great friends around here who love to get together and eat! Through the year we celebrate anything we can with a potluck dinner. It is definitely the way to go. Everyone brings something special and we always have a feast! Potluck dinners have the added advantage of easing the burden on the host and hostess. We marvel at how lucky we are to have such good friends and enjoy such wonderful feasts.

MORE FOOD HINTS: HERBS & GRAINS

Herbs: Fresh herbs can make an ordinary meal very special. Use them whenever you can. Many herbs are easily grown in a small area. Apartment dwellers can even have their herb garden, on their patio or windowsill, growing in containers. Otherwise, you can purchase herbs year-round at farmers' markets and good supermarkets. They are easy to preserve as well, freeze-dried or dried, or as vinegars, pestos, or herbed butters. In general, freeze-drying is better than drying, and quite easy. Parsley and dill are especially good like this: take fresh, clean and **dry** herbs, snip them and quickly pack into freezer bags. (They must be dry and you must get out all the air you can from the bag to prevent frost.) When you need some herbs in the winter just break off what you need and use! Freeze dried herbs won't be good in salads, since they do go limp when thawed, but they are great in any cooked recipe.

I often use one of three herb blends in my cooking. These are available in many health food stores and gourmet food shops. If you can't find them, you can make your own from the following "recipes":

Italian Herbs: Marjoram, Thyme, Rosemary, Savory, Sage, Oregano, Basil

Herbes de Provence: Oregano, Thyme, Bay Leaf

Fines Herbes: Dill, Sage, Thyme, Tarragon, Rosemary, Marjoram, Savory

One more herb blend I often use is **Beau Monde Seasoning**. Beau Monde is a blend of herbs and spices that is more like a natural flavour enhancer. It has a strong celery taste and is a bit like "Spike," and other blends. If you can't find it, it is easily omitted, but you may want to find something similar to use. It is an easy way to add richness to your dish, especially when you are in a hurry.

Whole Grains: Whole grains are the staff of life, the most basic of foods. They are healthier and less costly than their processed counterparts, and they taste better. We've been using them since the 1960s when they had a rebirth, and we wouldn't use anything else. Just a few years ago they were available only in health and natural food stores. Now many supermarkets carry them. If you don't use them already, try them and find out for yourself. Be sure to rinse them well before use, especially if they aren't organic: Place them in a colander and rinse with cold water, shake out excess moisture, and proceed with the recipe.

Brown Rice: Many of our favourite meals include brown rice. It is so tasty and chewy when properly cooked. Even though it is simple, there is a trick to it: Using twice as much water as rice, place water in a medium saucepan adding 1/2–1 tsp. salt per cup of rice. Bring to a rolling boil and slowly add your rice. Give it a good stir then put the lid on. Bring back to a boil, then turn the heat down until it is at a simmer, but do **not** lift the lid to check! Listen to

your pot. Keep it at a simmer, just barely bubbling, for 45 minutes to 1 hour. Do **not** lift the lid to check until 45 minutes have gone by; then you can peek and see how it is doing. Over time you'll recognize the proper bubbling noises emanating from your pot, and you'll know that patience will bring success.

Red River Cereal: An old-fashioned Canadian porridge rich in fibre and natural goodness. We've eaten Red River (also called three-grain cereal) since we first came to Canada 33 years ago. It is from the Red River Valley in Manitoba and is a blend of cracked wheat, cracked rye, and flax. It is available in most grocery stores in Canada. Ed Woodard, who helped us build our house, had us try it his way, with peanut butter and honey! Thank you, Ed. We've been eating it like that ever since. There is nothing better on a frosty morning.

APPETIZERS

PESTO CROSTINI

Crostini are "little crusts" embellished with different toppings. They are an easy and delicious beginning to any meal, and a great addition to buffets or potluck parties. The basis of crostini is toasted Italian or French bread. Any authentic French baguette is ideal. *Pesto* (p. 152-3) is my favourite topping, especially with freshly made pesto and vine-ripened tomatoes. There are many other possibilities: *Roasted Tomato Relish* (p. 77), or grilled mushrooms to name a few.

Crostini:
1 loaf French baguette, or 2 *Mock Sourdough Mini French Breads* (p. 242-3)
3–4 cloves garlic, cut in half
olive oil
freshly ground pepper

Topping:
1 recipe *Pesto* (p. 152-3)
½ lb. mozzarella cheese, thinly sliced
3–4 medium tomatoes, thinly sliced

Preheat oven to 375°F.

Slice the bread into slices ½" thick and place the slices in one layer on a cookie sheet. Toast them in the oven, about 5 minutes on each side or until they are crisp, crunchy, and just beginning to brown. While the toast is still warm, rub each slice on one side with the garlic, brush lightly with olive oil, and sprinkle with freshly ground pepper.

Top each slice of bread with a rounded teaspoon of the pesto and evenly spread it to edges. Follow with a slice of tomato and a slice of mozzarella cheese, then return to oven for 7–10 minutes, or until crostini are heated through and cheese is melted. Serve.

Yield: 20–24 crostini.

Variations:
Crostini con Funghi:
2 tbsp. olive oil
2 cloves garlic
2–2½ cups fresh mushrooms, chopped (chanterelles or fresh shiitake mushrooms, if possible)
⅓ cup green or red pepper, chopped fine
1 medium tomato, chopped fine
1 green onion, minced
2 tbsp. fresh parsley, minced
1 tsp. fresh thyme, minced
1 tsp. dried oregano
salt and pepper, to taste

Prepare "crostini" as above.

In a small skillet in the olive oil, sauté the garlic and pepper for 1–2 minutes. Add the mushrooms and cook about 5 minutes more or until the mushrooms are soft. Remove from heat. Add the tomato, green onion, parsley, thyme, oregano, salt, and pepper. Top the prepared crostini and serve. This is especially pretty in the late summer with chanterelles, green pepper, and fresh tomato.

Note: Chanterelles are beautiful gold-orange wild mushrooms which grow in Prince Edward Island in August. They are a relative of the oyster mushroom.

MARINATED MUSHROOMS

This recipe was in my first and second cookbooks, and I am including it again because it is still one of my favourite appetizers—great as part of an antipasto platter. The recipe came from an old friend we knew about 30 years ago in Chicago. I've been making it ever since.

⅔ cup olive oil
½ cup water
1 lemon, juiced
1 bay leaf
2 cloves garlic, smashed with the flat of a knife
salt and pepper, to taste
1 tsp. dried oregano
1 lb. small fresh mushrooms, cleaned and trimmed

In a non-reactive (stainless steel or ceramic) pot, combine the olive oil, water, lemon juice, bay leaf, garlic, salt, pepper, and oregano. Bring to a boil, lower heat, and simmer, covered, about 10 minutes.

Add the mushrooms and simmer 5 minutes longer, mixing gently so they cook evenly. Let mushrooms cool in their marinade. Chill until ready to serve. These mushrooms are better made one day in advance.

To serve: Bring to room temperature. With a slotted spoon, remove the mushrooms from the marinade, being careful to pick out the garlic cloves. Place in serving bowl with toothpicks alongside to "spear" the mushrooms.

Yield: Approx. 2 cups marinated mushrooms.

TZATZIKI

There's a wonderful Greek restaurant in Montreal where they smother all of their rolled stuffed pitas with tzatziki, with an extra dollop on each plate. The same restaurant sells it in tubs, which we brought home, where we discovered it is fantastic on so many things! I can't return to Montreal just for more tzatziki, so I tried to make it myself, with good success. I used no-fat yogurt and the result was excellent—and very healthy to boot! I don't think dill is used traditionally, but I find it a great addition.

2 cups no-fat yogurt

The night before, drain the yogurt: Line a strainer with a double thickness of cheesecloth. Set this over a pot, cover with a lid, and set in the fridge overnight.

⅓ English cucumber (seedless), peeled and coarsely grated (or ½ medium cucumber, peeled, seeded, and coarsely grated)
1 clove garlic, minced
2 tbsp. olive oil
1 tbsp. rice wine vinegar
salt and pepper, to taste
¼ cup fresh dill, minced (or to taste) (optional)

In the morning, place the yogurt in a serving bowl. Rinse out the cheesecloth and use this to drain the cucumber by placing the grated cucumber in the cheesecloth and squeezing out all excess moisture. When you think you have it all squeezed out, open, stir up the cucumber, and squeeze again! Place the grated cucumber on a cutting board and chop it into smaller pieces. Add this to the yogurt along with the garlic, olive oil, rice wine vinegar, salt, pepper, and dill, if desired. Mix it gently, cover, and chill until ready to use. This is better after it "mellows" a few hours.

Yield: 1½ cups.

Note: Try to get a yogurt that is completely natural with no added gelatin or emulsifiers. This will yield a much better tzatziki, as the whey will separate and drain far better.

Optional Suggestions: Tzatziki spread on bagels or focaccia with smoked fish (salmon or trout) on top makes an elegant appetizer. Tzatziki is also great in a pita roll with leftover chicken and Tabouli. A dollop of tzatziki alongside *Marinated Beet Salad* (p. 29-30) makes it special. I'm sure there are even more uses for this versatile condiment.

❀ WINTER CAPONATA ❀

Serve this appetizer on *Crostini* (p. 14-15) or with cut-up pita bread.

1 medium eggplant
2 tbsp. olive oil
1½-2 cups celery, finely chopped
1 onion, chopped
2 large cloves garlic, minced
½ can tomato paste (about 2 oz. of a 156 ml/5.5 oz. can)
½ cup red wine vinegar
¼ cup white wine
2 tsp. sugar
salt and pepper, to taste
2 tomatoes, chopped
½ cup Kalamata olives, pitted and sliced
¼ cup fresh basil leaves, minced (or 2 tsp. dried)
¼ cup fresh parsley, minced

Peel and cut the eggplant into ½" slices. Sprinkle lightly with salt on both sides and set aside for 15–20 minutes. Rinse slices and pat dry on paper towels. Cut into small cubes and set aside.

In a large saucepan heat the olive oil and in it sauté the celery, onion, and garlic, stirring, for about 5 minutes. In a small bowl mix the tomato paste, red wine vinegar, white wine, sugar, salt, and pepper. Add to the saucepan and bring to a simmer. Add the prepared eggplant and tomatoes and simmer for 15–20 minutes or until eggplant is tender. Remove from heat and add the olives, basil, and parsley. Mix gently, place in a serving bowl, and let cool to room temperature. Serve.

Yield: 8–10 servings.

ROASTED ZUCCHINI DIP

This is good as a vegetable dip or sandwich spread, and it's low-fat. I prefer it with dill, but other herbs may be used instead. Try **basil** for an Italian taste or **coriander** for a Mexican flavour. The results are better with small- to medium-sized zucchini, as the big ones tend to get a bit too juicy.

2 lbs. zucchini (small- to me-dium-sized), washed, halved, and cut into slices ⅛" thick.
2½ tbsp. olive oil
1 tsp. salt
1 large clove garlic, minced
⅓ cup plain low-fat yogurt (or
⅓ cup tahini plus 1 tbsp. lemon juice)
2 scallions, chopped
⅓ cup fresh dill, minced (or to taste)

Preheat oven to 500°F.

Lightly oil a large, shallow roasting pan. Spread out the zucchini slices in the pan, drizzle with the oil, and sprinkle with the salt. Toss to coat the slices evenly. Roast in the middle of the oven, turn-ing once, for about 20 minutes. Sprinkle the garlic over the zucchini and return to the oven for another 5 minutes.

Remove from oven and let cool in the pan. Scrape the contents of the pan into a food proces-sor, add the yogurt, and pro-cess for a few seconds, until well mixed. Remove to a bowl, stir in the scallions and fresh dill, and serve.

This spread keeps quite well in the fridge and gets better as the flavours mellow.

Yield: 2–3 cups.
Optional Suggestion: Replace the roasted zucchini with *Grilled Zucchini* (p. 83).

THAI FISH CAKES

I often make these for a potluck. They make tasty little tidbits of fish.

1 lb. haddock or cod
1 tbsp. soy sauce
2 cloves garlic, minced
2 tbsp. fresh cilantro, minced
1 tsp. grated fresh lemon peel
1 tbsp. fresh ginger, grated or finely minced
pepper, to taste
4–5 tbsp. vegetable oil, for frying (not olive)

Rinse fish and pat dry with paper towels. Cut into 1" pieces and place in a food processor along with the soy sauce, garlic, cilantro, lemon peel, ginger, and pepper. Process on and off for 10–20 seconds, or until the fish is chopped up but still chunky. Remove to a bowl. Heat oil in a cast-iron skillet. Scoop up about 2 tablespoonfuls of the fish mixture at a time and mould into little patties with your hands. (Wetting your hands with cold water makes this easier.) When oil is sizzling, place the cakes into the oil a few at a time and sauté until golden, about 4 minutes. Flip them once and continue sautéing until both sides are golden and fish is cooked through. Serve.

Yield: 15–16 fish cakes.

NOTES

SALADS & DRESSINGS

There is nothing better than a salad with fresh garden greens and a good dressing. Every winter, this is what we most look forward to again when the garden starts producing: a homegrown salad. And whenever we have fresh greens, we have a salad every day we possibly can.

There are many varieties of lettuce and greens, including gourmet varieties, which thrive in the often cool and damp climate of Prince Edward Island. Arugula, radicchio, and mesclun all love our climate. Lucky for us! When there is fresh arugula to be had, I cannot walk through the garden without picking a few leaves and popping them in my mouth. I love the peppery, pungent flavour. Lucky for me, arugula can survive light frosts, along with radicchio, which is even better when touched with frost.

With a bit of extra work, you can extend the life of fresh greens further with row covers, hot boxes, and so on. Our neighbour, Phil, is famous for his fresh salads. With a combination of greenhouse gardening, row covers, and searching the wilds for hardy wild greens like watercress, he can produce a fresh salad ten or eleven months of the year! He has even been known to dig through the snow to harvest hardy varieties of lettuce. Phil is the salad king around here for sure.

If you cannot grow your own greens, you can go to your local farmers' market for a quality product. Since we've been here, the quality of greens in most large grocery stores has risen dramatically. In the dead of winter, I can often find some excellent leafy green lettuce and locally grown hothouse tomatoes for a good salad.

If you want to extend a salad further, add croutons. They are a good way to use up stale bread and are also good in soup.

CROUTONS

3 tbsp. olive oil
1 clove garlic, bruised
2 slices **Homemade Wholewheat Bread** (p. 237-9), cubed
salt and pepper, to taste
1 tsp. fines herbes (or dried
thyme)

Heat olive oil in cast-iron fry-pan. In it sauté the bruised garlic until browned, mashing the juice out of it with a fork as it cooks. Remove and discard the garlic. In the oil sauté the bread cubes, stirring constantly, until they are evenly browned. During cooking, sprinkle with salt, pepper, and herbs. Remove to a paper towel and let cool.

❀ RASPBERRY VINAIGRETTE ❀

Good on a fresh salad that includes many different greens: radicchio, arugula, Bibb lettuce, red oak leaf lettuce, mustard greens, edible flowers, watercress, chives, parsley, etc. I find it is especially good with a salad containing lots of arugula. This dressing is best made at least ½–1 hour before serving. It does not keep well, so if you are having a smaller salad or if you prefer your salad lightly dressed, halve the recipe.

½ cup olive oil
4½ tbsp. **Raspberry Vinegar**
(p. 100)
1 tsp. salt
pepper, to taste
1 tsp. Dijon mustard
2 tbsp. sugar (or 1 tbsp. sugar and 1 tbsp. maple syrup, or 1½ tbsp. honey)
1–2 cloves garlic, minced

Place all ingredients in a jar and shake well. Let the dressing set at least an hour before serving. When salad is ready, shake dressing again, pour over salad, and toss. Try to include some green onions and parsley in your salad and a few fresh raspberries for garnish, if possible.

Yield: Enough for 1 large salad—6 servings.

GREEK SALAD AND DRESSING

One of our favourite salad dressings, especially in the summer with the beautiful fresh greens.

Dressing:
½ cup olive oil
juice of ½-1 lemon (2 tbsp.)
2 cloves garlic, minced
salt and pepper, to taste

In the morning put olive oil, lemon juice, garlic, salt, and pepper in a jar. Shake well and set aside.

Salad:
1 large head romaine lettuce (or equivalent amount of leaf lettuce)
1 tomato, diced
⅓–½ cup crumbled feta cheese
8–10 large black olives, pitted and sliced (Kalamata are best)
1–2 green onions, sliced (or 1 small red onion, sliced and separated into rings)

In large salad bowl, tear the lettuce into bite-sized pieces. Add tomato, feta, olives, and green onions. Pour dressing through a strainer over salad. Toss and serve immediately.

This makes a fairly large salad. For a smaller salad use about 4 tbsp. olive oil, the juice of ½ lemon (or less), and 1 clove garlic. The amount of lemon juice depends on the lemon—a big juicy one yields more juice, and you may need to adjust the amount of olive oil. Practice makes perfect.

Yield: 1 large salad.

Optional Suggestion: You may substitute ¼ **cup grated Parmesan cheese** or ⅓–½ **cup crumbled bleu cheese** for the feta. The results will be quite different.

GREEN SALAD WITH BERRIES

This is really special summer salad of fresh, crisp Bibb or Boston lettuce with either strawberries or raspberries in a piquant dressing.

Dressing:
½ cup olive oil
⅓ cup white sugar
¼ cup *Raspberry Vinegar* (p. 100)
½ tsp. salt (or to taste)
½ tsp. dry mustard
¼ cup minced green onions or chives (or to taste)
1½ tbsp. poppy seeds

In the morning (or several hours earlier) make the dressing. Place the oil, sugar, wine vinegar, salt, mustard, green onions, and poppy seeds in a jar and shake. Let dressing sit at room temperature.

Salad:
1 lb. greens—preferably with some Bibb or Boston lettuce
1 lb. fresh strawberries, trimmed and sliced, or raspberries, whole

At serving time, place greens in a bowl. Shake dressing again, really well, until it is all blended. Pour over greens and toss. Add the berries and toss again gently. Serve.

Yield: 1 large salad.

Optional Suggestions: If you do not have Bibb lettuce, **Romaine** will be fine. A mixture of spinach and lettuce would also work nicely. Also, **apples,** thinly sliced, can replace the berries in autumn.

TOMATO BALSAMIC VINAIGRETTE—
A CONNIE HEATTER ORIGINAL!

Connie is my sister who also loves to cook. Her recipes are always low-fat and heathy.

1 large ripe tomato, peeled, seeded, and chopped
1 small clove garlic, put through a press
1 white end of scallion, put through a press
½ cup tomato juice (Knudsen's Very Veggie is superb!)
¼ cup balsamic vinegar
¼ cup extra virgin olive oil
salt and pepper, to taste

Cook chopped tomato on medium-low in a non-reactive skillet until liquid evaporates. Add rest of ingredients and cool.

Yield: Approximately 1 cup.

Note: If making a large amount and storing in fridge, consider using vegetable oil, since olive oil hardens unattractively. (If you use olive oil, bring the dressing to room temperature before using.)

SALAD WITH BLEU CHEESE DRESSING

Top a mix of strong greens, preferably including some spinach and arugula, with this bleu cheese dressing for a robust, tangy salad. Romaine lettuce itself is fine.

3 sun-dried tomatoes
⅓ cup olive oil
2 tbsp. red wine vinegar
½ tbsp. lemon juice
1 clove garlic, minced or pressed
1 tsp. salt, or to taste
pepper, to taste
1 tsp. fines herbes
1 tsp. Dijon mustard
1 tbsp. maple syrup

8 cups total greens, preferably including spinach and arugula, washed and drained
½ cup bleu cheese, crumbled
1 tomato, diced
½ small red onion, halved, thinly sliced (or 1 green onion, minced)
1 hard-boiled egg, cooled and coarsely grated
1 tsp. capers

Place the sun-dried tomatoes in a bowl, cover with boiling water, and allow to soak for 5 minutes. Drain, cut tomatoes into slivers using scissors, and place them in a jar along with the olive oil, red wine vinegar, lemon juice, garlic, salt, pepper, fines herbes, Dijon mustard, and maple syrup. Shake well and set aside.

Place the greens in a salad bowl. Add the bleu cheese, tomato, onion, egg, and ca-pers and gently toss. Shake the dressing again, pour over salad, toss, and serve.
Yield: 4 servings.

Optional Suggestion: For a more traditional approach, substitute for the sun-dried to-matoes **3 slices bacon**, cooked until very crisp, drained, and broken into pieces. Toss the bacon in at the end. You may also use both bacon and toma-toes.

MOCK CAESAR SALAD AND DRESSING

Don't mock this salad dressing! It is much healthier than a tradi-tional Caesar salad, without sacrificing taste. It is good on salads or as a sauce over chicken, fish, etc. For a vegetarian version, sub-stitute sun-dried tomatoes for the bacon.

Dressing:
3 tbsp. olive oil
2 tbsp. low-fat mayonnaise
1 tbsp. Dijon mustard
2 tbsp. lemon juice
1 clove garlic, minced or pressed
2–3 tbsp. buttermilk or low-fat plain yogurt (3 tbsp. for salad dressing; 2 tbsp. for sauce)
salt and pepper, to taste
4–5 Kalamata olives, pitted and chopped (optional)
¼ cup grated Parmesan cheese

Place all ingredients in a jar and shake well.

Salad:
dressing, above
4 slices bacon, sautéed until crisp, drained, then crumbled (or 2 sun-dried tomatoes, soft-ened, drained, and cut into small pieces)
Croutons (p. 23)
1 large head Romaine lettuce
¼ cup grated Parmesan cheese

Toss the lettuce with the dress-ing. Top with the bacon, crou-tons, and Parmesan cheese and toss again. Serve.

Yield: Enough for 1 large salad.

PIQUANT TOMATOES

Nothing could be simpler. This recipe is a wonderful addition to many meals. I especially like it with **Creamy Macaroni and Cheese** (p. 168). Old, tired tomatoes benefit from this treatment.

2 medium tomatoes (or 1 large)
1 tbsp. red wine vinegar (or balsamic vinegar)
1 tsp. sugar

salt and pepper, to taste
Dice the tomatoes, place all ingredients in a serving dish, and gently toss together.

SLICED FRESH TOMATOES AND RED ONIONS WITH FRESH BASIL

Another simple and delicious fresh tomato side dish. You must have good vine-ripened tomatoes for this recipe. The amount of dressing you need depends upon the amount of vegetables. You don't need much—just a drizzle.

fresh tomatoes, sliced thick
(⅓–½" thick)
1 medium red onion, sliced thin
fresh basil leaves, torn
olive oil and red wine vinegar
(or balsamic vinegar), in a ratio
of 2:1
salt and pepper, to taste

On a serving platter arrange the sliced tomatoes and onions. Distribute the torn fresh basil leaves over the vegetables. In a small jar shake together the olive oil, red wine vinegar, salt, and pepper, and drizzle over all. Serve.
Optional Suggestions: Omit the vinegar and use just olive oil to drizzle. Try **fresh thyme**, finely minced, instead of basil.

FRESH TOMATO SALSA

Yet another simple tomato side dish. Try a fresh tomato salsa next time you have *Fajitas* (p. 143).

2–3 medium tomatoes, diced
1–2 cloves garlic, minced
1 green onion, chopped
¼ cup fresh cilantro, minced
1 tbsp. olive oil
2 tsp. fresh lime juice (or lemon juice, or white wine vinegar)
1 tsp. dried oregano
salt and pepper, to taste

Gently toss together the tomatoes, garlic, green onion, cilantro, olive oil, lime (or lemon) juice, oregano, salt, and pepper. Let it set together a short while before serving. If you make this ahead, cover with plastic wrap and keep in the fridge. Bring to room temperature before serving.
Yield: 2 cups

Optional Suggestions: Add 1 **tbsp. minced fresh or pickled jalapeño** for a zippier salsa.

MARINATED BEET SALAD

Fresh beets, one of the "earthiest" vegetables around, are underrated and underused in most kitchens. This is a good recipe to try if you are unsure of beets. It has an Eastern European taste to it, and is good as a side dish or in a buffet. When selecting beets for cultivation, consider **Forminova Beets**. This variety is long instead of round, which makes them look like fat purple carrots! Besides having excellent flavour and keeping well, the shape is quicker to cook, and perfect for slicing into rounds. This recipe is even better with a dollop of *Tzatziki* (p. 16) alongside.

5–6 medium beets
1 egg, hard-boiled, shelled, and sliced (optional)
½ cup olive oil
¼ cup apple cider vinegar, or *Dill Vinegar* (p. 100-1), if available
1 tsp salt (or to taste)
pepper, to taste
1–2 tbsp. fresh dill, minced (1–2 tsp. dried), or to taste
½ tsp. dry mustard
1 small red onion or shallot,

sliced and separated into rings (or 1 small white onion)

Wash beets. Trim the tops and bottoms. Leave small beets whole; halve larger ones. Put the beets in a medium saucepan and barely cover with water. Bring water to a boil and boil the beets gently until tender when pierced with a fork, about 30–40 minutes, depending on the size of the beets. Drain and let them cool.

In the meantime, in a small bowl, mix the olive oil, apple cider vinegar, salt, pepper, dill, and mustard. Beat gently with a fork.

When the beets are cool enough to handle, slip off the skins and slice into thin slices. Place them in a bowl, add the dressing and the red onion, and gently mix all together. Add egg, if used, and toss again. This is best if made ahead and left at room temperature for several hours. After that it may be kept in the fridge for several days. Let it warm a bit at room temperature before serving.

Yield: 4–6 servings. More if used in a buffet.

WARM POTATO SALAD WITH FRESH HERBS

Another simple salad made with fresh herbs—what could be better? Use one herb at a time and match it to your entrée—or to your mood.

1½ lbs. new potatoes
¼ cup canola or safflower oil
¼ cup olive oil
3 tbsp. red wine vinegar
1 tbsp. Dijon mustard
salt and pepper, to taste
3–4 tbsp. fresh tarragon or fresh basil or fresh dill, minced
2 tbsp. fresh chives, minced
2 tbsp. fresh parsley, minced

Scrub the potatoes and, if large, cut them into halves. Steam them in a steamer for about 15 minutes, or until tender.
In a jar place the oils, vinegar, Dijon mustard, salt, and pepper. When the potatoes are done, remove them to a bowl. Cut them with a knife into smaller pieces, if desired. Toss them gently with the dressing.

Add the herbs and toss again gently. Let the salad cool to room temperature and serve fresh.

Yield: 3–4 servings.

MARINATED SUMMER SQUASH SALAD

A great salad to serve in a buffet or to take along on a picnic, and a good recipe to use those ever-abundant zucchini in mid-summer.

⅓ cup olive oil
3 tbsp. red wine vinegar
2 tbsp. balsamic vinegar (or additional red wine vinegar)
salt and pepper, to taste
1 clove garlic, minced
1 young zucchini, 6–8" long
1 young yellow summer squash, 6–8" long (or an additional zucchini)
1 small red onion, minced
1 medium fresh tomato (or 6 sun-dried tomato halves, soaked in boiling water 10 minutes and drained)
1 small banana pepper (or ½ cup fresh red or green pepper), cored, seeded, and slivered

8–10 fresh basil leaves, slivered
⅓ cup fresh parsley, minced

In your serving bowl, gently mix the olive oil, red wine vinegar, balsamic vinegar, salt, pepper, and garlic with a fork.

Cut the squash lengthwise into thin slices, then cut these slices crosswise into pieces that resemble matchsticks. Add to the marinade and gently mix. Add remaining ingredients and again gently mix. Chill until serving time.

Yield: 4–6 servings.

MEDITERRANEAN ASPARAGUS SALAD

A delicious salad that is easy to make yet good enough to be served at the finest feast. It is best made in the morning, chilled, and then returned to near room temperature before serving.

1 lb. fresh asparagus (after trimming tough ends)

Cut the asparagus into 1½" lengths (approximately), putting the tips in one bowl and the stalk pieces in another. Bring a large saucepan with 2" of salted water to a boil. Drop in the stalk pieces and boil for 2 minutes. Add the tips and boil for an additional 2 minutes. Remove from heat, drain, and immediately rinse under cold water. Drain again very well and place pieces in your serving bowl.
Alternatively, if you have a steamer, cut asparagus into 1½" lengths and steam until tender, about 5 minutes. Rinse under cold water, drain well, and place in serving bowl.

Dressing and Assembly:
6 tbsp. olive oil
1½ tbsp. red wine vinegar
2 tsp. fresh lemon juice
2 tsp. Dijon mustard
1 clove garlic, minced
salt and pepper, to taste
1 ripe tomato, cut into bite-sized chunks
1 tsp. capers, drained
6 Kalamata olives, pitted and sliced (or more to taste)
½ cup fresh parsley, minced

Place the olive oil, red wine vinegar, lemon juice, mustard, garlic, salt, and pepper in a jar. Shake until all is blended. Pour over asparagus pieces and gently toss with a spoon. Add the tomato, capers, Kalamata olives, and parsley and again gently toss. Cover and refrigerate. Remove from refrigerator about 1 hour before serving so the salad can return to near room temperature. Gently toss again and serve.

Yield: 4–6 servings.

ASPARAGUS À L'ESTRAGON

Asparagus and tarragon have a great affinity for one another, perhaps because they are both in abundance in the early spring. This is another marinated salad best made in the morning and returned to almost room temperature before serving. It is ideal for your most elegant dinners.

1 lb. fresh asparagus (after trimming tough ends)

Leave spears whole and blanch in water until just tender. A smaller-bottomed, but tall, saucepan, with 1" of water works best for me. Place spears so the bottoms are in the water and the tips are not (so they can be gently steamed). Cover and cook until just tender. (Check after 5 minutes.) Immediately remove and place under cold running water to stop the cooking. Drain thoroughly and place in your serving dish. (Optional suggestion: Cut into lengths and steam as in preceding recipe.)

Dressing and Assembly:
⅓ cup olive oil
½ lemon, juiced
2 tsp. *Tarragon Vinegar* (p. 100)
1 tsp. Dijon mustard
1 clove garlic, minced
salt and pepper, to taste
3 tbsp. fresh tarragon, minced
3 tbsp. fresh garlic chives, minced

Place olive oil, lemon juice, tarragon vinegar, Dijon mustard, garlic, salt, and pepper in a jar and shake until well blended. Add the fresh tarragon and garlic chives and gently shake again. Pour over asparagus spears. Cover and place in the refrigerator until about 1 hour before serving. Remove from fridge and let the dish return to near room temperature. Serve.

Yield: 4–6 servings.

TABOULI

Still one of the best salads around. It is especially good in the summer when the tomatoes and herbs are right fresh. However, tabouli is an excellent winter salad as well, since good fresh parsley is available year-round.

1 cup bulghur (cracked wheat)
hot water (near boiling)
1–3 fresh tomatoes (depending on size), chopped into small pieces
1 large green onion, minced (or ¼ cup fresh chives, minced)
1 bunch fresh parsley
½ cup fresh mint, minced (or 3–4 tbsp. dried), or to taste
2 tsp. fresh oregano or fresh thyme, minced (or 1 tsp. dried oregano)
salt and pepper, to taste
6 tbsp. olive oil (or to taste)
juice of 1 lemon
fresh Romaine lettuce leaves, washed (optional)

Place bulghur in a large flat serving bowl. Add hot water until it is just covered. Let it stand about ½ hour. The bulghur absorbs the water and "plumps." Drain excess water if necessary.

Add the tomatoes, green onion, parsley, mint, oregano or thyme, salt, and pepper and mix gently. Add the olive oil and lemon juice and mix gently again. The amount of olive oil depends on the size and juiciness of the lemon and on your taste. When you get it to your liking, serve. You may use the Romaine leaves to scoop up the tabouli, but it is not necessary.

Yield: 4–6 servings.

PASTA-
VEGETABLE SALADS

In late summer when the vegetables come pouring in from the garden and the company comes pouring in from away, you don't want to spend your time in the kitchen, but you want to be serving all those fresh vegetables to your family and guests. Pasta and vegetables in various delicious combinations seem to have an affinity for each other. Prepared in advance, they benefit from time to sit and mellow in your fridge while you are out and about having fun. These salads are great to have around for lunches as well. I like to keep some handy all through the summer. When we're out working in the gardens, we can work up a big appetite very quickly. A bowl of pasta-vegetable salad is quick at hand and a reminder of why we spend all this time and effort in the gardens. These salads are all great for picnics and potlucks as well.

The following recipes have many variations and are meant to guide you along.

A few words about **tomatoes**: Most people agree, there is nothing to compare to a fresh, vine-ripened tomato. It is perfect in itself. For pasta salads, choose a variety of tomato that is smaller and sweeter—Early Cascade is one of my favourites. Paste tomatoes are excellent as well. Larger tomatoes tend to have more liquid, and this can make your pasta salad unappealing. If you have the time to peel and seed your tomatoes, this adds to any recipe, although, with fresh young tomatoes, it is not always necessary.

PASTA SALAD WITH GRILLED ZUCCHINI

Wholewheat pasta is good in this recipe.

1 recipe *Grilled Zucchini*
(p. 83)
1½ lbs. young, fresh vine-ripened tomatoes, diced
¼ cup olive oil
2 tbsp. red wine vinegar
salt and pepper, to taste
1–2 cloves garlic, minced
1 lb. pennette (small penne), or other medium-sized pasta (such as rotini, etc.)
½ cup Kalamata olives, pitted and coarsely chopped (or more to taste)
⅓–½ cup feta cheese, crumbled
½ cup fresh basil leaves, coarsely chopped

In a large bowl, combine the tomatoes, olive oil, red wine vinegar, salt, pepper, and garlic. Set aside.

Cook pasta according to package directions. Drain, rinse lightly, drain again very well, and add to the tomato mixture. Toss to blend. Add reserved zucchini to the pasta mixture along with the Kalamata olives, feta cheese, and fresh basil. Toss again and set aside for the flavours to mellow. Cover and chill if not eaten within 4 hours. If chilled, remove from fridge 1 hour before serving. Mix lightly and serve.

Yield: 6–8 servings.

Optional Suggestion: If you don't have a special pan for grilling vegetables, you can slice the zucchini into thick slices and grill right on the grill, turning and brushing often with olive oil mixed with herbs and garlic. Cut into cubes and add to the pasta, along with some fresh green onions and peppers, if desired. Or use *Roasted Zucchini*, following directions for roasted vegetables, page 83.

BROCCOLI-PASTA SALAD

An excellent summer dish. Easy to make ahead and serve for a light lunch or along with a soup and green salad for a cool summer dinner. Since this salad contains mayonnaise, it needs to be kept chilled until serving time.

Dressing:
1 or 2 cloves garlic (according to taste)
¼ cup light mayonnaise
salt and pepper, to taste
¼ cup olive oil
2 tbsp. *Tarragon Vinegar* (p. 100-1), or apple cider vinegar

In a food processor chop the garlic a few seconds. Add the mayonnaise, salt, and pepper and process a few seconds more. Add the olive oil and tarragon vinegar and again process a few seconds, or until the mixture is emulsified. Set aside.

Salad:
1 bunch broccoli, washed and broken into stalks for cooking
8 sun-dried tomato halves
250 g dried macaroni noodles (or other smaller pasta)
5–6 small to medium pepperoncini (Italian pickled peppers), coarsely chopped
2–3 tbsp. fresh tarragon
2–3 tbsp. fresh parsley

Steam the broccoli for 5 minutes, or until tender-crisp. Drain and rinse under cold running water. Drain again very well. Place broccoli in a bowl and coarsely chop it with a knife, right in the bowl. Set aside.

Cover the sun-dried tomato halves with boiling water for five minutes. Drain, cut into strips, and set aside.

Cook noodles according to package directions. Drain, rinse under cold water, and drain again very well. Place noodles in the serving bowl, add the dressing, and toss. Add broccoli and toss again gently. Add the sun-dried tomatoes, pepperoncini, tarragon, and parsley and again toss very gently. Serve or chill in the refrigerator until ready to serve.

Yield: 4 large or 6 smaller servings.

MEDITERRANEAN LOBSTER-PASTA SALAD

To some, a lobster-pasta salad is unthinkable. But before you condemn the idea, you might give it a try. Next time you have lobster, cook two extra and use the leftovers in this dish. Or use canned lobster in winter. This has the good taste of lobster without the large expense of a "feed."

2 cups dried small pasta (macaroni, bow ties, etc.)
2 lobsters, cooked and cooled, or 1 can (320 g/11.3 oz.) frozen lobster
1 can (396 ml/14 oz.) artichoke hearts, drained
1 stalk celery, diced (optional)
2 fresh tomatoes, cut in wedges

Boil the macaroni noodles according to package directions until done. Drain, run under cold water until cool, and drain again very well. Place in a large serving bowl.

Remove the meat from the lobster and cut up in bite-sized pieces. Cut the artichoke hearts into quarters. Add the lobster, artichoke hearts, celery (if desired), and fresh tomatoes to the pasta.

Dressing:
¾ cup mayonnaise
½ cup plain yogurt
2 tbsp. *Tarragon Vinegar* (p. 100-1)
2 tbsp. fresh tarragon leaves, minced (or 2 tsp. fresh)
¼ cup fresh chives, minced
½ cup fresh parsley, minced
2 tbsp. capers, drained and minced (optional)
salt and pepper, to taste

In a smaller bowl mix together the dressing ingredients and blend very well. Add to the pasta-lobster mixture and mix gently but thoroughly. Chill until ready to serve. This is better made one day in advance.

Yield: 4–6 servings.

Optional Suggestion:
Lobster-Asparagus Salad: Replace artichoke hearts with **1 lb. asparagus spears**, steamed and cut into bite-sized pieces. Proceed as above.

CURRIED ASPARAGUS-LOBSTER SALAD

Another lobster pasta salad. I think I like this one even better.

2 cups dried small pasta (macaroni, bow-ties, etc.)
2 lobsters, cooked and cooled (or 1 320 g/11.3 oz. can frozen lobster)
1 lb. asparagus spears, cut into bite-sized pieces and steamed
1 stalk celery, thinly sliced

Dressing:
¾ cup mayonnaise
½ cup plain yogurt
2 tsp. curry powder (or more to taste)
2 tbsp. fresh coriander
salt and pepper, to taste

Boil the macaroni noodles according to package directions until done. Drain, run under cold water until they are cool, and drain again very well. Place in a large serving bowl. Remove the meat from the lobster and cut up in bite-sized pieces. Add the lobster, the steamed asparagus, and the celery to the pasta.

In a smaller bowl mix together the dressing ingredients and blend very well. Add to the pasta-lobster mixture and mix gently but thoroughly. Chill until ready to serve. This is better made one day in advance.

Yield: 4–6 servings.

ITALIAN SAUSAGE-PASTA SALAD WITH SUMMER VEGGIES

Great for a potluck or for when company is coming. This is better made in the morning so the flavours can mellow. Keep it in the fridge. You may serve this chilled or bring it out a bit earlier to warm to room temperature.

Dressing:
½ cup olive oil
1 tbsp. water
1 tbsp. balsamic vinegar
⅓ cup red wine vinegar
1 tbsp. Dijon mustard
2 cloves garlic, minced

Combine all ingredients in a jar, shake, and set aside.

Salad:
1 lb. rotini or fusilli
⅔ lb. hot Italian sausage, casings removed
2 tbsp. olive oil
1 large onion, chopped
1 clove garlic, minced
3 cups broccoli florets
2 small (or 1 medium) zucchini, halved lengthwise and cut into ½" slices
¼ cup white wine
3 medium tomatoes, diced
1 cup fresh Italian parsley, minced
10 pepperoncini, chopped (optional)
½ cup Kalamata olives, pitted and sliced
½–⅔ cup grated Parmesan cheese

Cook pasta according to package directions. Drain well, run under cold water, and drain again very, very well. Place pasta in a bowl and toss with the dressing.

In a heavy skillet over medium heat sauté the Italian sausage, breaking it up with a fork and stirring it until it is browned and cooked. Remove with a slotted spoon to drain on a plate covered with paper towels. Drain any excess fat.

Return skillet to heat. Add the olive oil and in it sauté the onion and garlic for about 5 minutes. Add the broccoli, zucchini, and wine. Cover, lower heat, and "steam" veggies about 5 minutes or until tender. Return sausage to the skillet, add the tomatoes, cover, and cook an additional 1–2 minutes, just until tomatoes are heated through. Add to the pasta and toss until blended. Add the Italian parsley, pepperoncini, Kalamata olives, and Parmesan cheese and toss again. Cover and refrigerate for at least one hour before serving.

Yield: 6–8 servings.

COUSCOUS-SUMMER VEGETABLE SALAD

Couscous is tiny pasta that is the basis for a quick and delicious side dish when tossed with fresh vegetables and a light dressing. The couscous is very small, so this works best if all the vegetables are cut into very small dice.

1 cup water
1 tbsp. lemon juice
1 tbsp. olive oil
1 tsp. salt (or to taste)
pepper, to taste
¾ cup couscous
3 tbsp. olive oil
2 tbsp. red wine vinegar
1 small garlic shallot, minced
4–5 large fresh basil leaves, slivered
½ cup fresh parsley, minced
2 small to medium tomatoes, chopped small (Italian paste tomatoes, if possible)
1 small zucchini, cut into very small dice
½ small banana pepper (⅓ red or green pepper), finely diced
8–10 fresh snow peas, very thinly sliced (or frozen peas cooked and drained)

Bring the water, lemon juice, 1 tbsp. olive oil, salt, and pepper to a boil in a small saucepan. Remove from heat, add the couscous, cover, and let stand for 5 minutes.
Place cooked couscous in a serving bowl. Fluff with a fork. Add the 3 tbsp. olive oil, red wine vinegar, shallot, basil, parsley, tomatoes, zucchini, banana pepper, and snow peas, mixing gently after each addition. Serve.

Yield: 4 servings.

Optional Suggestion: Omit the **basil** and **peas**. Add instead ½ **tsp. cumin** and ⅓ **cup fresh coriander**, minced.

MEDITERRANEAN ASPARAGUS-PASTA SALAD

2 cups fusilli
1 lb. fresh asparagus (after trimming tough ends)

Cook the pasta according to package directions. Drain,

rinse under cold water, and drain again very well. Place pasta in a large serving bowl.

Cut the asparagus into 1½" lengths (approximately). If

you have a steamer, steam the asparagus pieces until tender. If not, put the tips in one bowl and the stalk pieces in another. Bring a large saucepan with 2" of salted water to a boil. Drop in the stalk pieces and boil for 2 minutes. Add the tips and boil for an additional 2 minutes. When finished, drain and immediately rinse under cold water. Drain very well, add to the pasta, and fold in gently.

Dressing and Assembly:
6 tbsp. olive oil
1½ tbsp. red wine vinegar
2 tbsp. water
2 tsp. fresh lemon juice
2 tsp. Dijon mustard
1 clove garlic, minced
salt and pepper, to taste
1 medium vine-ripened tomato, cut into bite-sized pieces

6 Kalamata olives, pitted and sliced (or more to taste)
½ cup fresh parsley, minced
½ garlic chives
½ cup crumbled feta cheese

Place the olive oil, red wine vinegar, water, lemon juice, mustard, garlic, salt, and pepper in a jar. Shake until all is blended and pour over pasta and asparagus. Gently toss with a spoon. Add the tomato, Kalamata olives, parsley, garlic chives, and crumbled feta cheese, and again gently toss. Cover and refrigerate. Remove from refrigerator about 1 hour before serving so the salad can return to near room temperature. Gently toss again and serve.

Yield: 4–6 servings.

TOMATO-PASTA SALAD AL FRESCO

One of the simplest and best summer pastas. But you must have fresh vine-ripened tomatoes and fresh basil, or the results won't be the same. This dish is great for picnics and potluck suppers since it is best at room temperature.

2 lb. fresh tomatoes
5 tbsp. olive oil
3 tbsp. red wine vinegar
¼ cup ground almonds
2 cloves garlic, minced (or to taste)
1 tsp. salt (or to taste)

pepper, to taste
1 tsp. sugar
¼ cup fresh basil, slivered (or more, to taste)
1 small red onion, thinly sliced (optional)
½ small jalapeño pepper, finely

minced (optional)
⅔ cup Kalamata olives, pitted and sliced (optional)
375 g wheat vermicelli, or other pasta, cooked and drained

Peel and chop the tomatoes: To easily peel tomatoes, bring a medium to large pot filled with 4–5" water to a boil. Add the tomatoes and simmer for 30 seconds. Drain into a colander and rinse immediately with cold water. Peel and chop the tomatoes. Add them to a large pasta bowl with the olive oil, red wine vinegar, almonds, garlic, salt, pepper, sugar, and basil and the onion, jalapeño pepper, and/or Kalamata olives, if desired. Gently mix and let this set at room temperature for at least an hour for flavours to mellow.

Cook pasta according to package directions. Drain and toss with the tomato mixture. Serve immediately. You can let it set at this point for a while before eating. If you are not going to use it for a few hours, put it in the refrigerator, but remove it and let it warm up a bit before serving. It tastes best at room temperature.
Yield: 4 servings.

Optional Suggestion: You can add the cooked noodles as soon as the vegetables are put together and let it all mellow together. The result will be a bit drier and more garlicky.

THAI NOODLE SALAD

A favourite for potlucks and large dinner parties. This recipe is easy to make and so delicious!

500 g rice or wheat vermicelli
½ cup tamari soy sauce

In the morning, or several hours earlier, cook the noodles according to package directions. Drain, rinse well under cold running water, and drain again very well. Place noodles in a large serving bowl, add the tamari soy sauce, and gently mix. Cover and place in the refrigerator for at least 2 hours.

Dressing and Assembly:
⅓ cup rice wine vinegar
⅓ cup sugar
¼ cup sesame oil
1–2 tbsp. sesame oil
2 tbsp. minced ginger
1 broccoli head, trimmed and steamed
½ red pepper, sliced and cut into small pieces
½ lb. fresh young snow peas, cut into bite-sized pieces
2 stalks celery, thinly sliced
2 green onions, thinly sliced (or ¼ cup garlic chives, minced)
¼ cup fresh cilantro, chopped (optional)

Remove noodles from the refrigerator. Place the rice wine vinegar, sugar, sesame oils, and ginger in a jar and shake well to combine. Pour over the noodles and toss gently.

Steam the broccoli until just tender. Drain, rinse quickly under cold water, drain again, and add to the noodles along with the red pepper, snow peas, celery, green onions, and cilantro (if desired). Toss gently and serve.

Yield: 6–8 servings.

Optional Suggestion: 1 lb. asparagus, steamed, may be used instead of the broccoli.

NOTES

SOUPS

SUMMER & FALL HARVEST SOUPS

In late summer there is a crispness in the air and we have an abundance of fresh produce, and that is the time I start to think of soup. Harvest soups are all wonderful to serve with some fresh bread and a good salad. Some soups can be made in season, with fresh veggies and herbs, and also in the winter, with some substitutions.

PISTOU

Pistou is a French provincial vegetable soup which is made in the summer when all of the vegetables and herbs are "right" fresh. It is one of the best soups you will ever eat. This recipe appeared in both of my previous cookbooks. It is slightly altered, and I am including it again because it is one of our all-time favourite recipes. I served it one summer while running a **Summer Kitchen** at a local health-food store and had one comment from a customer that made my day. He said he had travelled a lot and eaten in many restaurants in many countries, and the **Pistou** I served him that day was the best soup he had ever eaten!

1 cup dried kidney beans

Soak kidney beans overnight. In the morning drain them, cover with water, bring to a boil, lower heat, and simmer for 45 minutes to 1 hour, or until tender, adding more water during cooking if necessary. Drain, rinse, and set aside. (You may use 1 540 ml/19 oz. can kidney beans, drained and rinsed, instead.)

3 quarts water
3 cups new potatoes, scrubbed and diced
3 cups baby carrots, washed and diced
1½ cups leeks, white parts only, washed and sliced (or 1 cup onion, chopped)
2 tsp. salt
1 tsp. pepper, or to taste
2 cups young, small zucchini, sliced
1 green pepper, cut into slices
2 cups green beans, sliced
1 slice stale bread, crumbled

In a large soup pot bring to a boil the water, potatoes, carrots, leeks, salt, and pepper. Lower heat and simmer about 20 minutes.

Add the zucchini, green pepper, green beans, bread, and reserved drained kidney beans. Simmer another 10 minutes.

Pistou:
1 small can (156 ml/5.5 oz.) tomato paste
⅔ cup Parmesan cheese
½–1 lightly packed cup fresh basil leaves, minced (to taste)
4 cloves garlic, minced
⅓ cup olive oil

To make the Pistou: In a small mixing bowl combine the tomato paste, Parmesan cheese, fresh basil, and garlic and gently blend together. Using a whisk, gradually add the olive oil and blend it into the tomato mixture well. Add 1 cup of the soup stock, ¼ cup at a time, whisking after each addition. Now add the tomato mixture into the soup, stirring it well to blend all together. Serve.

Yield: 6–8 servings.

Note: This soup keeps well in the fridge for a few days, but does not freeze well. The potatoes get sort of weird and rubbery.

Optional Suggestion: Winter Pistou: Substitute a package of **pesto sauce mix** in place of the Parmesan cheese and fresh basil, and use frozen veggies for the ones you can't get fresh. Add less garlic (to taste) and proceed as above. The result won't be quite the same, but it will be good nonetheless.

CHILLED TOMATO-YOGURT SOUP

Perfect on a hot summer day! Make it in the morning. This recipe is from my sister, Connie, who prefers it with **fresh mint** instead of basil!

1 lb. (4 medium), or more, fresh ripe tomatoes, peeled, seeded, and chopped
2 cups non-fat yogurt
¼ cup chopped red onion
1 tbsp. sugar
3 tbsp. fresh basil (or fresh mint)
½ tsp. salt (or to taste)
good pinch of cayenne pepper
Blend in food processor until smooth. Refrigerate until served. Serve very cold.
Yield: 4 servings.

CREAMY-CHEESY GREEN HARVEST SOUP

An excellent fall soup when the potatoes are in and there is an abundance of fresh veggies on hand. There are two basic versions, **Green** and **Golden Rosy**. But don't be afraid of adding veggies you have and subtracting those you lack. This soup warms your soul on a cool fall day.

Soup Mixture:
4–5 cups chicken broth
4 medium potatoes, peeled and cut into chunks (2 large)
2 tbsp. olive oil
1 medium onion, chopped
½–1 green pepper, seeded and diced (optional)
2 cloves garlic, minced
1½–2 cups fresh broccoli or cauliflower (or both), chopped
1 stalk celery, chopped (optional)
3–4 cups (packed) shredded fall greens (kale, spinach, chard, etc.) (optional)
salt and pepper, to taste
½ tsp. powdered mustard
1–2 tsp. herbes de Provence or 2–3 tbsp. fresh dill, minced (or 2 tsp. dried)
1 tsp. celery seed

In a large saucepan begin cooking the potatoes in the chicken broth until just starting to get tender, about 15 minutes.

In a skillet in the olive oil, sauté the onion, green pepper, garlic, broccoli, and celery 5–10 minutes, or until the vegetables begin to brown. Add to the cooking potatoes and their liquid, along with the greens, salt, pepper, mustard, herbs, and celery seed. Continue to simmer 15–20 minutes. Set aside to cool.

Assembly:
1 cup milk, heated to scalding
2 cups coarsely grated Cheddar cheese (about ¼ lb.)
Croutons (p. 23)
½ cup green onions (optional)

Process the soup in batches in a blender or food processor until it is smooth, blending in the hot milk at this time. Return to saucepan and reheat, but do not boil. Stir in the grated cheese and continue cooking over low heat, stirring often, until heated through. Serve with croutons and green onions for garnish, if desired. If you are reheating leftover soup, be careful not to boil it, since the milk may curdle.

Yield: 4–6 servings.

Optional Suggestion: Use **vegetable broth,** homemade or from cubes, in place of chicken broth. Try **Gouda** or **Swiss cheese.** For an Italian version of the soup, use **½ cup grated Parmesan cheese** instead of Cheddar and **oregano** and/or **basil** for your herbs.

Variations:
Golden-Rosy Harvest Soup:
This soup uses a different crop of fall vegetables, but the basic recipe is the same. To the soup mixture add **1 large carrot** to cook with the potatoes. Use **red pepper** instead of green (if used). Omit broccoli, celery, and greens. Instead, add **2 cups fresh tomatoes**, seeded and chopped (**or 2 cups canned tomatoes**), and **corn cut from 2–3 ears (3–4 cups)**. Assembly as above.

CREAM OF FRESH TOMATO SOUP

An excellent soup to prepare in the fall when fresh tomatoes and thyme are still available but there is a chill in the air. Fresh thyme, if available, makes it special. If you want a totally amazing tomato soup, try the *Cream of Roasted Tomato Soup* variation, below.

Soup Mixture:
2 tbsp. olive oil
1 large onion, chopped
2 cloves garlic, minced
2 carrots, peeled and chopped
1 stalk celery, chopped
2 cup broth (chicken or vegetable)
4 cups fresh tomatoes, peeled, seeded, and roughly chopped
salt, to taste (if you use salted chicken stock, you may not need any)
freshly ground pepper, to taste
1 tbsp. fresh thyme (or ½ tsp. dried)
1 tsp. dried basil, or oregano
1 tsp. herbes de Provence

½ tsp. allspice
1 tsp. sugar
dash cayenne pepper (optional)

In a large saucepan heat the olive oil and sauté the onion, garlic, carrots, and celery until onion is soft, about 5 minutes. Add the broth, tomatoes, salt, pepper, thyme, basil, herbes de Provence, allspice, sugar, and cayenne, if desired. Cover and simmer about 20 minutes. Remove from heat and allow to cool.

Cream Sauce:
2 tbsp. butter
2 tbsp. flour
1½ cups milk
¼ tsp. nutmeg, freshly grated
(or allspice)

In a small saucepan melt the butter. Add the flour and blend well. Slowly add the milk, blending with a whisk, and continue cooking and whisking over low heat until mixture is smooth, thickened, and just beginning to bubble. Remove from heat, add the nutmeg or allspice, and set aside.

Assembly:
Purée the soup mixture in batches in a food processor. Return to pot. Bring back to a simmer. Add a couple ladlefuls of the soup mixture to the cream sauce, whisking it in. Slowly add the cream mixture into the soup. (Or, if you have a hand blender, buzz the vegetable mixture with the blender. Slowly add the cream sauce and keep buzzing. Be careful not to splash the hot mixture on yourself!) Do not boil after cream sauce is added. If reheating, do not boil—this may curdle the mixture.

Yield: 4–6 servings.

Variations:
Winter Cream of Tomato Soup: You may substitute **1 medium can (540 ml/19 oz.) tomatoes plus 8 softened and snipped sun-dried tomato halves** for the fresh tomatoes. You will have an excellent soup adults and children alike will enjoy.

Cream of Roasted Tomato Soup: Follow the preceding recipe using fresh tomatoes, but roast them first, following directions on page 76-7. Four cups of fresh tomatoes should yield **2–2½ cups roasted tomatoes**, coarsely chopped.

CREAM SOUP BASICS

The next three recipes are also cream soups. First, you cook the vegetables, then there are two ways to finish off the soup. You can use a food processor or blender to purée the soup, then add **a cream sauce** made using 2 tbsp. butter, 2 tbsp. flour, and 1½ cups milk; or you may heat 1½ cups milk to a simmer and add it to the vegetables while you purée the soup. I prefer the second method when using a hand blender, another kitchen utensil that is quite inexpensive and handy to have around. Adding just milk rather than cream sauce reduces the fat content and is quicker and easier. For this to be successful, two things are necessary to prevent curdling: potatoes in the soup and warming up the milk. After the milk is blended in **do not boil**. (I wouldn't use milk alone in cream of tomato soup. The high acidic content makes curdling easier, and blending in cream sauce is your best option.)

CREAM OF ASPARAGUS AND SPINACH SOUP

Quite simple to make and very delicious in early spring.

2½ cups vegetable stock
2–3 medium potatoes, peeled and cubed (2½ cups)
1–2 cloves garlic, minced
1 lb. asparagus, washed and cut into 1" lengths
½–⅔ lb. fresh spinach (or arugula), washed and chopped
salt and pepper, to taste

Finishing:
1½ cups cream sauce or heated milk (see *Cream Soup Basics,* above)
2 tbsp. fresh tarragon, minced (or fresh dill)
¼–½ cup fresh garlic chives, minced

In a large saucepan bring the vegetable stock to a boil. Add potatoes and garlic, cover, and simmer 15–20 minutes. Add the asparagus stalks, cover, and simmer an additional 5 minutes. Add the spinach (or arugula), cover, and simmer until greens are just wilted. Remove from heat, let soup cool a few minutes, and then process in a food processor, in batches, until mixture is smooth. Blend in the cream sauce or milk until smooth. Taste and add salt and/or pepper to taste. Keep warm. Reheat but do not boil. Stir in the fresh tarragon (or dill) and fresh garlic chives and serve.

Yield: 4 servings.

Optional Suggestion: In the fall try using **zucchini** instead of asparagus, and season it with **dill** rather than tarragon.

CREAM OF CAULIFLOWER SOUP

This is a great way to use up that cauliflower in the freezer.

4 cups chicken stock
6 cups frozen cauliflower (or florets from 1 large head)
3 medium potatoes, peeled and diced
2 tbsp. olive oil
1 large onion, chopped
2 stalks celery, chopped
2 cloves garlic, minced
1 tsp. fines herbes
2 tsp. dried dill weed (or 2 tbsp. fresh)
1 tsp. salt, or to taste
pepper, to taste
1½ cups cream sauce or heated milk (see **Cream Soup Basics,** above)
grated Cheddar cheese, for garnish

In a large saucepan heat the chicken stock to boiling. Add the cauliflower and potatoes and keep at a simmer. In a medium frypan heat the olive oil and in it sauté the onion, celery, and garlic until soft. Add the vegetables to the soup along with the fines herbes, dill, salt, and pepper. Cover and simmer until vegetables are tender, 20–25 minutes. Remove from heat, uncover, and let the soup cool down.

Blend the soup in batches in a food processor or all at once with a hand blender, adding the cream sauce or milk and blending until smooth. Reheat but do not boil. Serve with grated Cheddar cheese for garnish.

Yield: 4 servings.

CORN BISQUE

This soup is somewhere between a bisque and a chowder—and whatever you want to call it, it tastes delicious!

4 slices bacon, diced
1 tbsp. olive oil
1 large onion, chopped
1 stalk celery, diced
3½ cups water
2–3 medium potatoes, diced (approx. 2½ cups)
1 tsp. dried dill
1 bay leaf
4 cups corn (freshly cut off cob, frozen, or canned)
1 tsp. salt, or to taste
pepper, to taste
1½ cups cream sauce or heated milk (see *Cream Soup Basics*, above)

In a medium pot sauté the bacon, stirring, until crisp. Remove with a slotted spoon to some paper towels to drain. Set aside. Discard the bacon fat.

Add the olive oil to the pot and in it sauté the onion and celery for 5 minutes, or until soft and beginning to brown. Add the water, potatoes, dill, and bay leaf. Cover and simmer for 15 minutes. Add the corn, salt, and pepper. Cover and simmer another 10 minutes. Remove from heat. Discard the bay leaf.

If you have a hand blender, use it to purée the vegetable mixture, then continue blending while you add the milk. If you have a food processor, process the vegetables and cream sauce or milk in batches until smooth. Return to pan, add the reserved bacon, and reheat to a simmer, but do not boil. Serve.

Yield: 4 servings.

Optional Suggestions: Instead of dill, use **¼ cup fresh cilantro**, minced.

ROASTED RED PEPPER SOUP

In 2001 we had our hottest growing season ever, and, as a result, we had lots of red peppers—something we have never had before. This soup became a favourite. It is delicious either hot or cold, with *Croutons* (p. 23) or *Crostini* (p. 14-15).

4 red peppers, roasted and peeled

If you've never **roasted red peppers**, you might be surprised how simple it is. Preheat broiler. Cut the red peppers in half, remove their ribs and seeds, and gently flatten them a bit with your hands. Place them on a cookie sheet lined with foil. Broil until the skins are blackened and blistered all over. This takes about 10–15 minutes. You may need to turn the cookie sheet around or re-arrange the peppers to ensure even blackening. When they are all black, remove them to a plastic bag and close tightly (with a twist tie). Leave to "sweat" for 10 minutes, then remove from bag and peel the charred skin. Slice and set aside.

Soup:
3 tbsp. olive oil
1 large onion, chopped
2 small (4") zucchinis, diced
2 ears of corn, cut from the cob
reserved red pepper slices (above)

4 cups vegetable broth
½ cup white wine
3 tbsp. rice (Arborio if possible)
salt and pepper, to taste
¼ cup fresh basil, minced
¼ cup fresh parsley, minced
splash of red wine vinegar or balsamic vinegar

In a large saucepan in the olive oil sauté the onion for about 5 minutes. Add the zucchini and corn and sauté a few more minutes. Add the red pepper slices, vegetable broth, white wine, rice, salt, and pepper. Cover and simmer for 20–25 minutes or until the rice is tender. Stir in the basil and parsley and set aside to cool a bit. Then blend using a hand blender or in batches in your food processor. When ready to serve, reheat, add the splash of red wine or balsamic vinegar, and serve topped with homemade *Croutons* (p. 23) or *Crostini* (p. 14-15).

Yield: 4 servings.

WINTER SQUASH-APPLE SOUP

Perfect on a blustery fall day. Children will be surprised how delicious squash can be!

1 medium acorn squash
1 medium buttercup squash
4 tbsp. brown sugar (or honey)
4 tbsp. butter
2 tbsp. olive oil
1 medium onion, chopped
1 clove garlic, minced
1 tbsp. fresh ginger, minced (or 1 tsp. dried)
chicken stock or vegetable stock (or half and half)
1 cup apple cider
3 medium apples, peeled, cored, and diced
1 tsp. salt, or to taste
1 tsp. pepper (or more to taste—I like this soup peppery)
1 tbsp. cinnamon
½ tsp. freshly grated nutmeg

Preheat oven to 350°F.

Cut each squash in half and scoop out seeds. In each cavity place 1 tbsp. each of the brown sugar (or honey) and butter. Place in a shallow roasting pan and add hot water to the depth of 1". Bake in preheated oven for 1–1½ hours, or until squash is tender when pierced with a fork. Check occasionally during baking and add more water if needed. When squash is tender, remove from oven and set aside. Reserve any liquid.

In a large saucepan heat the olive oil and in it sauté the onion, garlic, and ginger for about 5 minutes, or until onion is soft. Drain the liquid from the baking dish and add chicken (or vegetable) stock to make 4 cups liquid. Add this liquid to the pot along with the apple cider, apples, salt, pepper, cinnamon, and nutmeg. Bring to a simmer. Scoop the squash from the skins and add to the pot. Simmer about 10 minutes or until apples are tender. Remove from heat and cool slightly.

Purée the soup in batches in the food processor or blender. Return to pot, reheat, and serve.

Yield: 4–6 servings.

Optional Suggestion: Instead of the cinnamon and nutmeg use **curry powder** to taste.

LATE FALL AND WINTER SOUPS

Late fall and winter weather inspires another host of soups. These rely more on canned vegetables and those readily available through the winter months, as well as beans and grains.

CURRIED LENTIL SOUP

This recipe is from my first cookbook, but this version is a bit thicker and a bit spicier! It is a good winter soup, since the ingredients are usually on hand, and since the hotness of the curry is extra good and warming on a cold winter day.

2 quarts water (or 1 quart chicken or vegetable stock and 1 quart water)
2 cups lentils, washed
1 tbsp. salt
2 tbsp. olive oil
1 large onion, chopped
3–4 cloves garlic, minced
1 stalk celery, diced
1 carrot, diced
2–3 tsp. curry powder
½ tsp. each cumin seed and coriander
¼ tsp. red pepper flakes (optional)
2 green onions
½ cup fresh coriander or fresh parsley, minced
½ tsp. *Garam Masala* (p. 196) (optional)

Bring the water (or stock and water) to a boil in a large saucepan. Add the lentils and salt and simmer, covered, for about 45 minutes.

Heat the olive oil in a cast-iron frypan over medium-high heat. Sauté the onion and garlic for about 3 minutes. Add the celery and carrot and sauté 5 minutes longer, stirring often. Add the curry powder, cumin, coriander, and red pepper flakes, if desired, and sauté a few minutes more, stirring the spices into the vegetables. Add to the simmering soup, cover, and simmer 30 minutes longer. If you want your soup thicker, remove from heat and process approximately half the soup in a food processor until smooth. Return to pot.

Just before serving, stir in the green onion and the fresh coriander or parsley. Ladle soup into bowls and sprinkle with garam masala, if desired. Serve.

Yield: 6 servings.

Optional Suggestion: Ten minutes before the soup is done, you can add **½ lb. fresh or frozen spinach** or **2–3 fresh tomatoes, chopped**.

ITALIAN LENTIL SOUP

A hearty and delicious soup, guaranteed to warm you up on a cold winter day. Using both chicken and beef broth makes it a very rich-tasting soup, but it is good with all chicken broth as well. You may also use good-quality dried chicken or beef base or both.

3 tbsp. olive oil
2 cups onion, chopped
2 cups celery, chopped
3–4 cloves garlic, minced (or to taste)
1 can (284 ml/ 10 oz.) condensed chicken broth
1 can (284 ml/10 oz.) condensed beef broth (or additional chicken broth)
water to make 8 cups liquid
1 large can (796 ml/28 oz.) tomatoes, diced, with their juice
1–1½ cups dried lentils, rinsed (more will make a thicker soup)
1 cup fresh parsley, minced
½ cup red wine
salt and pepper, to taste
¼ tsp. ground cloves
pinch of sugar

In a large soup pot heat olive oil. Add the onion, celery, and garlic and sauté over low heat, stirring occasionally, until vegetables are soft, about 10 minutes.

Add the chicken broth, beef broth, and water to make 8 cups liquid in all. Add the tomatoes and lentils. Bring to a boil, reduce heat, and simmer, uncovered, for about 20 minutes.

Add parsley, red wine, salt, pepper, cloves, and sugar. Stir well and simmer 30 minutes longer. Serve. This soup is ideal to make ahead and reheat.

Yield: 6–8 servings.

Variations:
Vegetarian Italian Lentil Soup: Substitute **vegetable broth** for the chicken and beef broth.

ITALIAN BREAD AND TOMATO SOUP

This is a quick and easy soup that is very delicious to eat! It is better made at least several hours before serving.

Soup:
2 tbsp. olive oil
1 large red onion, chopped
2 cloves garlic, minced
½ red pepper, diced
1 large can (796 ml/28 oz.) diced tomatoes
2 cups vegetable broth (homemade or made from good-quality cubes)
1 tsp. sugar
1 tbsp. red wine vinegar
red pepper flakes, to taste
salt, to taste (if needed)
2–3 tbsp. *Pesto* (p. 152-3), without cheese

In a large saucepan heat the olive oil and in it sauté the onion, garlic, and red pepper for about 5 minutes or until soft. Add the tomatoes, vegetable broth, sugar, red wine vinegar, red pepper flakes, and salt, if needed. Simmer soup for about 10 minutes. Add the pesto and simmer a few more minutes. Cool until needed.

Bread and Serving:
2–4 thick slices French or *Italian Bread* (p. 241-2) (any good homemade country bread is good also)
1 clove garlic cut in half
Parmesan cheese

Preheat oven to 375°F. Meanwhile, warm soup to a simmer.

Toast the bread slices on a cookie sheet in preheated oven for about 5 minutes on each side, or until they are very crisp on both sides. Remove from oven and immediately rub one side of each slice with a cut garlic clove. Place a piece or two of bread in each bowl. Ladle soup over the bread and serve with Parmesan cheese on the side.

Yield: 2 large or 4 small servings.

QUICK ITALIAN SAUSAGE SOUP

This recipe may be quick and easy, but if you let it sit for a few hours to "mellow," your guests will think you spent all day cooking. It is a good basic recipe that encourages improvisation.

1 tsp. olive oil
2–3 hot Italian sausages, casings removed
1 tbsp. olive oil
1 large onion, coarsely chopped
2 stalks celery, chopped
2 cloves garlic, minced
3 carrots, diced
1 large can (796 ml/28 oz.) Italian plum tomatoes
1 can (284 ml/10 oz.) condensed chicken broth, plus water to make 5 cups
salt and pepper, to taste
2 tsp. dried oregano
2 tsp. Italian herbs
1 tsp. sugar
½ cup orzo (or other very small pasta, like stars or alphabets)
1–2 cups frozen green beans or peas, or other vegetable
½ recipe *Pesto* (p. 152-3), or 3–4 tbsp. purchased pesto, or to taste
Parmesan or Romano cheese, grated, to serve

In a skillet, heat the 1 tsp. olive oil and in it brown the sausage, breaking it up with a fork until it is browned. Drain and set aside.

In a soup pot, heat the 1 tbsp. olive oil and in it sauté the onion, celery, and garlic until vegetables are soft. Add the carrots and sauté a few more minutes.

Place the tomatoes in a bowl and squish them into smaller pieces with your hands. Add the tomatoes, chicken broth, salt, pepper, oregano, Italian herbs, and sugar to the soup pot. Cover and simmer for 30 minutes. Add the orzo, cover again, and simmer an additional 10 minutes. Add the green beans (or other vegetable) and cook a few more minutes, or until the vegetables are cooked. Then stir in the pesto and let it set a few minutes. Pass the Parmesan or Romano cheese.

Yield: 4–6 servings.

Optional Suggestions: Add **½ green or red pepper**, diced, with the onions. Other fresh or frozen vegetables may be used. Try some **zucchini** or **canned artichoke hearts, diced. Frozen diced mixed vegetables** are good as well.

GRANDMA'S HAM AND BEAN SOUP

I was given this recipe by my mother-in-law years ago and it still remains one of our favourite winter soups and one of the best ways I know in which to use a ham bone.

1½ cups dried soup beans
6 cups water
2 tbsp. olive oil
1 cup onions, chopped
2 cloves garlic, minced
2 cups celery, chopped
1 cup carrots, diced
¼ tsp. ground cloves
2 bay leaves
4 cups chicken stock
salt and pepper, to taste
1 meaty ham bone
4 tbsp. apple cider vinegar

Soak beans in water overnight. The next day, drain beans and add 6 cups water. Bring to a boil and keep at a simmer.

In the olive oil in a skillet sauté the onion and garlic for about 5 minutes, or until they are soft and beginning to brown. Add the celery and carrot and sauté 5 minutes longer. Add vegetables to the soup along with the cloves, bay leaves, chicken stock, salt, pepper, and ham bone. Cover and simmer about 2–2½ hours or until beans are soft. Discard the bay leaves. Remove ham bone and when it cools enough to handle, cut all the ham off and return it to the soup. Add apple cider vinegar and serve.

Yield: 10–12 servings.

"UNBEETABLE" BEEF BORSCHT

When the wind is howling from the north and chills you to the bone, this is the soup to make. It does take a lot of time, but who wants to go out anyhow?

Roast the beets:
2 lbs. beets (4–5 medium), scrubbed, trimmed, and halved
Dill Vinegar (p. 100-1)

Preheat oven to 400°F.

Place the beets, cut-side up, on heavy-duty aluminum foil. Wrap them up tightly and bake in preheated oven for 45 minutes. Remove from oven, open up the package, and poke each cut side with a fork a few times.

Sprinkle 1 tsp. dill vinegar on each cut half. Reseal and return to the oven for at least 30 minutes longer, or until beets are tender when pierced with a fork. Open up and set aside to cool.

Soup:
1 tbsp. olive oil
1 onion, chopped
2 stalks celery, chopped
2 medium carrots, peeled and chopped
3 cloves garlic, minced
1 can (284 ml/10 oz.) condensed beef broth, plus water to make 5 cups
1 large can (796 ml/28 oz.) tomatoes, chopped
2 tbsp. olive oil, plus more as needed
2 lbs. stew beef, trimmed of excess fat
flour
reserved beets (above)
2 cups shredded cabbage
2 tbsp. red wine vinegar
2 tsp. sugar
¼ cup fresh dill, minced
salt and pepper, to taste
sour cream and additional minced fresh dill, to serve

In a large soup pot heat the olive oil and in it sauté the onion, celery, carrots, and garlic for about 5 minutes, stirring often. Add the beef broth and water. Drain the liquid from the canned tomatoes into the soup. Cut up the tomatoes and add them as well. Cover and bring to a simmer.

In a large frypan heat the 2 tbsp. olive oil. Dredge the beef lightly in the flour and sauté it in the olive oil in 2 or 3 batches, adding more olive oil as needed, until beef is lightly browned. Add to the soup, cover, and simmer for at least 1½ hours.

When the beets are cooled, peel them and coarsely grate them using a hand grater or a food processor. (If you do this by hand your fingers will turn a deep rose!) Add the beets and cabbage to the soup and simmer another 30 minutes.

Add the red wine vinegar, sugar, salt, and pepper to taste and simmer another 15 minutes. Serve with minced fresh dill and sour cream on the side.

Yield: 4–6 servings.

CHICKEN SOUP

There is nothing like a good homemade chicken soup when you are feeling a bit under the weather—or anytime, for that matter. This recipe is another of those basic ones to guide you along the way. There are so many ways to make a chicken soup—with leftovers, or with the bony parts of a large chicken. You can even use a package of chicken (or turkey) drumsticks. Once you have your stock, you can add a variety of vegetables and grains for different results. The following recipe is our favourite—a bit plain, but sometimes the simple things are the best.

Stock:
2–3 lbs. uncooked bony chicken pieces, or a meaty leftover carcass
1 large onion
2 carrots, cut into large chunks
1–2 stalks celery, cut into large chunks
2–3 sprigs fresh parsley
2–3 sprigs fresh dill (if possible), or 2 tsp. dried
1 tbsp. salt (or to taste)
freshly ground pepper, to taste

Put all ingredients in a large soup pot, cover with water (about 3 quarts)—you want the bones covered. Cover, bring to a boil, lower heat, and simmer about 45 minutes to 1 hour. Remove from heat, strain stock into another pot, and set aside. Remove the meat and bones. Discard the vegetables. When the bones are cool enough to handle, remove any meat from them and discard the skin and bones. Set meat aside.

Taste your stock and adjust seasoning. If the stock is weak, you may add some chicken bouillon powder or cubes (unsalted are best). If you can, let the stock cool down and refrigerate it. The fat will rise to the surface and congeal, so you can easily remove it.

Soup:
stock (about 2 quarts) (above)
½ cup pearl barley
2 carrots, peeled and chopped
1–2 stalks celery, chopped
1 medium onion, chopped
2 cloves garlic, minced
2 tbsp. fresh dill, minced (or 2 tsp. dried)
2 tbsp. fresh parsley, minced
2–3 medium potatoes, peeled and cut into small cubes
reserved chicken (above)

In a large saucepan over medium-high heat bring the chicken stock to a boil. Add the barley, lower heat to a simmer, cover, and gently simmer

for 30 minutes. Add the carrots, celery, onion, garlic, dill, and parsley and simmer, covered, for 15 minutes. Add the potatoes, cover, and simmer an additional 30 minutes. Add the reserved chicken and warm through. Serve.
Yield: 6–8 servings.

Optional Suggestions: Other vegetables to consider are **green beans, peas, fresh tomatoes, zucchini,** or **spinach (or other greens).** Add them to the soup so they will be done but not overcooked. (Greens should be added at the end and cooked just a few minutes.) **Rice** (added at the same time as the carrots, etc.) is good instead of some or all of the barley. **½ cup or more dried macaroni noodles or other small pasta** may be added instead of potatoes 10 minutes before the soup is done.

Variations:
Polish Chicken Soup with Kluskis: This is the version I grew up with and still is one of my favourites. Make chicken stock as above. Do not add any vegetables; instead make **Kluskis** and add them to the clear stock. You may double the recipe if desired.

Kluskis:
1 egg
¾ cup unbleached white flour
¼ cup water
pinch salt
scant ¼ tsp. baking powder

Mix the egg, flour, water, salt, and baking powder in a small bowl until it is smooth. Scrape all the batter into a food mill and force it through into the soup, stirring often during the process. Let the kluskis cook 2 minutes. Add the reserved chicken meat, heat through, and serve.

FALL HARVEST CHICKEN SOUP

Stock for *Chicken Soup* (above)
1 tbsp. olive oil
1 onion, chopped
1 clove garlic, minced
1 red or green pepper, chopped
4–5 large tomatoes, peeled, seeded and chopped
1 small zucchini, sliced

reserved chicken (from stock, above)
1 cup noodles (egg noodles or macaroni)
¼–½ cup fresh basil, slivered

Skim any fat from the chicken soup stock and bring stock to a simmer.

In a medium frypan heat the olive oil and sauté the onion, garlic, and pepper until soft. Add to the soup, along with the tomatoes and zucchini. Simmer about 10 minutes. Add the reserved chicken and noodles and simmer until the noodles are tender, about 10 more minutes. Add the basil, adjust seasonings, and serve.

Yield: 4–6 servings.

Optional Suggestion: If you don't want to go through the trouble of making fresh stock, you may substitute 2 cans (each 284 ml/10 oz.) of condensed chicken stock with 3 cans of water. Any leftover chicken may be added—or you may sauté 1–2 chicken breasts, sliced, if desired.

CREAM OF WILD RICE AND MUSHROOM SOUP

1 cup light cream (18%)
1½ tbsp. unbleached white flour
1 tsp. fresh thyme
1 tbsp. olive oil
1 shallot, minced
1 garlic clove, minced
3 cups chicken broth
¼ cup sherry
⅓ cup raw wild rice, rinsed and drained
½ lb. fresh mushrooms, cleaned and chopped (fresh shiitake mushrooms are best! Remember to remove the tough stems.)
salt and pepper, to taste

In a small bowl whisk together the cream, flour, and thyme. This can be warming to room temperature on the side while the rice is cooking.

In a medium saucepan heat the olive oil and quickly sauté the shallot and garlic for a minute or two. Add the broth, sherry, and wild rice. Bring to a boil, reduce heat, and simmer, covered, for about 50 minutes or until rice is tender. Whisk the cream mixture again then stir into the soup mixture and add the mushrooms. Bring to a simmer, taste, and add salt and pepper, to taste. Simmer, stirring frequently, until soup is thickened and bubbly. Serve.

Yield: 4 servings.

WELSH RAREBIT SOUP

Great on a cold, damp day with a good sandwich.

2–3 medium potatoes (5 cups)
3 cups water
1 tsp. salt
2 bay leaves
4–5 cloves garlic, chopped
2 tbsp. butter
2 tbsp. olive oil
2 large (approx. 2 cups) onions, chopped
1–2 stalks celery, chopped
pinch cayenne pepper
1 tbsp. flour
1 tsp. powdered mustard
1 bottle (341 ml/12 oz.) light beer
1 cup milk
1 can (284 ml/10 oz.) your favourite tomato soup, undiluted
½ lb. Cheddar cheese

In a medium saucepan, bring the potatoes to a boil in the water. Add the salt, bay leaves, and garlic. Cover and continue to simmer until potatoes are soft. Set aside but keep hot.

In a large saucepan heat the butter and olive oil together. Add the onions and celery and sauté a few minutes, or until vegetables are soft. Add the cayenne and sauté a few more seconds. Stir in the flour and powdered mustard, and then slowly add the beer and bring to a boil, stirring constantly. Add the milk, the potatoes, and all the cooking water and bring back to a simmer. Remove from heat. Remove and discard the bay leaves, then stir in the tomato soup. Process the soup in batches in a food processor until smooth. Return to a big pot and reheat. Add the cheese, stir until melted, and serve.

Yield: 4–6 servings.

FISH CHOWDER

I like this soup best on a fall day when you still have fresh thyme around to make it special. If you don't have fresh thyme you can use dried, or for a different flavour use **bay leaf** and **fines herbes**. You may omit the bacon. Sauté the vegetables in 1 tbsp. olive oil.

1 large onion, chopped
1 clove garlic, minced
1 stalk celery, sliced (or 3–4 fresh lovage leaves, minced)
3–4 sprigs fresh thyme (or 1 tsp. dried), or 1 tsp. fines herbes and 1 bay leaf
1 cup white wine
salt and pepper, to taste
1–1½ lbs. fresh fish—cod, haddock, etc. (or frozen and thawed)
4 slices bacon, diced
1 small onion, sliced
1 stalk celery, chopped
1 clove garlic, minced
3–4 cups potatoes, peeled and diced
1 carrot, thinly sliced

Cream Sauce:
3 tbsp. butter
3 tbsp. flour
3 cups milk
1 tsp. salt
pepper, to taste
3 tbsp. fresh thyme, minced, to sprinkle on top (don't use dried thyme)
¾ cup grated aged Cheddar cheese (smoked Cheddar adds another dimension)

In a large frypan, scatter the onion, garlic, celery, and fresh or dried thyme. Add the wine, salt, and pepper, to taste. Cover the pan and let it come to a boil. Add the fish. Cover pan again, lower heat and poach fish until it flakes, 5–8 minutes depending on the thickness of fish. Remove from heat and let fish cool in the broth until you need it.

Heat a large saucepan over medium-high heat. Add the bacon and sauté 5 minutes, stirring constantly, to render the fat. Drain excess fat. Add the onion, celery, and garlic. Lower the heat and gently sauté the mixture, stirring occasionally, until the bacon is brown and the onion is soft. Add 1 tbsp. olive oil if needed.

Gently remove fish from the broth and set it aside. Strain the broth into a large measuring cup and add water to make 2 cups liquid. Discard the vegetables. Add the broth to the bacon mixture and bring to a boil. Add the potatoes and carrot. Cover and cook until potatoes are tender, 15–20 minutes. Remove bay leaf, if used.

While potatoes are cooking, make a light cream sauce: Melt the butter in a small saucepan, add the flour, and stir until blended. Slowly add the milk, whisking often, and bring mixture to a boil. Remove from heat.

When the potatoes are done remove from heat and stir the cream sauce into the soup mixture. Flake the fish and gently stir into the soup. Add the fresh minced thyme and the grated Cheddar cheese. Cover and let it sit 5–10 minutes and serve.

Yield: 4 large or 6 smaller servings.

Optional Suggestions: Use **mussels or clams** for some of the fish. Steam them in the same wine broth, remove from shells, and add to the chowder. Omit cheese. If using canned clams, drain them, measure the liquid, add ½ **cup white wine** and **water** to make the needed 2 cups broth. **Scallops and/or crab** may also be substituted for some of the fish.

NORTH SHORE BOUILLABAISSE

A beautiful soup to serve for the first course of a summer feast—full of fish and shellfish!

2 dozen fresh soft-shell clams
4 dozen fresh mussels
½ cup dry white wine
¼ cup olive oil
1 large onion, chopped
1 large red or green pepper, seeded and diced
4 cloves garlic, minced
1 tsp. paprika
½–1 tsp. red pepper flakes
1 tbsp. fresh rosemary, minced
1 tbsp. fresh thyme, minced
2 bottles clam juice (approx. 4 cups)
1½ cups water
1 cup dry white wine
1 large can (796 ml/28 oz.) diced tomatoes, juice included
1 lb. fresh scallops, halved if large
2 lbs. fresh firm-fleshed fish (cod, haddock, halibut, monkfish—a mixture if possible)
½ cup fresh parsley, minced
½ cup fresh basil, slivered
juice of ½ lemon

Scrub mussels and clams if necessary. Place in a large pot with ½ cup white wine. Cover, bring to a boil, and cook over medium-high heat for 5 minutes. Halfway through the cooking stir by lifting the shellfish at the bottom to the top. Remove from heat and set aside to cool.

In a very large saucepan heat the olive oil and in it sauté the onion, pepper, garlic, paprika, and red pepper flakes, stirring often, for 5 minutes. Add the rosemary, thyme, clam juice, water, 1 cup white wine, and tomatoes. Bring to a boil and cook, covered, for 5 minutes. Remove from heat.

Strain clam and mussel cooking liquid into stock. Remove most of the mussels and all of the clams from the shells, discarding any unopened mussels or clams. (Leave about 1 dozen mussels in the shells, for garnish, if desired.) Set aside.

Bring soup back to a boil. Slice the fish into large chunks. When the soup is boiling again add the scallops and cook 2 minutes. Add the fish and cook, stirring often, just until fish is cooked through, about 3 minutes. Add the reserved clams and mussels and cook just until heated through again. Remove from heat, stir in the fresh parsley and basil, and serve.

Yield: 10–12 servings.

VEGETABLES

Vegetables (and fruits) are a central theme in this cookbook, and in my cooking, and should be looked at in themselves. You've probably figured out by now that we grow and raise as much of our food as we can. And we do it organically, and have for nearly 30 years. Why? And is it worth the effort? (And it *is* a lot of effort!)

To answer the first question, why we grow our food and do it organically: We enjoy working on the land, digging, building up the soil, planting, and harvesting. It helps to keep us fit. It is a joy on a beautiful day to be out working in the garden. It costs less to grow your food organically, without the cost of chemicals. It tastes great!

Is it worth the effort? Most definitely, for all the above reasons. I have the added pleasure of having an amazing garden at my beck and call for every meal. I don't know what could be better for someone who loves to cook.

I do realize gardening is not for everyone, and you folks are lucky as well, since you can now purchase your local produce at farmers' markets. I don't go often enough, but whenever I do go I am thrilled to see the good food available to everyone, and I stock up myself, with locally produced eggs, sausages, fish, and more.

Perhaps the best reason to start with good produce is because your meals will be delicious, and you and your family will be healthier.

Once you have your good vegetables, you want to cook them properly, right?

Several basic cooking methods are used, and are interchangeable. I find **steaming** vegetables the easiest and quickest method of cooking (or precooking) vegetables. If you don't have a steamer, you should consider getting one. They are inexpensive and are designed to fit into different-sized pots. On hot days, steaming is quick and easy.

Another quick indoor method is **stir-frying and "steaming"**: Start by sautéing onions, peppers, garlic, etc., in a frypan; add more vegetables (mushrooms, green beans, snow peas, etc.); sauté a few minutes more; then splash in a tablespoon or two of white wine (or other liquid). Cover and "steam" the vegetables until just done.

On cooler days, you may enjoy **roasting** your vegetables in the oven, and warming up your kitchen at the same time. Roasting adds flavour and is very healthy, since it locks in all those good vitamins. To roast vegetables: Preheat oven to 400°F. Oil a cookie sheet with olive oil. Cut up the vegetables into bite-sized pieces, place in a bowl, drizzle with olive oil, sprinkle with salt and pepper and herbs to taste, and toss gently. Spread the vegetables out on the cookie sheet and roast in preheated oven for 20 minutes, or until tender. Stir the vegetables a few times with a spatula. (Cool before adding to any pasta salad or cold dish.)

Grilling adds even more flavour to your vegetables. Not everyone has a grill, and fewer still have grilling woks, which are readily available in the summer and worth considering if you like to grill. We have become enamoured of grilled fresh garden vegetables. The directions are on page 83. Grilling can be used to bring out the best in vegetables that are getting a bit tired.

No matter which method you choose to cook your vegetables, be sure to start with the freshest you can find.

CREAMED SPRING SPINACH

This is delicious in the spring with fresh spinach, dill, and chives. "Pan steaming" spinach is an excellent way to prepare it for any recipe that needs cooked, drained spinach, and if steamed until just wilted it remains a bright green that looks like spring itself.

1 lb. fresh spinach

Sauce:
2 tbsp. butter
2 tbsp. flour
¾ cup milk
salt and pepper, to taste
½ cup fresh dill, minced
½ cup fresh garlic chives, minced

Wash spinach well, shake off excess moisture, coarsely chop, and "pan steam" using a large frypan with a lid. Place spinach in pan, cover and "steam," stirring often, until spinach is just wilted. Remove from heat and drain.

While spinach is cooking, prepare the cream sauce: In a small saucepan melt the butter, stir in the flour and gradually add the milk, stirring constantly until sauce is smooth and bubbling. Remove from heat, add salt and pepper, to taste, and stir in the dill and garlic chives. Add the cooked and drained spinach, mix in thoroughly, and serve.

Yield: 2–4 servings.

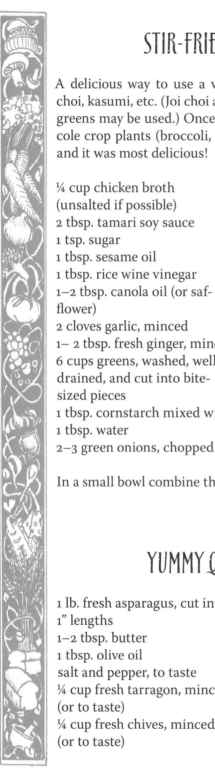

STIR-FRIED SPRING GREENS

A delicious way to use a variety of spring greens—spinach, joi choi, kasumi, etc. (Joi choi and kasumi are oriental greens—other greens may be used.) Once when we had an abundance of young cole crop plants (broccoli, cabbage, and the like), we used them, and it was most delicious!

¼ cup chicken broth (unsalted if possible)
2 tbsp. tamari soy sauce
1 tsp. sugar
1 tbsp. sesame oil
1 tbsp. rice wine vinegar
1–2 tbsp. canola oil (or safflower)
2 cloves garlic, minced
1– 2 tbsp. fresh ginger, minced
6 cups greens, washed, well drained, and cut into bite-sized pieces
1 tbsp. cornstarch mixed with
1 tbsp. water
2–3 green onions, chopped

In a small bowl combine the chicken broth, tamari soy sauce, sugar, sesame oil, and rice wine vinegar.

In a wok, heat the canola oil. Add the garlic and ginger and sauté for a few seconds. Add the prepared greens and stir-fry a minute. Add the broth mixture, cover, and "steam" 1–2 minutes or until greens are wilted. Stir in the cornstarch mixture and cook until thickened, 20–30 seconds. Gently mix in the green onions and serve.

Yield: 2–4 servings.

YUMMY QUICK ASPARAGUS

1 lb. fresh asparagus, cut into 1" lengths
1–2 tbsp. butter
1 tbsp. olive oil
salt and pepper, to taste
¼ cup fresh tarragon, minced (or to taste)
¼ cup fresh chives, minced (or to taste)

¼ cup freshly grated Parmesan cheese

Steam the asparagus until just tender. (This may be done in advance.)

In a medium skillet heat the butter and olive oil. Add the

asparagus and sauté a few minutes, or until tender-crisp and heated through. Add the salt, pepper, tarragon, chives, and mix together well. Place in a serving bowl, top with the Parmesan cheese, and serve.

Yield: 2–4 servings.

KAREN'S GINGERED WAX BEANS

Karen Berrouard came up with this great recipe for a dinner party one day. It is so simple and so delicious, you'll want to serve it often.

1 lb. fresh wax beans, trimmed and cut into serving pieces
3 tbsp. butter
1 tbsp. fresh ginger, grated
salt and pepper, to taste

Precook beans by steaming just until they are tender-crisp, 3–4 minutes. Drain well in a colander. (This may be done in advance.)

In a large skillet melt the butter, add the ginger and the beans, and sauté a few minutes until the beans are coated and heated through. Season to taste with salt and pepper and serve.

Yield: 4 servings.

ITALIAN STIR-FRIED BROCCOLI

2 tbsp. olive oil
2 cloves garlic
1 head broccoli, cleaned and cut into bite-sized pieces
½ red or green pepper (optional)
2 tbsp. balsamic vinegar
1–2 tbsp. white wine
salt and pepper, to taste
1 green onion, chopped

2 Italian plum tomatoes, diced (or 2 medium-small tomatoes)

Heat the olive oil in a wok. Stir-fry the garlic for 20 seconds. Add the broccoli and pepper, if used, and continue to stir-fry for 1 minute. Add the balsamic vinegar, 1 tbsp. white wine, salt, and pepper. Lower the heat,

cover the wok and let the veggies "steam" for about 5 minutes (or until broccoli is tender-crisp). Check a few times, and if the liquid is evaporating too quickly add an additional tablespoon of white wine. Add green onion and tomatoes and stir-fry an additional minute, or until the tomatoes are heated through. Serve.

Yield: 3–4 servings.

PIQUANT BROCCOLI

A simple recipe to perk up a tired broccoli.

1 head broccoli
3 tbsp. olive oil
1 tbsp. red wine vinegar (or balsamic vinegar)
1 clove garlic, minced
salt and pepper, to taste
3 tbsp. Parmesan cheese

Steam broccoli until tender-crisp, remove to a bowl, and toss with dressing. While broccoli is cooking place olive oil, red wine vinegar, garlic, salt, pepper, and Parmesan cheese in a food processor and pulse until garlic is chopped fine (or mince garlic very finely, then blend ingredients in a small bowl using a whisk). Pour over the drained broccoli and serve.

Yield: 3–4 servings.

ROASTED TOMATOES

This summer I discovered the joys of roasted tomatoes. Roasting is a very simple way to make something even more special from a beautiful, sun-ripened tomato. The process of slow roasting brings out the tomatoes' flavour while it reduces the juices, rendering the tomatoes quite delightful for use in many recipes. Try them instead of a sauce for pizza, or in many recipes calling for diced tomatoes—or just eat them! Tomatoes that are less than perfect (toward the end of the season) also benefit from slow roasting.

tomatoes

Preheat oven to 300°F.

Line a cookie sheet with aluminum foil. (This step is important, since the juice roasting tomatoes can dissolve non-stick coatings from some pans!)

Wash and dry the tomatoes. Trim them of any bad spots, and slice them in half horizontally. Arrange the halves, cut-side up, on the prepared sheet and place them in the oven for 1¼–1½ hours, checking them occasionally and rotating the pan at least once. As they are cooking, you might wish to press them lightly to release the juices. If they are large,

juicy tomatoes, you might need more cooking time. Remove from the baking sheet with a metal spatula and use as desired.

Optional Suggestion: Pack the tomatoes into small, well-sealed plastic containers and freeze. Add to soups, stews, pastas, pot roasts, and other dishes during the winter!

Variations:
Garlic-Lovers' Roasted Tomatoes: Proceed as above, but sprinkle the tomato halves with **minced garlic,** to taste, and drizzle with olive oil. Baste and press lightly to release juices a few times during baking.

ROASTED TOMATO RELISH

1½–2 cups roasted tomatoes (above) cooled and diced
1 tbsp. red wine vinegar
1 tsp. sugar

salt and pepper, to taste

Gently toss all ingredients together and serve.

CORN SAUTÉ

An end-of-summer dish. This is good at room temperature. It is more of a relish than a side dish and is good with fish or poultry or as part of a Mexican meal.

1–2 tbsp. olive oil
1 tbsp. butter
4 cups corn (cut from 6 cobs)
2 medium tomatoes, chopped
salt and pepper, to taste
1½ tbsp. sugar
juice ½ lime
3–4 tbsp. fresh cilantro, minced

In a large skillet heat the olive oil and butter and in it quickly sauté the corn and tomatoes for about 5 minutes, or until the corn turns colour. Add salt and pepper, to taste. Stir in the sugar and lime juice, sprinkle with the chopped cilantro, and let cool to room temperature. Serve.

Yield: 4 servings.

SUMMER SQUASH MEDLEY

Everyone needs a recipe to use a lot of zucchini or yellow summer squash (or both!) when they are in abundance. This is my attempt. When it is zucchini season, try to keep on top of your crop by harvesting them when they are young, small, and tender. If you have leftovers try heating them up and putting them in an omelet, topped with cheese! There are many variations to this recipe depending on the herbs used.

3 tbsp. olive oil
1 onion, chopped
½ cup fresh sweet pepper, chopped
1 clove garlic, minced
½ small jalapeño pepper, finely minced (optional)
1 medium-sized zucchini (about 6–8" long), cut into chunks

1 medium-sized yellow squash (about 6–8" long) (or additional zucchini), cut into chunks
3–4 small fresh tomatoes, chopped
salt and pepper, to taste
fresh or dried herbs (or both), to taste:

Italian: fresh basil, fresh parsley, fresh or dried oregano
Greek: fresh or dried oregano, cinnamon, green onions
Mexican: fresh or dried oregano, cumin, fresh coriander (add coriander just before serving)

Preheat oven to 350°F.

In a large skillet sauté the onion in the olive oil over medium heat for a few minutes. Add the sweet pepper, garlic, jalapeño pepper (if used), and sauté a few minutes longer.

Add the squash and sauté an additional 5 minutes, stirring often. Add the tomatoes, salt, pepper, and herbs of your choice. Sauté a few more minutes, stirring gently.

Transfer vegetable mixture to an ovenproof casserole (or leave in the skillet if it is ovenproof and has a cover). Cover and bake for 30 minutes. Remove and serve, or let it cool to room temperature and serve.

Yield: 4–6 servings.

"DILLICIOUS" ZUCCHINI GRATIN

Another way to use up those abundant zucchini. This is best made with small to medium zucchini. If you do use large ones, press out some of the excess moisture after you grate the zucchini; otherwise your gratin will be a bit soggy. You may serve this as a vegetable side dish, or, cut into smaller pieces, as an appetizer. It keeps well in the fridge for several days and is excellent cold for lunch.

2 lbs. zucchini (small to medium), washed and coarsely grated
3 large eggs
3–4 scallions, thinly sliced
½ cup fresh parsley, minced
½ cup fresh dill, minced
1 cup mozzarella, coarsely grated
¼ cup feta cheese, crumbled

1 tsp. salt, or to taste
pepper, to taste
1¼ cup unbleached white flour
1 cup fresh breadcrumbs (made in a food processor)
¼ cup Parmesan cheese
¼ cup butter, cut into bits

Lightly butter a 9" x 13" baking dish. Preheat oven to 375°F.

Place the grated zucchini in a large mixing bowl. Add the eggs, one at a time, and beat them in with a mixing spoon. Add the scallions, parsley, dill, mozzarella, feta, salt, and pepper. Blend the mixture well. Sprinkle in the flour, mixing gently, until the mixture is well blended. Spread in prepared baking dish.

In a small bowl toss the breadcrumbs with the Parmesan cheese and sprinkle over the zucchini. Dot with butter and bake in preheated oven for 35–40 minutes, or until top is nicely browned. Serve.

Yield: 8–10 servings, or more as an appetizer.

ZUCCHINI "FRITTERS"

These little tidbits are not exactly fritters, because fritters are deep-fried and these are sautéed in oil. But they are similar in intent—a tasty mélange of vegetables, herbs, eggs, and flour. I often make them to round out a meal when zucchini are available.

¾–1 lb. fresh zucchini, coarsely grated (3–4 cups)
2 eggs
½ cup green onions, minced
½ cup fresh dill, minced
salt and freshly ground pepper, to taste
⅓ cup grated Parmesan cheese
½ cup flour
4 tbsp. olive oil

Grate the zucchini into a bowl, add eggs, and beat gently until well blended. Add the onions, fresh herbs, salt, and pepper, and mix well. Add the grated Parmesan cheese and stir gently but thoroughly. Add the flour and again stir gently.

Heat the oil in a cast-iron frypan. When it is hot drop heaping tablespoonfuls of the "batter" into it and flatten a bit if necessary. Sauté for about 3–4 minutes on each side, or until golden-brown. Remove and drain on paper towel-lined plate. Continue until all the batter is used up, adding more oil to the pan if necessary. You should get about a dozen "fritters." Serve.

Yield: 12 "fritters."

Optional Suggestions: You may use some fresh **carrot**, coarsely grated, in place of half of the zucchini. Other fresh herbs may be used in place of dill, although we definitely prefer dill in this recipe. **Fresh basil, thyme,** or **tarragon** goes well with **parsley.** This recipe is also delicious without the cheese.

PUMPKIN "FRITTERS"

Another vegetable "fritter" that is lightly sautéed rather than deep-fried. Try this as a side dish with roast chicken or beef, or as

part of a buffet.
½ cup flour
1 tsp. salt
¼–½ tsp. each cinnamon, ginger, cloves (or to taste)
2 tbsp. sugar
2 cups cooked pumpkin, mashed
2 eggs, lightly beaten
canola or safflower oil

In a small bowl mix together the flour, salt, spices, and sugar. In a larger bowl place your mashed pumpkin. Add the flour mixture and eggs and stir together to blend well.

Heat the canola oil, to a depth of ¼" in a medium cast-iron skillet over medium-high heat. Drop the batter by spoonfuls and sauté until lightly browned on each side. Add more oil, if necessary. Drain on paper towel and serve.

Yield: 16 "fritters."

THYMELY (OR UNTHYMELY) CORN FRITTERS

These tasty little things are more like the traditional fritters than the preceding two recipes. The addition of fresh thyme makes them special. If you don't have fresh thyme, **don't** use dried. I tried it once and found the dried thyme overpowering! Try fresh cilantro or parsley instead.

2 cups corn kernels (cut from 2 cobs) (or frozen corn, cooked and drained)
2 eggs
⅔ cup flour
1 tsp. salt, or to taste
1 tsp. paprika
1 tbsp. sugar
2 tsp. baking powder
½ jalapeño pepper, seeded and minced (optional)
1 small red onion (or 1 green onion), minced
2–3 tbsp. fresh thyme, minced (or fresh cilantro or parsley)
canola or safflower oil

Place the corn and eggs in a food processor. Process on high for a few seconds, just until the eggs are blended in. (You want the corn to remain chunky.) Transfer mixture to a medium bowl. In a small bowl mix the flour, salt, paprika, sugar, and baking powder. Add to the first mixture and beat just until blended. Gently stir in the jalapeño pepper (if used), onion, and fresh thyme.

In a medium-sized cast-iron skillet heat enough canola oil to measure ½" up the side of the pan. When it is very hot, drop the batter in by tablespoons and "fry" 3–4 minutes on each side, or until the fritters are golden-brown. Remove with a slotted spoon to a paper towel-lined plate to drain. Don't crowd the fritters in the oil. Repeat frying, adding more oil if necessary, until finished. Serve.

Yield: 4 servings.

GRILLED VEGETABLES

To make these grilled vegetables you need a gas grill and a grilling "wok," which is available at many hardware stores. (They come square or round. Ours is shaped like a small round wok, with a flat bottom and holes throughout.) Grilled vegetables are fantastic! You can use whatever you have on hand, as long as the vegetables are large enough not to fall through the holes. We always include onions for their flavour and find mushrooms a great addition. Avoid tomatoes—they are too juicy.

vegetables: (4–6 cups)
onions, halved or quartered
red or green peppers, cut into chunks
broccoli and/or cauliflower, rinsed, dried, and cut into bite-sized pieces
zucchini, cut into 1½" cubes
green beans, cut in half
¼ cup olive oil
1 clove garlic, minced
salt and pepper, to taste
1 tsp. fines herbes (or your choice of herbs)
mushrooms
snow peas

Toss together the vegetables (all except the mushrooms and snow peas) with the olive oil, garlic, salt, pepper, and herbs. This is best done at least ½–1 hour before you plan to cook.

When you are ready to grill, oil the special pan lightly with olive oil. Heat it up on the barbecue over medium heat, add the vegetables, and close the barbecue lid. Check and stir the mixture every 5 to 10 minutes. Add the mushrooms and snow peas after 15 minutes. After about 30 minutes, check for tenderness. The vegetables should be tender-crisp and ready to eat. Serve.

Yield: 4–6 servings.

GRILLED CORN

Simple and delicious.

corn on the cob
butter

Prepare your barbecue (or fire)

Grill the corn, basting very lightly with butter, turning often, until the corn is lightly browned. Serve.

EAST INDIAN GRILLED EGGPLANT

This was given to me by Rita Sahajpal. Rita herself raves about this recipe—it was one of her favourites, I believe.

1 large fresh eggplant
3 tbsp. butter
1 medium onion, minced (or 2 green onions, minced)
1 tbsp. fresh minced ginger
1 clove garlic, minced (optional)
¼ tsp. cumin seed
½ tsp. ground coriander
¼ tsp. crushed foenugreek seed
⅛ tsp. turmeric
¼ tsp. hot pepper (or cayenne), or to taste
1 medium tomato, diced

Char your eggplant on the barbecue (or over an open flame), turning often until the skin is blackened all over. Rinse under cold water to remove the skin, dice into ½" cubes, and set aside. (Treat this eggplant as you would red peppers when you char them.)

In a medium skillet melt the butter and sauté the onion, ginger, and garlic (if desired), until browned. Add the cumin seed, coriander, foenugreek, turmeric, and hot pepper. Cook and stir an additional minute or two. Add the tomato and the reserved eggplant. Cover and cook over low heat for 5–10 minutes. Serve. This is also good served at room temperature.

Yield: 4 servings.

NEW POTATOES AND BASIL

This recipe proves that the simplest things are often the best! The potatoes must be really "new"—the first of the season when the skins come off with a little scrubbing. And the basil must be fresh.

new potatoes
fresh basil leaves, minced (¼ cup per 4 cups potatoes), or to taste
butter, to taste

salt and pepper, to taste

Wash the new potatoes and gently scrub them to remove most of the skins. (Don't worry if some skins remain.) Halve or quarter the potatoes (depending on size—some may even be left whole) and cook in a small to medium saucepan in ½" of water, stirring often, until they are just tender. This will take 5–10 minutes, depending upon the size of the potato pieces and the quantity cooked. (Alternatively, steam until tender.)

Drain any excess water, add the butter, salt and pepper to taste, and fresh basil. Gently mix and serve.

POTATO CAKES

I like to make extra and have the leftovers the next morning for breakfast, topped with a fried egg.

2 pounds medium potatoes, scrubbed (about 6 medium potatoes)

In the morning steam potatoes until half done, or cook the potatoes in boiling water to cover for 10 minutes. Drain. Cool the potatoes and refrigerate until later. They should be in the fridge for at least 4 hours. If you can't do this in the morning, the night before is fine.

1 small onion, finely minced
salt and pepper, to taste
2 tbsp. olive oil
2 tbsp. butter
1–1½ tbsp. milk
1½ tbsp. additional butter, softened

Peel and coarsely grate the potatoes into a large bowl. Add the onion, salt, and pepper and gently toss with a fork.

Heat a medium-sized cast-iron griddle or frypan over high heat. Add the olive oil and butter and when it is sizzling add the potato mixture using your hands and a spatula to shape and flatten it into a large round pancake (about 10" diameter). Immediately turn the heat down to low and let it cook for 20 minutes or until the bottom is nicely crusted. (You may need to move the griddle around the burner to have it brown evenly.) If your heat is low enough, there is no danger of it burning. When the bottom is browned, sprinkle the milk over the surface,

spread the additional butter on top, and flip the "pancake" over. (I find it easiest to cut it into quarters with a sharp knife and flip each quarter.)

Continue cooking 10–15 minutes, or until the bottom is nicely browned. Serve in quarters.

Yield: 4 servings.

GARLIC-ROASTED POTATOES

A delicious accompaniment to lamb chops, roast chicken, and many more main dishes. These potatoes smell absolutely fantastic when roasting. They are not as good reheated and should be served immediately. This recipe may be expanded, but do not crowd the potatoes in the frying pan or they won't be as crispy. If you don't have a large pan, use two, or halve the recipe.

¼ cup olive oil
8–10 medium sized potatoes
2 cloves garlic, minced
salt and pepper, to taste

Preheat oven to 400°F. Preheat a large cast-iron frypan with the olive oil in it in the oven.

Prepare potatoes by scrubbing them very well and trimming them of any eyes or bad spots. If you have "new" potatoes and they are thin-skinned, you can forego the peeling. Cut potatoes into chunks ¾"–1" in size.

When your frypan is hot, remove it from the oven and set it over medium-high heat. Add potatoes and gently toss them in the olive oil with a

spatula until all the potatoes are lightly coated. Bake in the lower ⅓ of your oven for 15 minutes, turning the potatoes with the spatula after 7–8 minutes. Sprinkle the garlic, salt, and pepper over the potatoes and return to oven for another 10 minutes. Remove pan from oven and again gently turn potatoes with a spatula. (They may stick somewhat to the pan, but this gets easier as they cook.) Continue cooking and turning potatoes for another 15–20 minutes, or until they are golden-brown and tender when pierced with a fork. Serve.

Yield: 4 servings.

PERFECT HASH BROWNS

A lower-fat version of an old favourite. I always make a large batch and keep some to cook up for breakfast the next day, with a fried egg on top.

6–8 medium-large potatoes, scrubbed
1 medium onion, chopped
1 or 2 cloves garlic, minced
salt and pepper, to taste
Cajun or Creole spice mixture (optional)
2 tbsp. olive oil
1 tbsp. butter
½ cup fresh parsley, minced (optional)

Steam (or boil) the potatoes until they are almost tender. They should still be a bit firm when poked with a fork. Drain and cool.

Peel and slice the potatoes. Set aside.

Over medium heat in a large frypan (cast-iron if possible) with a lid, heat the olive oil and sauté the onion and garlic a few minutes. Lower heat, cover, and cook a few more minutes or until the onion is soft. Add and melt the butter. Add the potatoes and sprinkle to taste with salt, pepper, and Creole or Cajun spice, if desired. Press down with a spatula, cover, and cook about 10 minutes, or until bottom is nicely browned. Turn potatoes, press down again with a spatula, and cook, uncovered, an additional 10 minutes, or until nicely browned. Sprinkle with the parsley, if desired, and serve.

Yield: 4–6 servings.

BEETS MASHED WITH SOUR CREAM (OR YOGURT)

A very simple, delicious, and beautiful way to serve beets. The beets turn a beautiful magenta colour when the sour cream (or yogurt) is added.

5–6 medium beets (or 2–3 larger ones)
salt and pepper, to taste
1 cup sour cream (or yogurt)

Wash and trim the beets. (It isn't necessary to peel them, since the peels slip off easily after the beets are cooked.)

Cook beets by steaming or boiling until very tender. Drain and cool until you can handle them. Peel beets and mash. Return to a pot and warm them gently over low heat. Add the salt and pepper, to taste and mix in the sour cream (or yogurt). Heat through, but do not boil Serve.

Yield: 4–6 servings.

Variation:
Beets Mashed with Tzatziki: Proceed as above, using homemade or purchased *Tzatziki* (p. 16) instead of the yogurt or sour cream. It is surprisingly delicious.

BUTTERNUT SQUASH "CHUTNEY"

This is a delicious accompaniment to many meals and excellent as part of a potluck dinner. It is best served at room temperature.

2½–3 lbs. butternut squash (5–6 cups)
1 tbsp. olive oil
salt and pepper, to taste
½ cup pecan pieces, toasted
2½ cups fresh or frozen whole cranberries
1 cup orange juice
⅓ cup sugar
2–3 tbsp. pickled jalapeño slices, or to taste, minced (optional)

Preheat oven to 400°F.

Peel and seed the squash, cut into 1" cubes, place in a bowl, and toss with the olive oil, salt, and pepper. Spread the squash on an ungreased cookie sheet and bake in preheated oven for 40–45 minutes, stirring occasionally, until squash is tender and browning.

When the squash is finished, remove from oven and lower temperature to 350°F. Spread the pecans on a baking pan and toast them in the oven for 5–7 minutes. (Be careful not to burn them.) Remove from oven and set aside.

While the squash is baking, prepare the sauce: Place the cranberries, orange juice, and sugar in a small saucepan. Bring to a boil and simmer about 5 minutes, or until the cranberries pop.

When the squash is finished baking, place it in a large serving bowl, pour the sauce over, and mix well. Fold in the minced jalapeño, if desired. Let mixture cool to room temperature.

Just before serving stir in the reserved toasted pecans and serve.

Yield: 6–8 servings

WINTER SQUASH BAKED IN HONEYED APPLE CIDER

Any winter squash can be used in this recipe; however, it is easier to peel a smooth-skinned squash such as butternut or buttercup rather than acorn or Hubbard.

8 cups raw winter squash, peeled and cut in 1" cubes
1 onion, coarsely chopped
¼ cup apple cider
3 tbsp. butter
2 tbsp. honey
salt and pepper, to taste
½ tsp. each freshly grated nutmeg and ginger

Preheat oven to 400°F.

Put the squash cubes in a large buttered baking dish (7" x 11") and sprinkle chopped onion evenly over the squash. Combine apple cider, butter, honey, salt, pepper, nutmeg, and ginger in a small saucepan and heat just until the butter and honey are melted. Pour over squash, mix with a spoon, place in preheated oven, and bake 20 minutes. Remove from oven and again mix with a spoon. If the squash seems to be drying out too much, cover with foil. Return to oven and bake an additional 20 minutes, removing foil (if used) for last 5 minutes.

Yield: 6–8 servings.

QUICK CABBAGE-NOODLE STIR-FRY

A great side dish that is quick and easy to make. Do not try this with old cabbage.

2 tbsp. butter
2 tbsp. olive oil
1 small onion, chopped
1 carrot, coarsely grated
1 small green or red pepper, chopped
1 small cabbage (about 4 cups), slivered (savoy is best)
½ cup chicken stock
2 tbsp. white wine
salt and pepper, to taste
⅓ cup sour cream
⅓ cup fresh dill, minced
⅓ pkg. rice or wheat vermicelli, broken into pieces, cooked according to package directions and drained

In a large frypan heat the butter and olive oil. In it sauté the onion, carrot, and pepper until soft. Add the cabbage, chicken stock, white wine, salt, and pepper and bring to a simmer. Cover and cook over medium-low heat until cabbage is cooked, about 10 minutes. Stir a few times during the cooking.

Remove from heat. Stir in the sour cream and dill. Return to heat and heat through, but do not boil. Stir in the cooked noodles and continue cooking a few minutes, or until noodles are heated through. Serve.

Yield: 4 servings.

SAVOY CABBAGE AND APPLES IN CIDER

Full of fall flavours and quick to prepare, this is a good side dish for sausage or roast meats.

4 tbsp. butter
1 medium onion, thinly sliced
½ medium-sized savoy cabbage, cored, and thinly sliced (approx. 4 cups)
1 cup apple cider
pinch of ground cloves
grating of nutmeg
½ tsp. celery seeds

1 tsp. salt, or to taste
pepper, to taste
2 tart apples, peeled, cored, and thinly sliced

In a large saucepan melt the butter, add the onion, and sauté for 5 minutes, or until it is soft. Add the savoy cabbage and sauté a few more minutes, stirring constantly. Add the apple cider, cloves, nutmeg, celery seeds, salt, and pepper. Bring to a boil, lower heat to a simmer, cover, and cook about 10 minutes. Add the apple slices, cover, and cook an additional 2–3 minutes. Serve.

Yield: 4 servings.

SWEET AND SOUR RED CABBAGE

3 slices bacon, diced
1 medium onion, thinly sliced
1 small head red cabbage, or ½ a large red cabbage, quartered, cored, and thinly sliced
1 apple, peeled, cored, and chopped
3 tbsp. red wine vinegar
2 tbsp. honey
2 tbsp. red wine (or apple cider or juice)
salt and pepper, to taste
½ tsp. caraway seed (optional)

In a medium saucepan cook the diced bacon over medium-high heat, stirring, until beginning to get crisp, about 5 minutes. Drain excess fat. Add the onion and sauté 5 minutes more, stirring, until onion is beginning to soften. Add the cabbage, apple, red wine vinegar, honey, and red wine. Cover and simmer about 30 minutes, stirring occasionally. Taste and add salt and pepper, if needed, and the caraway seed, if desired. Cover and simmer an additional 15 minutes. Serve.

Yield: 4 servings.

NOTES

PUTTING UP
THE HARVEST

Whether you live in the country and have a large garden, or in the city and use your local farmers' market, you may want to preserve the local produce available in abundance in the summer for the long winter months ahead. This section contains some basic recipes that I have developed over the years to try to cope with huge amounts of produce such as tomatoes. It also includes more exotic ideas for preserving herbs and fruits. Anything of the harvest you freeze, can, dry, or otherwise "put up" can enhance the winter menu, especially if you live in a place where fresh produce is expensive and sometimes of dubious quality.

A FEW GENERAL "RULES" FOR FREEZING

Berries: Strawberries and raspberries should be sprinkled with sugar (to taste), gently mixed and spooned into plastic bags, sealed, and frozen. The sugar inhibits enzyme action, which is what spoils the fruit. Raspberries freeze extremely well and taste fantastic all winter long. Strawberries, on the other hand, lose their flavour after a few months. Blueberries freeze well without sugar, as does rhubarb, cut into pieces.

Vegetables: Peas, green beans, spinach, and corn (cut off the cob) all freeze very well. They must first be blanched to stop the enzyme action. Get your largest pot and put in about ½" of boiling water. Prepare your vegetables and "steam" them until they turn colour, mixing gently to move the vegetables from top to bottom, so they cook evenly. Drain, chill vegetables quickly to prevent further cooking, put into plastic bags, and seal. Green beans lose their flavour first, but they are always good in soups and stews.

Berries for "Jamming": If you don't have time to make jam in the summer, measure the berries; freeze whole, very lightly sugared; mark the amount on your freezer container; and freeze. When you have time for berries, just thaw your frozen berries (in a bowl large enough to hold them and all the juice as they thaw). Add the proper amount of sugar and continue as usual.

TOMATO SAUCE FOR FREEZING

This is a general recipe for making a tomato sauce when you have an abundance of tomatoes. There are no quantities because when I make it I use all the tomatoes that need to be processed that day (a lot when you have between 30 and 40 tomato plants!) and add onions, garlic, peppers, herbs, and spices to taste. I have better-tasting results when I add a lot of onion, garlic, and peppers, since frozen tomatoes, no matter what you do, seem to get bitter. If you don't want to take the time to seed the tomatoes, I wouldn't even bother as the result will be bitter and not very tasty. When you thaw out a batch you can adjust the seasonings to suit what you are making that day.

fresh ripe tomatoes
onions
garlic
peppers
celery (optional)
olive oil, for sautéing
salt and pepper
oregano, Italian herbs, basil
sugar
tomato paste
wine, either red or white (optional)
fresh basil to taste (I add a good handful), slivered

Wash tomatoes. Cut off the tops and any bad spots. Remove any peels that come off easily. Cut them in half horizontally. Set a strainer over a bowl and squeeze the seeds from the tomato halves into the strainer. (You need to remove the seeds because they will make your sauce bitter if you don't.) Put the seeded halves into a food processor along with the juice in the bowl beneath the strainer and any pulp you can mash through the strainer. Buzz some of the tomatoes in your food processor until smooth and place them in a large stockpot. Continue buzzing batches of tomatoes until all are processed. Bring tomatoes to a boil. Lower heat and simmer, skimming any foam that comes to the surface.

While your tomatoes are coming to a boil, continue processing quantities of onion, garlic, peppers, and celery (if desired) in your food processor. Sauté these lightly in olive oil, if possible. Add them to the tomato mixture. Season to taste with salt, pepper, oregano, Italian herbs, basil, and about 1 tbsp. sugar for every 2 quarts of tomatoes.

You may add approximately one 156 ml/5.5 oz. can of tomato paste per 2–3 quarts to help thicken the sauce up. Some wine, either red or white, can be added also. Continue cooking until mixture reaches desired thickness. When you have reached the desired thickness, remove from heat, stir in the basil, and let it cool down. Cooking time varies greatly depending on the type of tomatoes used and the amount of liquid in the tomatoes. (Plum tomatoes require less cooking time—as do smaller tomatoes. The large, juicy beefsteaks take longer.)

When your sauce is cool, ladle into plastic containers, cool further, label, and freeze.

It is handy to freeze sauce in different sizes. The 500 g yogurt containers are good for several pizzas, whereas lasagna or spaghetti sauce would need at least a litre (quart) container.

Optional Suggestion: When you are about halfway finished cooking, you can add additional tomatoes that have been peeled and seeded then coarsely chopped. This will give you a chunkier sauce.

WINTER SAUCE

I always have some of the following sauce frozen in the freezer to have on hand for spaghetti, lasagna, pizzas, and other recipes.

1 onion, chopped
2 cloves garlic, minced
1 tbsp. olive oil
1 1-litre container sauce from above recipe
1 large can (796 ml/28 oz.) tomato sauce
1 small can (796 ml/28 oz.) tomato paste
½ cup red or white wine
1 tbsp. each dried oregano and Italian herbs
1 tsp. salt (or to taste)
pepper, to taste

1 tsp. sugar
1 lb. ground beef
2–3 Italian sausages, casings removed
½ recipe frozen **Pesto** (p. 152-3), without the cheese (or ½ cup purchased) (optional, but very preferable)

In a large saucepan, heat the olive oil and in it sauté the onion and garlic until soft. Add the homemade sauce, can of tomato sauce, tomato paste, wine, oregano, Italian herbs, salt, pepper, and sugar. Bring to a simmer.

In a cast-iron skillet, brown the ground beef. Drain excess fat and add to the sauce. Sauté the sausage until browned and add to the sauce also. Contin-ue to simmer the sauce until it is nicely thickened. Serve or cool down and place in either 500-gram or 1-litre plastic containers. Chill down and then freeze.

Yield: 3 litres, approximately

SALSA

Another recipe that uses a lot of tomatoes! This is canned instead of frozen. It takes a lot of time but is well worth the effort. The following recipe can be doubled, tripled, or even quadrupled if you have a bumper crop—and a large enough pot! (My biggest pots hold 2½ batches.)

8 cups tomatoes, chopped and processed in a food processor, measured after processing
4 cups peppers (a combination of red, green, and yellow if possible), cleaned, seeded, and chopped
1 cup jalapeño peppers (or less, to taste)
2 cups chopped onions
4 cloves garlic, minced
1 cup apple cider vinegar
1 small can (796 ml/28 oz.) tomato paste
2 tbsp. sugar
1 tbsp. salt
2–3 tsp. paprika
1 tbsp. dried oregano
¼ cup chopped fresh coriander

Process the tomatoes in batches in a food processor as in the preceding recipe, but leave them chunkier. Place them in a large pot and slowly bring them to a boil. Lower heat and keep at a simmer. Skim foam from time to time. In the meantime, process the peppers and add them to the pot. Next chop the jalapeños, discarding the seeds if you want your salsa milder, keeping some seeds for a hotter version. Add the onions, garlic, cider vinegar, tomato paste, sugar, salt, paprika, and oregano, and simmer the mixture for about one hour, or until it reaches desired thickness, continuing to skim any foam that rises

to the surface. (It will thicken a bit more when cooled.) A larger batch will require more cooking time.

When the salsa is thick enough, stir in the fresh coriander. Simmer an additional 5 minutes.

While the salsa is cooking, sterilize your canning jars. One batch will fill 3 or 4 1-quart jars. Ladle the salsa into the sterilized jars, seal with new lids, and process them in a boiling water bath for 20 minutes. Remove and let them cool, tightening lids if needed as they cool.

The salsa needs a few days at least to fully develop its flavour. If you cannot find any fresh coriander it won't be quite the same, but it still will be good. If you have access to fresh coriander earlier in the season, make some **Coriander Pesto** (p. 152-3) and add 2 tbsp. per batch!

Yield: 3 qts., approximately.

OVEN SUN-DRIED TOMATOES

Making your own dried tomatoes is easier than you think. They are delicious snipped into any tomato sauce or soup. Or use in any recipe calling for sun-dried tomatoes.

Italian paste tomatoes, ripe but not too soft, with no blemishes
salt

Wash and dry the tomatoes. Halve them, or quarter them if large, and cut out the stem and surrounding hard tissue. Place the tomatoes, cut-side up, on a drying rack. Sprinkle them lightly with salt and place them in your oven. Turn the oven on to 200°F and leave the tomatoes for 30 minutes. Turn the oven off and leave them.

(Best not to open the oven door.)

If you have a propane oven, keep the tomatoes in it until you reach desired dryness. You may want to hasten the progress of the drying by turning on your oven to 200°F for 20–30 minutes every 4 hours, or whenever you can. This will take several days if you want to store the tomatoes dry. If you have an electric oven, you will have to turn your oven on and off more often, or leave it on low and prop open the oven door.

When they are totally dry, store in a sterilized jar in a cool place. If there is any moisture left, the tomatoes may grow mould.

Another method is to dry them until they are half dried, following above directions, but store them in a sterilized jar filled with olive oil. Add a sprig of fresh rosemary or thyme, if possible. These are ready to snip into salads or to use as a pizza topping, and store in a cool dark place.

FROZEN HERBED BUTTER ROLL

A great way to preserve some fresh herbs for those long winter months, since you can easily cut off the needed amount from your butter roll and return the rest to the freezer. The combination of herbs in this recipe is one of my favourites. Other herbs would be good as well—dill, parsley, and chives. Or maybe you have your favourite combination! (My editor, Jane, swears by a combination of basil, coriander, and mint!)

1 lb. butter, room temperature
10 tbsp. fresh tarragon leaves, minced
10 tbsp. fresh chives, minced
5 tbsp. fresh parsley, minced
5 tbsp. fresh thyme, minced
10 tsp. *Tarragon Vinegar* (p. 100-1)
salt and pepper, to taste

Mix all ingredients, form into a roll, wrap with several layers of plastic wrap, and freeze.

Yield: 1 lb. herbed butter

Suggestions for Use: Try stirring 4 tbsp. into a finished *Risotto* (p. 104-6). Spread 1 tbsp. over a **fresh, broiled fish steak or filet**. Toss 5–6 tbsp. with **fresh cooked pasta, 1 lb. sautéed shrimp or scallops**, and a **sautéed small zucchini and 2 tomatoes (or ½ lb. cooked asparagus)**!

RASPBERRY VINEGAR

Great in salads and so easy to make!

4 cups fresh raspberries
3 cups distilled white vinegar

Place berries and vinegar in a sterilized 2-quart canning jar. Cover jar and set in a large saucepan with water halfway up the jar. Bring water to a boil, lower heat to a simmer, and process in this hot-water bath for 20 minutes. Remove from water and set jar aside. Let berries set in vinegar for at least two weeks. Give the jar a shake every few days.

Strain vinegar into a sterilized 1-quart canning jar, seal, and store. (A coffee filter works quite well for straining.)
Yield: 1 quart.

Optional Suggestion: If you don't have time in the summer to do this, freeze 4 cups of fresh clean raspberries, mark the bag, and proceed to make the vinegar in winter when you have more time.

FRESH HERB VINEGARS

Herb vinegars are another great way to preserve fresh herbs for winter use, and they require a minimum of effort. I always make at least one quart each of **tarragon** and **dill** vinegar, using a good handful of the fresh herbs for each batch. The more herbs used, the stronger the flavour will be in the vinegar, so this should be done to taste. I prefer a very strong flavour. Try basil, rosemary, chives, or your favourite herb—or a combination.

a good handful of fresh herbs
4 cups distilled vinegar

Bring vinegar to a boil. In the meantime, sterilize your jars and lids and prepare your herbs. Remove any brown or mottled leaves. The herbs must

be fresh, clean, and dry. Place the herbs in the sterilized jars. Bring the vinegar to the boiling point, pour it over the herbs in the jars, seal jars, and set aside for several weeks.

Strain into sterilized quart jars, seal, and store.

HONEY-APPLE SPREAD

2½ cups fresh apple cider
1 cup honey
¼ cup molasses
1 tbsp. cinnamon
1 tsp. ginger
½ tsp. allspice
5 lbs. apples (a combination of McIntosh and Cortland if possible)

In a large saucepan, bring to a boil the apple cider, honey, molasses, cinnamon, ginger, and allspice. Reduce heat, and keep it at a simmer while you add the apples. Peel, core, and chop the apples. (If you have a food processor, use the coarse-grate blade. A manual food chopper will work as well.) When all the apples have been added, continue cooking for 45 minutes to 1 hour, or until the mixture is thick.

In the meantime, sterilize five pint jars. When the apple mixture is of desired consistency, ladle it into the sterilized jars, removing any air space with a small spoon. Seal with new lids, screwing on until just finger-tight. Place jars in canner. Fill canner with water up to the lids, cover canner, bring water to a boil, and process 10 minutes. Remove and let jars cool, tightening lids occasionally. Store in a cool dark place.

Yield: 5 pints

NOTES

RICE

RISOTTO POSSIBILITIES

Risotto is a wonderful Italian creation whose essential ingredient is Arborio rice, a special Italian rice. Towards the end of the cooking, or after the cooking is complete, bite-sized pieces of vegetables, seafood, or herbs—or a combination—can be added. Risotto can be a main dish or a side dish, depending on what you add. The possibilities are almost endless, the results always wonderful! Don't be afraid to experiment. Choose one of the possibilities mentioned, or make one of your own. Our favourite is the *Pesto Risotto*.

BASIC RISOTTO

1 can (284 ml/10 oz.) condensed chicken broth
1 cup white wine (or additional chicken broth)
water to make 5 cups liquid
1 tsp. salt, if desired
pepper, to taste
2 tbsp. olive oil
1 or 2 clove garlic, minced
1 medium onion, chopped
1½ cups Arborio Rice—do **not** rinse rice

In a medium saucepan, heat the chicken broth, white wine, water, salt, and pepper, if desired. Heat to the boiling point and keep at a simmer.

In a large cast-iron frypan heat the olive oil over medium-high heat. Add the garlic and onion, stir, and sauté 5 minutes. Add the rice and sauté, stirring constantly, until the rice is just browning, about 5 minutes. Add ½ cup of the hot liquid, stirring constantly until it has been absorbed. Continue adding the hot liquid ½ cup at a time, stirring constantly each time until the liquid is absorbed. This should take about 25–30 minutes in all. The rice will be creamy, but slightly al dente.

Servings: 4–6 servings.

Possibilities:
Pesto Risotto: One of the simplest risotto, and perhaps one of the best. This has become one of our favourite winter side dishes. It is excellent with frozen pesto. Prepare the basic risotto and simply add ¾–1 **cup *Pesto* (p. 152-3), fresh or frozen, with Parmesan cheese** to the cooked risotto.

Spring Green Risotto: With 15 minutes cooking time remaining add **½ lb. fresh asparagus,** cut into ½" lengths. When rice is finished, but before you remove it from the heat, add **3 cups fresh spinach**, washed, excess water shaken off, and cut into slivers. Stir it into the rice until it is just wilted and heated through. Remove from heat and gently stir in **1 green onion (or fresh chives),** minced, **¼ cup fresh parsley**, minced, and **2 tbsp. fresh thyme, dill, or basil.**

Broccoli Risotto: Add florets from **1 large head broccoli,** cut into bite-sized pieces, and **½ red or green pepper,** diced, with the rice and sauté. Stir in **½ cup Parmesan cheese** at the end.

Tomato Risotto: With about 10 minutes cooking time remaining add **2 cups fresh tomatoes,** coarsely chopped, and **1 tbsp. (or more) fresh basil or rosemary,** minced. Or if fresh tomatoes and herbs are unavailable, substitute **1½ cups canned tomatoes,** chopped, and **1½ tsp. dried basil or rosemary or Italian herbs.** Add **½ cup grated Parmesan cheese.**

Fall Harvest Risotto: After 10 minutes cooking time add **1 large tomato,** diced. After all the liquid has been absorbed, add **4 cups spinach,** cut in ribbons. Let this melt in, while stirring. Then add **1 recipe** *Pesto* (p. 152-3) and **1 green onion,** chopped.

MEXICAN RISOTTO

1 can (284 ml/10 oz.) condensed chicken broth
1 cup white wine (or additional chicken broth)
water to make 5 cups liquid
1 tsp. salt, if desired
pepper, to taste
1 tsp. chili powder
1 tsp. cumin
1 tsp. dried oregano
1 tsp. dried thyme
½ tsp. cinnamon

2 tbsp. olive oil
1 or 2 cloves garlic, minced
1 large onion, chopped
½ red or green pepper, chopped
1 jalapeño pepper, minced (optional)
1½ cups Arborio rice—do **not** rinse rice
2 tomatoes, diced
1 cup corn

In a medium saucepan heat the chicken broth, white wine, water, salt and pepper (if desired), chili powder, cumin, oregano, thyme, and cinnamon. Heat to the boiling point and keep at a simmer.

In a large cast-iron frypan heat the olive oil over medium-high heat. Add the garlic, onion, pepper, and jalapeño pepper, if desired. Sauté about 5 minutes. Add the rice and sauté, stirring constantly until the rice is just browning. Add ½ cup of the hot liquid, stirring constantly until it has been absorbed. Continue adding the hot liquid ½ cup at a time, stirring constantly each time until the liquid is absorbed. This should take about 25–30 minutes in all. When approximately half the liquid is used, add the tomatoes and the corn. When it is finished the rice will be creamy, but slightly al dente.

Servings: 4–6 servings.

MEXICAN RICE

This is similar to the rice dish served alongside meals at Mexican restaurants. It complements chicken, beef, and fish as well. Save leftovers and reheat—they are even better!

2 cups brown rice
4 cups chicken stock—with salt and pepper, to taste
1 large onion
2 cloves garlic
¼ cup olive oil
1½ cups tomato sauce (or 1 398 ml/14 oz. can)
1–2 tsp. dried oregano
1 green onion, minced (optional)
½ cup fresh coriander or parsley, minced (optional)

One and one half hours before serving: Cover rice with hot water and let it stand for 15 minutes. Drain and rinse well in cold water. Drain very well and let it set to dry for a while.

About 1 hour before serving (if possible): Purée the onion and garlic with ½ cup of the stock and set aside. In a medium saucepan sauté the rice in the olive oil until it is golden, stirring frequently. Add the onion purée, remaining chicken stock, tomato sauce, and oregano. Taste and adjust seasoning if needed. Bring to a boil, cover, and let simmer 1 hour, or until most of the liquid is absorbed. Garnish with green onions and fresh coriander (or parsley), if desired. Serve.

Yield: 6–8 servings.

THAI FRIED RICE

Try with salmon steaks that have been grilled and basted with Thai sweet red chili sauce.

1¼ cups basmati rice
2½ cups water
1 tsp. salt
1 tbsp. canola or safflower oil
1 medium onion, sliced
4 cups cut-up fresh vegetables (a combination of broccoli, carrot, green or red pepper, celery, and Chinese cabbage)
1 tbsp. canola or oil
2 cloves garlic, minced
1 tbsp. fresh ginger, minced
½ tsp. turmeric
2 tbsp. Thai sweet red chili sauce
1 tbsp. tamari soy sauce
1 tbsp. hoisin sauce
1 tsp. sesame oil
2 eggs, lightly beaten
2 green onions, thinly sliced
½ cup fresh cilantro leaves, if possible

In the morning cook the rice: Wash the basmati rice and drain it well. Bring the water and salt to a boil in a medium saucepan. Add the rice, turn down heat, and simmer until rice is done, about 25 minutes. Let it cool, fluff with a fork, and refrigerate for at least one hour.

Stir-fry: Heat a wok. Add 1 tbsp. oil and when it starts to smoke add the onion and stir-fry for 1 minute. Add the prepared vegetables, stir-fry for a minute, add 2 tbsp. water, cover wok, and "steam" vegetables for 4–5 minutes. Remove veggies to a bowl, wipe out wok with a paper towel, and return to heat.

Add the other tablespoon oil and when it starts to smoke add the garlic, ginger, and turmeric and stir-fry 1 minute. Add the rice and stir-fry until rice is heated through. In a small bowl mix together the Thai sweet red chili sauce, tamari, hoisin sauce, and sesame oil. Slowly add this mixture to the rice, stirring constantly until heated through.

Add the vegetables and gently mix them in. Make a hole in the middle of the rice mixture, add the eggs, and slowly incorporate the rice into the eggs as they cook. Sprinkle with the green onions and cilantro and serve.

Yield: 4 servings.

RICE PILAF

A simple dish that is good when you want your rice to be a little special.

1 tbsp. butter
1 tbsp. olive oil
1 garlic shallot, minced
1 small carrot, grated
1 clove garlic, minced
2 cups chicken broth, seasoned with salt and pepper, to taste
1 cup basmati rice, rinsed and drained
½ tsp. cinnamon (or more to taste)
½ tsp. allspice (or more to taste)
½ cup raisins
½ cup pistachios, shelled (optional)

In a saucepan heat the butter and olive oil and sauté the garlic shallot, carrot, and garlic until soft, about 4–5 minutes. Add the chicken broth, cover, and bring to a boil. Add the basmati rice, cinnamon, allspice, and raisins. Cover and cook about 20–25 minutes, or until rice is tender and liquid is absorbed. Add the pistachios, if desired, and serve.

Yield: 3–4 servings.

WILD RICE PANCAKES WITH SUN-DRIED TOMATOES

Delicious as an accompaniment to grilled fish steaks.

2⅔ cup water
1 tsp. salt
1 cup wild rice
5–6 sun-dried tomato halves, not in oil
2 eggs
¾ cup milk
2 tsp. tamari soy sauce
1 medium carrot, washed and grated
1 garlic shallot, minced
1 green onion, finely chopped
2 tbsp. fresh tarragon, minced (or 1 tsp. herbes de Provence)
1 cup unbleached white flour
olive oil

In a saucepan bring to a boil the water and salt. Rinse the wild rice very well under running water, drain, and add to the boiling water. Lower heat to a simmer and simmer the rice, covered, for 50 minutes, or until rice is tender and water is absorbed. When it is finished, drain well, transfer the rice to a large mixing bowl, and let it cool to room temperature.

Cover the sun-dried tomatoes with boiling water and let them soak for 10 minutes. Drain and, using scissors, cut into slivers. Set aside.

Beat together the eggs, milk, and tamari soy sauce. When the rice is cool, stir this mixture into the rice. Add the grated carrot, garlic shallot, green onion, and herbs and fold the mixture gently together. Stir in the flour until the mixture is blended.

Heat a medium-sized griddle over medium-high heat, add 1 tbsp. olive oil, and tilt it so the oil covers the surface. Add the batter by heaping tablespoonfuls and smooth each with the back of the spoon. Cook about 4–5 minutes on each side, or until they are golden-brown. When you flip them the first time, flatten them gently with the spatula. Continue cooking, adding additional olive oil as needed. As you finish the pancakes, keep them warm on a platter in the oven (200°F). Serve immediately.

Yield: About 15 pancakes.

Variation:
Wild Rice Pancakes with Shiitake Mushrooms: For the sun-dried tomatoes, substitute **5–6 dried shiitake mushrooms,** soaked in water, drained, and cut into slivers. (Discard tough stems.)

NOTES

EGGS AND
CHEESE DISHES

BLINTZES WITH STRAWBERRIES

These are special enough to serve on Christmas morning! Strawberries or **blueberries** are the more traditional fruits to serve with blintzes, but **raspberries** are just as good, if not better! This recipe was given to me by Reda Scher, a good friend when we lived in Boston many years ago. It had been in her family for years and was in my first cookbook. I am including it again because I wanted to make blintzes for Christmas this year—and this was the only recipe I could find!

Cheese Filling:
1 lb. farmer's cheese or ricotta (cottage cheese may be used also, but it should be pressed through a sieve before mixing)
1 egg
¼ tsp. salt
½ tsp. cinnamon
1 tsp. flour
⅓ cup sugar (or ¼ cup honey, melted)

With a fork, mix together well the cheese, egg, salt, cinnamon, flour, and sugar. Set aside.

Batter:
¾ cup unbleached white flour
1 heaping tsp. potato starch
¼ tsp. salt
1 cup water
2 eggs
butter for frying
2–3 cups sliced strawberries, sweetened to taste (or 2–3 cups frozen strawberries)
1 cup sour cream (optional)

Preheat oven to 350°F. Butter an oblong baking dish (9" x 13").

Mix and sift the flour, potato starch, and salt. Add water and blend well using a whisk. Add the eggs, one at a time, whisking well after each addition.

Over medium-high heat, place a crêpe pan, omelette pan, or curved skillet, and heat the pan until butter will sizzle when added. Add 1 tsp. butter, and when it sizzles add about 2 tbsp. batter while you tilt the pan so the batter spreads into a circle (5–6"). I find it helpful to use my ¼ cup measuring cup (about half-full with batter) for pouring the batter with my left hand while my right hand manoeuvres the pan. (After a few blintzes you will find it is not as difficult as it sounds.) Once you have the batter in the pan, let it cook just 1–2 minutes, flip it gently with a thin spatula, and cook the other side 1 more minute. If your pan is hot enough, the blintz should be lightly golden.

Remove the blintz to a plate where you place about ¼ cup of the cheese filling down the middle, roll it, and place it in the buttered baking dish. (You can fill and roll it after you get your next crêpe started.) Add an additional 1 tsp. butter to your pan and get it sizzling before frying each blintz. Continue in this manner and place the blintzes side by side in the pan until all the batter is gone.

When all the blintzes are made, bake the dish is the preheated oven for 25–30 minutes. If the blintzes are browning too quickly, cover with foil. Serve with the berries and sour cream, if desired.

Yield: 16 blintzes (4 servings).

PUFFED PANCAKE WITH CINNAMON AND HONEY

Another recipe from my first cookbook, and still one of our favourites. It is a comforting dish, excellent on a cold winter morning and great for children.

¼ cup butter
1 cup unbleached white flour, sifted
2 tbsp. brown sugar
½ tsp. salt, or to taste
3 eggs
2 cups milk
warm honey and cinnamon

Preheat oven to 375°F.

Place butter in a 9" ovenproof skillet. Place skillet in oven as it preheats.

In a large mixing bowl mix the flour, sugar, and salt. In another bowl beat the eggs and milk with a rotary beater for a few minutes. Add egg mixture to flour mixture and beat together well.

Remove skillet from the oven. The butter should be quite "frothy" and hot. Pour mixture into skillet. Immediately return to oven and bake for 30 minutes or until pancake is puffed and lightly browned.

Serve in wedges. Drizzle honey over and sprinkle with cinnamon.

Yield: 4 servings.

SURPRISE VEGETABLE PANCAKE

Try this interesting dish for brunch. It is another one of those recipes that lends itself to adaptation. Different vegetables and different cheeses can be used with great success. I have even used a frozen vegetable mixture in mid-winter when fresh ones were scarce. The trick is to cook the vegetables a minimum amount of time, and drain them well. Crumbled cooked sausage or bacon can be added for extra flavour.

Vegetable Mixture:
2 tbsp. olive oil
2½ cups broccoli, washed and cut into bite-sized pieces
1 or 2 cloves garlic, minced
½ cup green or red pepper, chopped (or bottled roasted red pepper, added with the green onions)
1 tbsp. white wine
1 medium tomato, chopped
salt and pepper, to taste
1 tsp. dried thyme (or 2 tsp. fresh)
2 green onions, minced

In a medium skillet heat the olive oil over medium-high heat. Sauté the broccoli, garlic, and green or red pepper (if using fresh) a few minutes, stirring constantly. Add the white wine, lower heat, cover, and steam about 5 minutes, or until tender-crisp. Add the tomato, salt, pepper, and thyme. Cover and steam about 2 more minutes. Remove from heat, add green onions (and bottled roasted red pepper, if used) and set aside.

Pancake and Assembly:
2 tbsp. butter
¾ cup milk
3 eggs
¼ cup wholewheat flour
½ cup white flour
½ tsp. salt
1 tsp. herbes de Provence, or other dried herbs
2 cups grated Cheddar cheese (about ½ lb.)

Preheat oven to 425°F.

Put butter in a 10" omelette pan or pie pan and place in oven until the butter is sizzling.

In the meantime prepare your batter: In a medium mixing bowl beat together the milk, eggs, wholewheat flour, white flour, salt, and herbs with a whisk for about 3 minutes. The batter should be well-blended and slightly frothy.

Remove pan from the oven, swirl the butter around, pour in the batter, and gently swirl it around as well. Immediately return to the oven and bake for 12 to 15 minutes, or until golden-brown and slightly puffed. Distribute about 1 cup of the cheese over the pancake, arrange the vegetable mixture over the cheese, and top with remaining cheese. Return to oven for 5 more minutes, or until cheese is melted. Serve immediately.

Yield: 4 servings.

Optional Suggestions: Try **Swiss cheese** instead of Cheddar. Other veggies such as **zucchini**, diced and sautéed briefly, or **cauliflower**, lightly steamed, may be used for some or all of the broccoli.

SPINACH-WILD RICE TORTA

Elegant if wild rice is used. It is also good at room temperature, or leftover cold the next day. Good for picnics and lunches.

½ cup brown rice
1 cup water
½ tsp. salt
½ cup wild rice
2 cups water
½ tsp. salt
1 lb. fresh spinach
2 tbsp. olive oil
1 clove garlic, minced
3 eggs
4 tbsp. Parmesan cheese
1–2 fresh green onions, or ½ cup fresh chives, minced (or 1 small onion minced and sautéed in 1 tbsp. olive oil)
2 tbsp. fresh dill, minced (1 tsp. dried)
3 tbsp. fresh parsley, minced
salt and pepper, to taste

Cook brown rice in 1 cup boiling water with ½ tsp. salt about 30–35 minutes Set aside to cool.

For the wild rice, bring the 2 cups water and second ½ tsp. salt to a boil. Rinse the wild rice well and slowly add to boiling water. Cover and cook for 45–50 minutes. Drain if necessary. Set aside to cool.

Preheat oven to 400°F.

Wash the spinach, shake off excess water, and cut into strips. In a large skillet, sauté the garlic in the olive oil for 1 minute, add the spinach, a handful at a time, and cook, stirring occasionally, until it is just wilted. (Covering the skillet with a lid for a minute or two will speed the process along.) Set aside to cool a few minutes.

In a large bowl combine the brown and wild rice. Add the eggs, cheese, onions, herbs, and salt and pepper, to taste. Add the spinach and gently incorporate it evenly in the rice mixture.

Oil a quiche dish and spread mixture evenly in pan. Sprinkle additional Parmesan cheese on top, if desired. Bake in preheated oven for about 20 minutes. Serve.

Yield: 6–8 servings.

ROASTED POTATO-VEGETABLE FRITTATA

This is one of those recipes that is great to experiment with. The basics are simple, and the results are hearty and satisfying. Leftovers are also excellent, if you are lucky enough to have some.

Roasted Potatoes:
2 tbsp. olive oil
3 medium potatoes, peeled and cut into ½" cubes
1–2 cloves garlic, minced
salt and pepper, to taste.

Preheat oven to 375°F.

Heat a medium-sized cast-iron frypan over medium-high heat. Add olive oil. When it is almost smoking, add the potatoes and sauté a few minutes, using a spatula to turn the "chunks" so they are evenly coated. Place in oven and bake, turning the potatoes with a spatula every 5 minutes. After 10 minutes sprinkle potatoes with the garlic, salt, and pepper and bake an additional 15 minutes or until potatoes are tender when pierced with a fork. Remove from oven and let them cool. This step can be done the night before—in fact, it is better if it is.

Frittata:
1 tbsp. olive oil
1 medium onion, sliced
1 small head broccoli, cleaned and cut into bite-sized pieces (3–4 cups)
2 cups mushrooms, cleaned and sliced
1 tbsp. white wine
2 tbsp. olive oil
8 eggs
½ cup low-fat cottage cheese
salt and pepper, to taste
1 tsp. herbes de Provence (or rosemary and thyme)
roasted potatoes (above)
¼ cup **Roasted Red Pepper** (p. 56), diced (optional)
½ cup freshly grated cheese (Cheddar, mozzarella, fontina, etc.)
a few sprigs of parsley, minced, for garnish

Preheat oven to 400°F.

Heat 1 tbsp. olive oil in a medium skillet. Add the onion and sauté a few minutes. Add the broccoli and mushrooms and continue sautéing a few more minutes. Add the white wine, cover, and steam until tender, about 7–8 minutes. Uncover and set aside.

Heat 2 tbsp. olive oil in a large size cast-iron frypan over medium-high heat until it is hot—just beginning to smoke. Beat the eggs, cottage cheese, salt, pepper, and herbs together lightly. Add to the frypan, and cook 1–2 minutes or until bottom begins to set. Turn down the heat to medium-low and add the potatoes and red peppers (if used), spreading them evenly and gently over the eggs. Distribute the sautéed vegetables over the potatoes and gently press them into the eggs. Cook on top of the stove a few minutes more until eggs are beginning to set. Place in oven and bake until the eggs are all set, 10–15 minutes. Sprinkle cheese on top, return to oven and bake a further 5 minutes, or until it is slightly puffed and cheese is melted. Sprinkle parsley on top and serve.

Yield: 6–8 servings.

Optional Suggestions: This is another recipe that is very flexible. Many other vegetables may be used instead of the broccoli and mushrooms. If you are having vegetables for dinner the night before, just set a few aside. Some possibilities:

cauliflower pieces—steamed lightly and cut into small pieces
asparagus spears—lightly steamed (add tarragon and chives to the egg mixture)
artichoke hearts—canned or marinated, sliced
tomatoes—thinly sliced (do not sauté, arrange on top before broiling)
Kalamata olives—pitted and sliced (do not sauté)
red or green pepper—sliced and lightly sautéed (instead of roasted red pepper)
With different vegetables, try different herbs. **Fresh tarragon** is an excellent addition with **cauliflower**. **Chives** would be a good addition to almost any combination.

Variations:
Western Frittata: One of our favourites, a Western includes **ham, onion,** and **red or green pepper**.

Italian Frittata: A more traditional and elegant combination: **asparagus** and **prosciutto** with **fontina cheese.**

PASTA FRITTATA

Easier and quicker to prepare than the previous recipe. Good for brunch or lunch.

1 cup pasta (such as fusilli), cooked according to package directions and drained
1 tbsp. olive oil
1 medium onion, chopped
½ green or red pepper, chopped (optional)
1 clove garlic, minced
4 eggs
½ cup low-fat creamed cottage cheese
¼ cup milk
salt and pepper, to taste
¼ cup fresh parsley, minced
2 tbsp. fresh dill, minced (or 1–2 tsp. dried)
2 tbsp. olive oil
1 cup grated Cheddar cheese (or cheese of your choice)

Preheat oven to 350°F. Place cooked pasta in a bowl. Heat the olive oil in a medium (9") skillet and sauté the onion, pepper, and garlic until soft, about 5 minutes. Remove vegetables to the bowl with the cooked pasta. Mix. Clean out the skillet.

In a medium bowl beat together the eggs, cottage cheese, milk, salt, pepper, parsley, and dill, using a whisk until well blended. Return the skillet to medium-high heat, add the 2 tbsp. olive oil. and when it is smoking add the egg mixture. Turn down the heat and cook eggs without disturbing for a few minutes, or until the bottom is set. Add the noodles and vegetables to the skillet, gently distributing them over the eggs. Cook a few more minutes without disturbing. Sprinkle the cheese over the top and place in preheated oven for 15–20 minutes, or until eggs are set and cheese is melted and bubbling. Serve.

Yield: 4 servings.

Optional Suggestions: This is a great basic recipe. It can be doubled for a crowd, in which case you will need a large skillet to cook it in. You can add 1–2 cups of other vegetables to cook with the onion: **zucchini, asparagus, broccoli**—or add some **cooked ham, sausage, or other meat.** You may vary the herbs and the cheese and omit the cottage cheese, or substitute finely diced **tofu.**

SPRING PASTA-ASPARAGUS FRITTATA WITH TARRAGON AND CHIVES

1 cup fusilli, cooked according to package directions and drained
½ lb. fresh asparagus, cooked until just tender and drained
4 eggs
½ cup cottage cheese
¼ cup milk
salt and pepper, to taste
2–3 tbsp. fresh tarragon, minced
⅓ cup fresh chives, minced
1 tbsp. olive oil
1 cup grated Jarlsberg cheese

Preheat oven to 350°F.

In a bowl beat the eggs with a whisk, add the cottage cheese, milk, salt, pepper, tarragon, and chives and blend all together well with a fork.

Heat a cast-iron skillet over medium-high heat, add the olive oil, and swirl it around. When it is sizzling add the egg mixture and cook, without stirring, until the bottom is setting. Distribute the cooked pasta and the asparagus over the egg mixture, pushing it in gently with your hands or the back of a spatula. Cook a few more minutes without disturbing. Sprinkle the cheese on top and place in preheated oven for 15–20 minutes, or until eggs are set and cheese is melted. The frittata will be slightly puffy. Serve immediately.

Yield: 4 servings.

SMOKED SALMON AND ASPARAGUS QUICHE WITH FRESH HERBS

Crust:
1½ cups unbleached white flour
½ tsp. salt
½ cup cold butter
scant ⅓ cup ice water, or buttermilk

Assembly and Baking:
⅔ lb. fresh asparagus spears, washed, trimmed, and cut into 2" lengths
⅓ lb. smoked salmon, cut into slivers
3 tbsp. fresh tarragon, minced
1 tbsp. fresh thyme, minced
¼ cup fresh chives, minced

1½ cups light cream (18% coffee cream)
3 egg yolks
salt and pepper, to taste (easy on the salt, since smoked salmon is often salted)
⅓ cup Gruyère cheese, grated

Prepare an 11–12" pastry shell, using a quiche pan if available. (Otherwise a large pie pan will do.) In a medium bowl mix the flour and salt with a fork. Cut in the cold butter with a knife and, using a pastry blender (or two sharp knives), cut into the flour and butter until the mixture is mealy. Add the ice water or buttermilk, 1 tbsp. at a time, stirring after each addition, until the dough sticks together. Form it into a ball, wrap in wax paper, and chill for at least 1 hour. (Or make dough in a food processor: Place flour and salt in the processor, add the butter, cut into pieces, and pulse a few times until dough is mealy. Process on slow, adding the water or buttermilk down the funnel until dough sticks together. You'll need less liquid if you use this method.)

On a lightly floured surface roll out the dough to fit the pan. Prick the bottom of the crust with a fork and chill for 30 minutes.

In the meantime steam (or cook in 1" water in a saucepan) the asparagus spears until just tender. Rinse under cold water and drain very well. Set aside.

Preheat oven to 450°F.

Cover the pastry shell with aluminum foil, fill the foil with dried beans, and bake in the preheated oven for 8 minutes. Remove from oven, remove the foil and beans, return the shell to the oven and bake an additional 5 minutes. Remove and set aside to cool slightly.

Reduce oven to 375°F.

Carefully arrange the asparagus spears in the pie shell. Distribute the smoked salmon evenly on top and sprinkle with the fresh herbs. In a small bowl lightly beat together the cream, egg yolks, salt, and pepper. Carefully pour over the asparagus-salmon filling. Sprinkle with the Gruyère cheese and bake in oven for 35–40 minutes, or until lightly browned.

Yield: 6–8 servings.
Variation:
Prosciutto-Asparagus Quiche: Substitute a scant ¼ **lb. prosciutto**, slivered, for the smoked salmon; omit fresh tarragon and thyme and use

instead **1 tsp. Italian herbs**. Substitute **½ cup grated mozzarella mixed with 4 tbsp.** **grated Parmesan cheese** for the Gruyère. Proceed as above.

ORIENTAL ZUCCHINI-CHICKEN "OMELETS"

A different side dish to offer with other Chinese dishes. The sesame oil adds a distinct flavour that can become addictive.

1 lb. fresh zucchini
½ tsp. salt (or to taste)
pepper, to taste
4 tbsp. flour
6 eggs, lightly beaten
½–1 tsp. sesame oil (to taste)
½ lb. ground chicken
1 tbsp. chives, minced
2 tbsp. canola oil

Coarsely grate the zucchini into a large bowl. (Or use the grating disk or your food processor.)
Add the salt, pepper, flour, eggs, sesame oil, chicken, and chives.

Heat the oil in a medium or large cast-iron skillet (or heavy frypan). Drop the batter by the spoonful into the oil. You want the omelets to be 3–4" in diameter. Sauté, flipping once or twice, until nicely browned on both sides. Use more oil if needed. Serve with dipping sauce.

Optional Suggestion: Add ¼ **cup fresh coriander**, minced, to the batter.

Dipping Sauce:
¼ cup light soy sauce
1 tbsp. white wine vinegar
1 tsp. sugar
½ tsp. sesame oil (or more to taste)
1 tbsp. chives, minced

Mix all together in a small bowl.

Yield: 4 servings, or more if used with other dishes.

SPINACH PIE

This recipe is good cut into wedges and served as a luncheon dish or cut into squares and served as an appetizer or as part of a pot-luck.

1 tbsp. olive oil
1 shallot, minced (or a small onion, minced)
250 g fresh mushrooms, sliced ¼" thick
1 tsp. **Dill Vinegar** (p. 100), or lemon juice
½ tsp. salt (or to taste)
pepper, to taste
1 pkg. (300 g/10 oz.) fresh spinach, washed, if necessary, and chopped (or 1 pkg. frozen chopped)
grating fresh nutmeg
1 tbsp. fresh chives (or 1 green onion), minced
¼ cup fresh dill, minced
2 eggs, lightly beaten
1 cup low-fat cottage cheese
1 cup mozzarella cheese, shredded
½ cup Parmesan cheese

Preheat oven to 375°F. Oil a 9" pie pan and set aside.

In a large skillet, heat the olive oil over medium heat. Add the shallot and mushrooms and sauté a few minutes. Add the dill vinegar, salt, and pepper and sauté until the liquid has evaporated, about 5 minutes. Add the spinach and nutmeg, cover, and "steam" 1–2 minutes, or until spinach is wilted. Remove cover and cook a few minutes more, until the spinach is cooked and excess liquid has evaporated. Remove from heat and stir in the chives and dill. Cool slightly.

In a medium bowl combine the eggs, cottage cheese, and mozzarella. Blend well and add to the cooled vegetable mixture. Pour into the prepared pie pan, sprinkle with the Parmesan cheese, and bake in the preheated oven for 25–35 minutes, or until the top is lightly browned and the pie is set. Cut and serve.

Yield: 6–8 luncheon servings.

Variation:
Connie's Low-Fat Version: Substitute ¼ **cup "Egg Beaters"** for the eggs, and use **low-fat mozzarella**. Reduce the **olive oil** to **1 tsp.** Process in a food processor until it looks like "green tweed" and proceed as above. Serve the Parmesan cheese on the side.

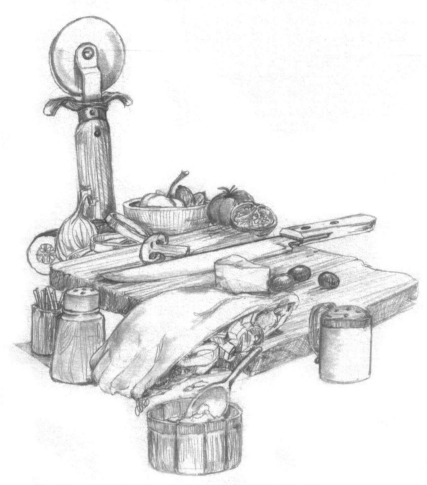

PIZZAS, PITAS, AND OTHER FILLED DELIGHTS

HOMESTYLE PIZZA POSSIBILITIES

There are some recipes that are impossible to pin down—there are just too many possibilities. Pizza is one of those recipes. The following is my attempt at a basic recipe on which to build. There are advantages to this approach—you can make several varieties at once, such as a pizza for meat eaters and one for vegetarians. The following recipe makes 2 large or 3 smaller pizzas. If you don't have pizza pans, you may use large frypans, or even cookie sheets.

Dough:
1⅓ cups warm water
1 tsp. salt
1 tbsp. olive oil
2 cups wholewheat flour
1 tbsp. instant yeast
1⅓–1½ cups unbleached white flour

In a medium-sized bowl mix the warm water, salt, and olive oil. Add the wholewheat flour and the instant yeast. Beat for a few minutes until well-mixed and smooth. Add 1 cup white flour and beat with a spoon until the dough is sticking together. Spread about ⅓ cup of the remaining flour on a board and knead the dough until it is smooth and satiny, using remaining flour if necessary. Place in a clean, oiled bowl in a warm spot until doubled in bulk, about 1 hour.

Basic Easy Sauce:
This sauce is easy to prepare and readily available any time of the year. (Of course,

a homemade sauce would be the best, especially in summer with fresh tomatoes.) This makes enough for 2–3 pizzas.

1 small can (156 ml/5.5 oz.) tomato paste
1 can water
1 tsp. salt, or to taste
½ tsp. sugar
2 cloves garlic, minced (more or less to taste)
1–3 tsp. dried herbs—a combination of oregano, basil, Italian herbs, etc. (fresh herbs, if available, are better)
black pepper, to taste, or red pepper flakes for a hotter pizza

Mix all ingredients together in a small bowl and set aside.

Toppings:
Prepare all of your toppings while the dough is rising. The following list offers several possibilities and could go on forever! **My favourite** includes some sausage or pepperoni (or both), caramelized onions, a

little red pepper, mushrooms, and Kalamata olives.

Italian sausage—removed from casings, sautéed until cooked through, and drained well
pepperoni—sliced, sautéed, and drained on paper towel
bacon—diced, sautéed until crisp, and drained on paper towel
chicken–1 breast grilled, sautéed, or barbecued (or leftover) and cut into small pieces
ham—leftover, or a good packaged ham, diced
prosciutto—slivered
fresh mushrooms—sliced (Wild or special mushrooms such as portobello, sliced and sautéed, are excellent!)
onions (white, red, or green)—sliced
caramelized onions—(Sauté 2 onions in 2 tbsp. olive oil until lightly browned. Add 2 tbsp. balsamic vinegar and cook 1 minute longer. Add salt and pepper, to taste.)
olives—pitted and cut in slivers (Kalamata are best!)
peppers (green, red, hot, or sweet)—sliced
bottled roasted red peppers, bottled jalapeño peppers, or pepperoncini—drained and sliced
zucchini—thinly sliced and sautéed
eggplant—thinly sliced and sautéed

fresh tomatoes—thinly sliced
green tomatoes—thinly sliced
artichoke hearts—canned or bottled marinated, drained and sliced
broccoli—a few spears thinly sliced and sautéed
clams—drained (If you are lucky enough to have some **PEI bar clams**, use them!)
spinach or radicchio—about 2 cups fresh, washed, dried, and finely shredded
asparagus—steamed and cut into 1–2" lengths (especially good with prosciutto)

Cheese:
¾–1 lb. mozzarella cheese, grated

Mozzarella is traditional, but other cheeses are good as well. Try half **Cheddar**, or **Monterey Jack,** or substitute some freshly grated **Pecorino** or **Parmesan** for some of the mozzarella. Match your cheese with your fillings. **Cheddar** or a **Swiss** cheese would be good with ham and broccoli.

Prepare pans, assemble, and bake:

Preheat oven to 475°F.

Lightly oil pans with olive oil. (A cookie sheet makes 1 large pizza. A large cast-iron frypan makes one medium.)

When dough is doubled, punch down, break off proper amount, and shape as required. If the dough is being uncooperative, let it rest a few minutes, then try shaping it again. Place in pan.

Cover dough generously, but not too generously, with the tomato sauce. Arrange your toppings and distribute the cheese evenly on top. Bake in preheated oven for 15–20 minutes, or until crust and cheese are lightly browned. Cut into pieces and serve.

Yield: 2 large or 3 smaller pizzas, 4–8 servings.

Variations:
Pesto Pizza: Instead of tomato sauce, spread *Pesto* (p. 152-3) thinly over crust. Process as in basic recipe. This is good with fresh **tomatoes** and **zucchini** thinly sliced and arranged over the pesto, and **mozzarella cheese** (about 2 cups mixed) sprinkled over all.

Winter Pesto Pizza: **Sun-dried tomatoes** (plumped, drained well, and sliced), **Kalamata olives** (pitted and sliced), **green onions** (minced), and **bottled roasted red peppers** (sliced), covered with the grated mozzarella, as above.

Mexican Pizza: Use pizza dough. Add some **salsa** to the sauce and top with **sliced jalapeño pepper, sliced red or green pepper, Kalamata olives,** and **sliced tomatoes.** Cover with **2 cups Monterey Jack cheese** and bake as above.

STUFFED AND DEEP-DISH PIZZAS

The next section is full of ideas for stuffed and deep-dish pizzas. They both use the same dough, with a slight variation: stuffed pizza dough includes a bit of cornmeal, while the deep-dish pizza does not. They both use the same type of sauce, thicker and chunkier, and I have included two for you to choose between. You may use the fillings I suggest or develop some of your own. Whatever you do, the result will be a delicious, hearty pizza designed to warm both body and spirit.

Stuffed Pizza Dough:
1 cup warm water
1 tsp. salt
¼ cup olive oil
1 cup wholewheat flour (or 1 cup unbleached white flour)
½ cup cornmeal
1 tbsp. instant yeast
1½ cups white flour, more for kneading

Mix the warm water, salt, and olive oil in a large bowl. Add the wholewheat flour, cornmeal, and instant yeast and beat well for a few minutes with a whisk. Using a spoon, mix in 1½ cups white flour, ½ cup at a time, and continue beating dough for another few minutes.

Sprinkle some of the remaining ¼ cup white flour on a clean surface, turn out dough, and knead until dough is smooth and elastic, adding more flour if necessary.

Place dough in a clean, oiled bowl. Turn dough to coat it all with oil, cover with plastic wrap, and set in a warm place to rise until double in bulk, about 1 hour. In the meantime prepare the filling.

Deep-Dish Pizza Dough: Follow the method above but replace the ½ cup cornmeal with ½ cup unbleached white flour.

Sauces for Stuffed or Deep-Dish Pizzas

You may use 2 cups of your favourite ragu spaghetti sauce, with or without meat. The sauce must be quite thick, though, so if your sauce is too thin, thicken it up by cooking it down, or add 1–2 tbsp. tomato paste and simmer a few minutes. Putting it through a food processor can thicken a sauce also. Or use the following recipes.

Regular Tomato Sauce:
1 tbsp. olive oil
1 small onion, chopped
1 clove garlic, minced
1 can (398 ml/14 oz.) stewed tomatoes
1 tsp. dried oregano
1 tsp. Italian herbs
salt and pepper, to taste

In a small saucepan heat the olive oil and in it sauté the onion and garlic a few minutes. Add the stewed tomatoes, oregano, Italian herbs, and salt and pepper, to taste. Cook over medium-high heat, stirring often, for about ½ hour, or until sauce is thickened up. Set aside to cool.

Roasted Tomato Sauce:
2 cups *Roasted Tomatoes* (p. 76-7), chopped
¼ cup fresh basil, chopped
½ red pepper, diced and sautéed quickly
1 small red onion, chopped
1 clove garlic, minced
1 tsp. dried oregano
salt and pepper, to taste

Combine all ingredients in a bowl and gently toss.

MEATBALL-STUFFED PIZZA

This is a double-crust pizza stuffed with meatballs. It is best served after the pizza has rested and cooled for at least 30 minutes: It will be easier to slice and the filling will have "set." Great party and picnic food.

Meatballs—your favourite or:
1 lb. lean hamburger
½ lb. hot Italian sausage
1 clove garlic, minced
1 small onion, finely chopped
½ cup fine dry breadcrumbs
¼ cup Parmesan or Romano cheese
1 tsp. dried oregano
1 tsp. Italian herbs
2 tbsp. fresh parsley, minced
½ tsp. salt, or to taste
pepper, to taste
1 tbsp. olive oil

Mix together the hamburger, sausage, garlic, onion, breadcrumbs, cheese, oregano, herbs, and salt and pepper. Use your hands to blend the mixture well. Shape the mixture into 1" balls. Place them on a plate. Heat the olive oil in a medium-large skillet and sauté the meatballs, turning frequently, until they are evenly browned. Turn down the heat and continue cooking for about 15–20 minutes, turning occasionally, until meatballs are cooked through. Remove with a slotted spoon to drain on paper towels.

Assembly and Baking:
1 recipe *Stuffed Pizza Dough* (above)
meatballs (above)
2 cups tomato sauce, either *Regular Tomato* or *Roasted Tomato Sauce* (above)
¾ lb. mozzarella cheese, grated
1 tbsp. olive oil

Preheat oven to 450°F for at least 15 minutes.

With olive oil, oil well a heavy 15" skillet or pizza pan with sides.

Punch dough down and divide into two pieces, one a bit larger than the other. Roll out the larger piece on a lightly floured clean surface to a circle about 16" in diameter. Place in the oiled pan and be sure the dough goes up the sides about 1½" to 2".

If your meatballs are large, cut them in half. Arrange meatballs over the dough, cut-side down, and top with the tomato sauce and the mozzarella cheese. Roll out remaining dough to a circle of 14"– 15". Place on top of filling. Fold the bottom edge of the dough over the top piece and crimp the edges together using your fingers. Be sure to create a good seal. Slash the top of the pizza in a few places and let it set in a warm place for 15–20 minutes.

Brush the surface of the pizza generously with olive oil, place in the preheated oven, and bake for 15 minutes, or until golden-brown.

Remove pizza from pan and let it cool on a wire rack. (I find it easiest to place a wire rack over the pizza, flip it over onto the rack and quickly flip it back onto a second rack.) When cool, transfer to a large cutting board and cut into serving pieces with a large serrated knife. (You may cut smaller pieces if this is to be served to a crowd.) Serve.

Yield: 6–8 servings.

ROASTED TOMATO AND SAUSAGE-STUFFED PIZZA

1 recipe *Stuffed Pizza Dough* (p. 127)
1 recipe *Roasted Tomato Sauce* (p. 128)
1 lb. hot or sweet Italian sausages
1 tbsp. olive oil

Cut the sausage into bite-sized pieces and quickly sauté in a skillet with the olive oil until browned and cooked through. Drain on paper towels and set aside.

Follow directions in preceding recipe for forming and baking the pizza.

RICOTTA, PESTO, AND VEGETABLE-STUFFED PIZZA

This is fast becoming one of our favourite dinners. It is even better left over for lunches and is great for travelling and picnics.

1 recipe *Stuffed Pizza Dough* (p. 127)
1 container (500g) ricotta cheese (low-fat if possible)
½ recipe (or ½ cup) *Pesto* (p. 152-3), without cheese
2 cloves garlic, minced
1 tbsp. olive oil
½ red pepper, diced (optional)
2–3 cups broccoli, cut into bite-sized pieces
½ lb. mushrooms, sliced thick
splash of red or white wine
1 small red onion, sliced into rings and separated
½ cup sun-dried tomatoes (either in olive oil or dried and soaked in hot water until soft), snipped
⅓ lb. mozzarella, grated
3–4 tbsp. Parmesan cheese

olive oil, for brushing on the crust

Make the pizza dough following directions in previous recipe. While it is rising, prepare the filling.

In a small bowl combine the ricotta cheese, pesto, and garlic. Set aside.

In a medium skillet heat the olive oil and sauté the red pepper a few minutes. Add the broccoli and sauté a few minutes more. Add the mushrooms and again sauté a few more minutes. Add a splash of wine, cover, and steam vegetables until tender-crisp. Remove from heat, drain any excess liquid (if necessary), and set aside.

Preheat oven to 450°F for 15 minutes at least.

With olive oil, oil well a heavy 15" skillet or pizza pan with sides.

Punch dough down and divide into two pieces, one a bit larger than the other. On a lightly floured clean surface, roll out the larger piece to a circle about 16" in diameter. Place in the oiled pan and be sure the dough goes up the sides about 1½" to 2".

Spread the ricotta mixture over the bottom. Distribute the broccoli, mushrooms, roasted red peppers, red onion rings, and snipped sun-dried tomatoes evenly over the surface and top with the mozzarella and Parmesan cheeses.

Roll out remaining dough to a circle of 14"–15". Place on top of filling. Fold the bottom edge of the dough over the top piece and crimp the edges together using your fingers. Be sure it is well sealed. Slash the pizza top in a few places and let it set in a warm place for 15–20 minutes.

Brush the surface of the pizza generously with olive oil, place in the preheated oven, and bake for 15 minutes, or until golden-brown.

Remove pizza from pan and let it cool on a wire rack. (I find it easiest to place a wire rack over the pizza, flip it over onto the rack, and quickly flip it back onto a second rack.) When cool, transfer to a large cutting board and cut into serving pieces with a large serrated knife. You may cut smaller pieces if this is to be served to a crowd.

Yield: 6–8 servings.

Optional Suggestions: Try **chopped fresh spinach, artichoke hearts,** or **asparagus** for some or all of the vegetables. **Kalamata olives,** pitted and sliced, are also a good addition.

PESTO PROVENÇAL PIZZA

½ recipe **Stuffed Pizza Dough** (p. 127)
olive oil
¾ cup **Pesto** (p. 152-3)
1 small jar (179 ml/6 oz.) marinated artichoke hearts, sliced ⅓" thick
2 medium tomatoes, seeded and chopped
¼ cup Kalamata olives, pitted and sliced
1 small red onion
⅓ lb. mozzarella cheese, thinly sliced

Make half the recipe for the dough, following the directions in recipe.

Preheat oven to 450°F.

Oil a large heavy frypan (or cookie sheet) with olive oil. Roll and pull the dough until it fits the pan. Spread the pesto evenly over the surface. Top with the artichoke hearts, tomatoes, olives, red onions, and mozzarella cheese. Bake in preheated oven for 15–20 minutes. Serve.

Yield: 4 servings.

DEEP-DISH PIZZA

If you are lucky enough to have a deep-dish pan (15" in diameter and 1½" deep), you are all set. I recently bought one but was very disappointed in the recipe I found. Several pizzas later, success! It was delicious! If you don't have a pan, use a cast-iron frypan.
1 recipe **Deep-Dish Pizza Dough** (p. 127)

1 recipe **Regular Tomato** or **Roasted Tomato Sauce** (p. 128)
1 tbsp. olive oil
1 stick pepperoni, sliced
½ lb. Italian sausage, casings removed
1 small sweet onion, chopped
½ red pepper, chopped
¾–1 lb. mozzarella cheese, grated

dried oregano

Prepare all the filling ingredients while dough is rising. In a frypan heat the olive oil and sauté the pepperoni about 5 minutes. Remove to a paper towel-lined plate to drain. In the same pan sauté the sausage, breaking it up with a fork, until it is cooked through.

Remove to another paper towel-lined plate to drain. Add 1 tbsp. more olive oil, if needed, and quickly sauté the onion and red pepper a few minutes. Set aside to cool.

Preheat oven to 450°F. If you have a pizza stone, place it in the middle of the oven. Oil the deep-dish pan very well with olive oil.

After the dough has risen, punch it down and roll, stretch, and so on until it fits the pan. Gently settle it in, being sure the dough goes up the rim. Cover loosely and let it rest for about 20 minutes.

Cover the bottom with the sauce. (You may not want to use all of the sauce.) Distribute the pepperoni, sausage, onion, and peppers evenly over the pizza. Top with the cheese and sprinkle with oregano.

Bake in upper third of preheated oven for 15–20 minutes. Remove from oven, let it cool a few minutes, remove from pan, cut, and serve.

Yield: 8 large slices pizza.

DEEP-DISH CAJUN PIZZA

This creation was a joint venture between my son John and me. It was definitely one of the best pizzas we've ever had.

Chicken:
2–3 chicken breasts, depending on size
1 cup ketchup
1 tbsp. Dijon mustard
2 tbsp. honey
2–3 cloves garlic, minced
1 tbsp. Worcestershire sauce
1 tbsp. Creole/Cajun spice, or to taste
1 tbsp. red wine vinegar
1 tbsp. chili powder, or to taste
cayenne pepper, to taste

Day before (this chicken is best marinated a day in advance, or at least for a few hours): Trim chicken breasts of excess fat, if necessary.

Place ketchup, Dijon, honey, garlic, Worcestershire sauce, Creole/Cajun spice, red wine vinegar, chili powder, and cayenne in a small saucepan and simmer about 10 minutes, or until nicely thickened and blended. Cool and pour over chicken breasts. Cover and place in fridge overnight.

Next day: Remove chicken from marinade and grill, turning and basting, until cooked through (when juices run clear). Cool slightly and cut into bite-sized pieces. Set aside.

Shrimp:
⅓ lb. shrimp, deveined
2 tbsp. olive oil
1 tbsp. white wine
1 clove garlic, minced
dried oregano
salt and pepper, to taste
1 tbsp. olive oil

Marinate the shrimp for at least 1 hour in the olive oil, white wine, garlic, oregano, salt, and pepper. Quickly sauté it in the 1 tbsp. olive oil until pink. Remove from heat and cut into bite-sized pieces.

Assembly and Baking:
1 recipe *Deep-Dish Pizza Dough* (p. 127)
1 recipe *Regular Tomato Sauce* (p. 128)
2 Cajun sausages, removed from casings, cooked through, and drained on paper towels
½ red pepper (or less), chopped and sautéed in olive oil a few minutes
prepared chicken (above)
prepared shrimp (above)
¾–1 lb. Monterey Jack cheese
dried oregano

Preheat oven to 450°F. If you have a pizza stone, place it in the middle of the oven. Oil the deep-dish pan very well with olive oil.

After the dough has risen, punch it down and roll, stretch, and so on until it fits the pan. Gently settle it in, being sure the dough goes up the rim. Cover loosely and let it rest for about 20 minutes.

Cover the bottom with the sauce. (You may not want to use all of the sauce.) Distribute the sausage, red pepper, chicken, and shrimp on the top. Top with the cheese and sprinkle with oregano.

Bake in upper third of preheated oven for 15–20 minutes. Remove from oven, let it cool a few minutes, remove from pan, cut, and serve.

Yield: 8 large slices pizza.

PESTO CALZONE

The **Stuffed Pizza Dough** (p. 127) can also be used to make calzones, and the possibilities for stuffing calzone are numerous! The recipe is enough for 6 large or 8 smaller calzones.

Dough:
1 recipe dough for **Meatball-Stuffed Pizza** (p. 128-9)

Proceed as in the above recipe through the first rising.

Filling:
340 g/12 oz. ricotta cheese
1 recipe **Pesto** (p. 152-3)
100 g/3.5 oz. mozzarella cheese

Mix together the ricotta cheese, pesto, and mozzarella cheese

Assembly and Baking and Serving:
dough, after first rising
filling (above)
2 cups your favourite marinara or meat sauce

Grease 2 cookie sheets with olive oil.

Punch down the dough and divide into 6 or 8 portions (depending on whether you prefer smaller or larger calzones). Knead each portion into a small, round ball and roll out each ball into a circle about 5–6" across. Divide filling between the calzones, placing the filling on one side of the circle and spreading it out to within 1" of the edge. Wet one half or the circle rim with water and carefully fold the dough over the filling. Roll the edges over twice, to bury the seam. Pinch the dough together well with your fingers as you do a pie rim. The calzones will be shaped like half moons. As each one is finished place it on a prepared cookie sheet and cover loosely with a cloth or plastic wrap.

Preheat oven to 450°F for 15 minutes. Let the calzones rise for 15 minutes.

Prick each one a few times with a fork and bake in preheated oven for 15 minutes, or until browned. Serve with the marinara sauce on the side.

Yield: 8 servings.

Optional Suggestions: Before you fold over the dough and seal, arrange slices of **marinated artichoke hearts** and **Kalamata olives** over the pesto filling.

The possibilities are quite endless for calzone fillings. Try your favourite **marinara sauce** in combination with cooked **sausage, veggies, etc.**, topped with some grated cheese, usually mozzarella. (**Sausage and broccoli** is a good combo.)

Variations:
Ham, Cheese, Sun-Dried Tomato, and Broccoli Calzone: Combine ½ lb. ricotta cheese, ½ lb. Swiss cheese (grated), ¼ lb. ham (diced), ½ cup sun-dried tomatoes (soaked in hot water 5 minutes, drained, and minced), and 1 cup broccoli (steamed and chopped).

Shrimp and Pesto Calzone: Combine 1 lb. fresh shrimp (peeled, deveined, and sautéed), 1 cup fresh plum tomatoes (chopped), ½ cup pesto, and ½ lb. mozzarella cheese (grated).

Chicken and Broccoli Calzone: Combine **1 whole chicken breast** (grilled and diced), **1 cup broccoli florets** (steamed), **½ lb. mozzarella** (grated), and **1 cup fresh tomatoes** (chopped).

Meatball Calzone: Use ½ recipe **meatballs** from the *Meatball-Stuffed Pizza* (p. 128-9), only make them smaller. After they are cooked combine them with **2 cups thick tomato sauce** and **½ lb. grated mozzarella cheese.**

Summer Garden Calzone: In the summer try to include a mixture of **2 cups veggies (broccoli, spinach, zucchini, etc.)** that have been lightly sautéed, cooled, and mixed with **1 cup fresh tomato sauce** seasoned with fresh herbs (either **basil** or **tarragon** mixed with **parsley and/or chives,** or your favourite combination), and topped with grated **mozzarella cheese.**

MELLOW MIDDLE EASTERN PITA

The combination of hummus, arugula, and coriander is a favourite lunch for us. Hummus is easy to make and good to have in the refrigerator.

Hummus:
1 cup dried chick peas (garbanzo beans), soaked and cooked, or 1 can (540 ml/19 oz.), drained

¼ cup liquid from beans, or less for a thicker spread
juice of ½–1 lemon, depending on the size and juiciness of the lemon and your taste

½–1 tsp. honey, depending on sourness of the lemon
½ cup tahini
1 clove garlic (or 2 for a very garlicky hummus)
salt and pepper, to taste
½–1 tsp. cumin powder

Place the drained cooked or canned beans in a food processor along with some liquid, if desired, and lemon juice, tahini, garlic, salt, pepper, and cumin. Process until smooth.

Assembly:
fresh rounds *Pita Bread* (p.247-8)
hummus (above)
2–3 leaves fresh arugula per half sandwich
3–4 sprigs fresh coriander leaves per half sandwich
fresh tomato slices

Cut pita rounds in half, open each half, and spread hummus on one side. Top with arugula and fresh coriander and serve.

FELAFEL

One of our favourite vegetarian meals of all time. Made-from-scratch felafel are worth the effort.

1 cup dried chick peas
pinch baking soda
¼ cup bulghur
2 cloves garlic
3 tbsp. fine breadcrumbs
1 egg, beaten
1 tsp. cumin
salt and pepper, to taste
¼ tsp. cayenne pepper (optional)
1 tbsp. fresh coriander
white flour
olive oil

Soak chick peas overnight. Drain, place in a saucepan, and cover again with fresh water. Add baking soda, cover, and bring to a boil. Lower heat and simmer until beans are tender, 45 minutes–1 hour. Set aside to cool.

Cover the bulghur with boiling water and let it set for 10 minutes to "plump." Drain any excess water.

In your food processor place the drained cooked chick peas, plumped bulghur, garlic, breadcrumbs, egg, cumin, salt, pepper, and cayenne, if desired. Process until smooth. Remove to a bowl.

Heat a little olive oil in a cast-iron skillet. Take a heaping

tablespoonful of the chick pea mixture and plop it into a flat-bottomed bowl with flour in it. Roll the ball around to coat it with flour, pick it up, and flop it between your hands a few times to shape it into a 2"

patty. Gently place it in the frypan. Cook each patty about 5 minutes on each side, or until nicely browned. Remove to a serving plate. Continue until all the mixture is used. You should have 14–16 felafel.

TAHINI SPREAD AND RELISH

½ cup tahini
½ tsp. salt
1 clove garlic, minced
dash cayenne pepper
⅛ cup lemon juice
2 tbsp. fresh coriander
1 tbsp. olive oil, or more to taste

Place all ingredients in a small serving dish and mix gently with a spoon until smooth.

2 tomatoes, finely chopped
½ red or green pepper, chopped
1–2 green onions, chopped
½ cup fresh parsley, minced
3 tbsp. olive oil
2 tbsp. lemon juice
1 tbsp. dried mint

Combine all ingredients in a serving bowl and mix together gently.

Serving:
4 rounds *Pita Bread* (p. 247-8)
felafel (above)
tahini spread (above)
relish (above)
1 cup plain yogurt

Place all ingredients on the table and have everyone help themselves. We usually cut the pita rounds in half, split them open to have pockets, spread some of the tahini spread on the bottom, place two felafel in each half, spoon on some relish, and top with yogurt. You will need plenty of napkins when you eat felafel!

Yield: 4 servings.

Optional Suggestions: Instead of the relish, you may use Tabouli, and *Tzatziki* (p. 16) is good instead of the plain yogurt.

KOFTA KEBABS WITH VEGETABLE RELISH AND TZATZIKI

A delicious meal we had in Montreal inspired this recipe. Grilled lamb kebabs (or grilled chicken) are the traditional (and perhaps better) fillings, but kofta kebabs with ground lamb are more economical. Combined with **relish** and *Tzatziki* (p. 16), you have a delicious and healthy dinner pleasing to the palate as well as the pocketbook.

Relish:
2 tomatoes, chopped
1 small red onion, minced
1 cup fresh parsley, minced
½ cup Kalamata olives, sliced
1 tbsp. olive oil
1 tbsp. lemon juice
salt and pepper, to taste

Combine all ingredients in a serving bowl and mix gently with a spoon.

Kofta Kebabs:
1 lb. ground lamb
1 clove garlic, minced
1 shallot, minced
2 tsp. herbes de Provence
½ tsp. cinnamon
3–4 tbsp. fresh parsley, minced

Combine all ingredients and form into "cigars" around skewers. Grill on an outdoor barbecue, turning frequently, until cooked through. (If you don't have skewers, you may form the meat into small patties. And if you don't have a grill, you may broil the patties.)

Serving:
Pita Breads (p. 247-8)
kofta kebabs (above)
1 recipe relish (above)
1 recipe *Tzatziki* (p. 16)

If you are lucky enough to get large pitas, split each into two circles, place some of the kofta kebab down the centre of each half, top with some of the vegetable relish, smother with the tzatziki, roll up, and serve.

If you have smaller pitas, cut in half, open and fill each half with some of the kofta kebab and relish, and smother with the tzatziki. Serve either version with plenty of napkins.

Yield: 4 servings.

Optional Suggestion: Substitute **grilled chicken breasts,** sliced, or **leftover chicken** for the kofta kebabs, and top with either the relish or Tabouli.

BEEF BURRITOS

One of our favourite Mexican dinners. Have your fillings and condiments ready on the table so everyone can make their own burritos to taste. Great for a relaxing Saturday-night dinner. This recipe is for four hungry adults but can easily be expanded by estimating the amount needed for each person. One-third to one-half pound meat per person is average. Be sure to have enough of your other ingredients ready.

1 pkg. large flour tortillas (burrito size)
1½ lb. good, tender steak (sirloin, etc.), grilled to taste and thinly sliced
2 cups *Mashed Frijoles* (p. 142), or canned refried beans
1½ cups *Fresh Tomato Salsa* (p. 29), or your favourite purchased salsa
2 cups grated Cheddar or Monterey Jack cheese
1 cup sour cream
1 large tomato, chopped
2 large green onions, chopped
½ cup Kalamata olives, pitted and sliced

Preheat oven to 375°F. Lightly oil a large cookie sheet. Arrange all ingredients in the centre of the table.

For each burrito: Place one large flour tortilla on a plate. Place a bit of each ingredient on tortilla. (It is best first to put about 3 tbsp. mashed frijoles down the centre of the tortilla to within 1½" of the edge. Distribute remaining ingredients evenly along the centre.) Do not overfill, as they will not roll properly and will be difficult to eat.

Roll tortilla up: Fold about ⅓ of the tortilla over the filling. Fold edges in about 1", roll up, and place seam-side down on cookie sheet. When all burritos are made, cover with aluminum foil. Bake in preheated oven for 20–25 minutes, or until burritos are heated through. Serve with plenty of napkins and water.

Yield: 4 large servings.

Variations:
Chicken Burritos: Omit beef, use instead **1–1½ lbs. grilled chicken breasts.**
Shrimp Burritos: Omit beef, use instead **1–1½ lbs. grilled shrimp.**
Vegetarian Burritos: Omit beef, use instead **1 lb. broccoli spears,** steamed or **1 medium zucchini,** sliced thin and sautéed.

Picadillo Burritos (one of our favourites): Use following recipe for *Picadillo (Beef, Chicken, or Pork)* and proceed as above.

PICADILLO (BEEF, CHICKEN, OR PORK)

A picadillo is a Mexican basic used to fill burritos, tacos, etc. This is what you get when you use the packaged taco mixes. Home-made, as usual, is better. There are many options in this recipe, so use what appeals to you. If you have chipotle peppers, one can add a lovely smokey accent.

2 tbsp. olive oil
1 onion, chopped
1–2 large red or green peppers (or 1 of each)
1 or 2 cloves garlic, minced
1½ lbs. lean ground beef (or ground chicken—or turkey, or lean ground pork)
1 tbsp. flour
½ cup red wine (white wine if you use ground chicken or turkey), or tomato juice
1 large or 2 small tomatoes, chopped
2 canned jalapeño peppers or pickled jalapeños, minced (if desired), or 1 chipotle pepper, minced
¼ cup raisins (optional)
¼ cup olives (green or black), pitted and slivered (optional)
salt and pepper, to taste
1 tbsp. chili powder (or more to taste)

dash of cinnamon
½–1 tsp. ground cumin
1 tsp. dried oregano
1 tsp. thyme

Heat the oil in a medium-sized heavy frypan. Sauté the onion, peppers, and garlic until soft and browning. Add the ham-burger and continue sautéing, breaking the meat up with a fork. Remove from heat and drain excess fat. Return skillet to heat. Blend in the flour and then stir in the red wine (or tomato juice) and cook about 5 minutes. Add the tomatoes, ja-lapeño peppers, raisins, olives, salt, pepper, chili, cinnamon, cumin, oregano, and thyme. Simmer gently, uncovered, for about 20 minutes longer.

Yield: 4 servings, or enough for 1 dozen tacos or 10 bur-ritos.

MASHED FRIJOLES

I don't know the Mexican word for mashed, but I am sure it would sound better in the title! This recipe to me is a basic one for many Mexican dishes. It is a variation of the traditional **frijoles refritos,** or refried beans, where the cooked beans are mashed in lard and fried. Perhaps the flavour is not the same, but this version is healthier, easier, and very tasty.

2 cups pinto beans (kidney beans may be used although the result is different)
2 onions, chopped
2 cloves garlic, minced
1 tsp. dried oregano
salt and pepper, to taste
2 additional cloves garlic, minced
1–2 tsp. ground cumin (or to taste)
¼–½ cup pickled jalapeño peppers, minced (or fresh jalapeños)
red pepper flakes, to taste (optional)
¼ cup olive oil
¼ cup canola oil

Wash beans and soak overnight covered in cold water. The next day drain the beans, place in a large saucepan, cover with cold water, add the onions and garlic, cover, and bring to a boil. Reduce heat and simmer gently for 45 minutes to 1 hour, or until beans are tender.

Drain excess liquid and set aside. Mash the beans in the pot with a potato masher and add the oregano, salt and pepper, 2 more cloves garlic, cumin, peppers, and red pepper flakes, if desired. Keep mashing, beating occasionally with a large spoon, adding the olive oil, canola oil, and some reserved liquid if needed. (You want a heavy paste.) Taste the beans and adjust seasoning if needed. The beans are now ready for tacos, tortillas, nachos, burritos, etc.

Leftovers freeze well in plastic containers. When I make these beans I make extra to freeze in pint-sized containers such as yogurt containers. These seem to hold the perfect amount for many Mexican dishes.

BEEF FAJITAS

Fajitas are even simpler to make than burritos! You need flour tortillas, grilled onions, and peppers (if desired). Place the ingredients on the table and everyone can assemble their own.

2 tbsp. olive oil
2 tbsp. butter
3–4 medium onions, sliced
1 green or red pepper, sliced (optional)
1 pkg. flour tortillas (extra thick, if possible)
1½ lbs. tender steak, grilled to taste and sliced
2 cups *Mashed Frijoles* (above), or canned refried beans, warmed
1½ cups salsa
2 cups grated Cheddar or Monterey Jack cheese
1 cup sour cream
1–2 fresh tomatoes, chopped (optional)
½ cup Kalamata olives, pitted and sliced (optional)
pickled jalapeños or banana peppers (optional)

In a medium cast-iron frypan, heat the olive oil and butter and sauté the sliced onions and peppers, if desired, slowly for 10 minutes, stirring occasionally.

Heat the tortillas according to package directions.

Arrange the grilled onions and peppers, tortillas, grilled steak, refried beans, salsa, cheese, sour cream, tomatoes, olives, and pickled peppers on the table. Have everyone help themselves, making a pocket of their tortilla and filling with the ingredients of their choice. Again, have plenty of water and napkins on hand.

Yield: 4 servings.

Optional Suggestion: Indoor Version: Sauté the beef strips in the skillet, remove, and sauté the onion and pepper until tender. Return beef to skillet and sauté a few minutes longer or until beef is heated through.

Variations: Chicken or Shrimp Fajitas: You may replace the beef with **grilled chicken breast** or **shrimp** marinated prior to its cooking in **garlic and olive oil**.

Hamburger Fajitas: Substitute *Hamburger Picadillo* (p. 141) for the grilled meat.

BARBECUED "MUSHU" PORK FAJITAS

A delicious combination of meat and winter veggies rolled up in wholewheat flour tortillas—which serve as an excellent substitute for the traditional Chinese pancakes. Marinate the pork in the morning for best results. This is easier to prepare if two people are involved in the process. One prepares the veggies and pancakes while the other grills the meat outdoors.

Pork Marinade:
1 lb. centre-cut pork tenderloin, cut ½" thick
2 tbsp. hoisin sauce (or 1 tbsp.
hoisin and 1 tbsp. Thai sweet
red chili sauce)
1 tbsp. soy sauce
1 tbsp. white wine vinegar
1 tbsp. ketchup
1 tsp. sesame oil
1 tsp. sugar
1–2 cloves garlic, minced

Trim the pork of all fat. Combine remaining ingredients in a small bowl. Add the pork and turn until pork is well coated. Cover and place in fridge until needed.

Pancakes and Grilling Meat:
12 wholewheat flour tortillas
sesame oil

Preheat oven to 350°F. Prepare the "pancakes" by brushing one side of each tortilla lightly with sesame oil, placing brushed sides of two tortillas together, and stacking them on a large sheet of aluminum foil. When the "pancakes" are all prepared, seal the foil and place them in the oven for about 10 minutes.

In the meantime grill the pork over low heat, on an outdoor barbecue if possible. Turn and baste often, until pork is cooked through, about 20 minutes. Slice and keep warm.

Sauce and Vegetable Stir-fry:
¼ cup chicken broth
2 tbsp. white wine
2 tbsp. soy sauce
2 tbsp. hoisin sauce
1 tsp. sugar

1 tbsp. olive or canola oil
1 large sweet Spanish onion, thinly sliced
3–4 large cloves garlic, minced
3–4 cups cabbage, thinly sliced
1 carrot, coarsely grated
½ red pepper, thinly sliced
2 stalks celery, thinly sliced
½ lb. fresh mushrooms, thinly sliced
1 tbsp. cornstarch dissolved in 2 tbsp. water

Combine the chicken broth, white wine, soy sauce, hoisin sauce, and sugar in a bowl and set aside. In a small cup combine the cornstarch and water and set aside.

In a large skillet heat the olive oil. Add the onion and garlic and stir-fry a few minutes until onion is softened. Add the cabbage, carrot, red pepper, celery, and mushrooms and stir-fry another minute.

Add the chicken broth sauce, cover, and "steam" for about 5 minutes. Uncover, add the cornstarch and water, and continue cooking over medium-high heat, stirring often, until the vegetables are tender and the sauce is thickened, 3–4 more minutes. Place in a bowl and serve with the pork and pancakes. Let everyone make their own servings by placing some meat and vegetables on a pancake and rolling it up to eat. Serve with lots of napkins!

Yield: 4 servings.

Optional Suggestions: In the summer you may use **bok choy** or **Chinese cabbage** instead of the regular cabbage and add some sliced **snow peas.**

BOXING DAY ENCHILADAS

Leftover turkey never tasted so good!

Sauce:
2 tbsp. olive oil
1 large onion, chopped
2 cloves garlic, minced
½ green pepper, diced
2 cups canned or bottled tomato sauce (smooth, not chunky, sauce)
1 cup salsa
⅓ cup white wine
2 tsp. dried oregano

In a medium saucepan heat the olive oil and in it sauté the onion, garlic, and green pepper for about 5 minutes, stirring often. Add the tomato sauce, salsa, white wine, and oregano and cook about 15 minutes, or until slightly thickened. Set aside.

Filling:
¾ cup sour cream
⅔ cup red onion, chopped
½ cup *Roasted Red Pepper* (p. 56), finely chopped
½ cup pickled jalapeño peppers (optional)
⅓ cup Kalamata olives, pitted and minced (optional)

Mix all ingredients and set aside.

Preparing Tortillas and Assembly:
½ cup canola oil
12 corn tortillas (6–7")
2–2½ cups leftover turkey or chicken, chopped
filling (above)
sauce (above)
3 cups grated Cheddar cheese (medium or old)

In a small cast-iron frypan heat the oil over medium-high heat until hot. Using tongs to manoeuvre tortillas, cook each tortilla as follows: Place in oil for 4 seconds. Turn and cook 3 more seconds. Remove with tongs and let excess oil drain. Place on paper towels spread over a cookie sheet. (My cookie sheet holds 6 tortillas, so I layer paper towels on top of the first layer and continue.) Cooking in hot oil softens the tortillas.

Preheat oven to 350°F.

Down the middle of each tortilla place about 2 tbsp. filling, 2–3 tbsp. turkey, and 2 tbsp. grated Cheddar cheese. Roll up: Use both hands to tuck and roll one end under the filling and then roll the tortilla up and place seam-side down in an oblong baking dish (9" x 13"). Pour the sauce over the enchiladas, sprinkle remaining cheese over all, and bake in preheated oven for 15–20 minutes, or until cheese is melted and sauce is bubbling. Serve.

Yield: 4 servings.

Variations:
Beef Enchiladas: Substitute **grilled steak**, sliced, for the turkey. (One small steak will suffice.)
Vegetarian Enchiladas: Substitute *Mashed Frijoles* (p. 142) for the turkey.

CHICKEN QUESADILLAS

My first quesadillas were in the Montreal train station, and they were some of the yummiest Mexican foods I had ever had the pleasure to partake of. When I got home I attempted to recreate the dish, and although my method may not have been the same, the result was totally devoured.

1½ lb. chicken breast
salt and pepper, to taste
1 red pepper, or ⅔ cup bottled roasted red pepper, chopped
½ cup sour cream
½ lb. Monterey Jack cheese, grated
1 medium red onion, chopped
1–2 pickled jalapeño peppers, minced (if desired)
½ cup fresh coriander, minced (optional)
10 thick 10" flour tortillas (one package)
olive oil for brushing
additional sour cream
salsa

Grill the chicken breast until the juices run clear. Slice the chicken, season with salt and pepper to taste, and set aside. Leaving the red pepper whole, grill it at the same time, turning often, until it is charred. Place the red pepper in a plastic bag for a few minutes, then rub off the charred skin. Remove the seeds, slice the pepper, and set aside.

Preheat oven to 375°F.

In a bowl, mix together the sour cream, Monterey Jack cheese, red peppers, red onion, pickled jalapeños, and coriander, if desired.

Lightly oil 2 cookie sheets. On a large surface spread out all of the tortillas (if possible—if not, do them in two shifts). Place some of the sour cream mixture on each tortilla. Place some of the chicken on each tortilla also. Wet the edge and fold the tortilla in half, pressing the edges together to seal them as well as possible. You won't get (or need) a tight seal. Place the half-moon shaped quesadillas on a baking sheet, brush lightly with olive oil, and bake in the preheated oven for 10–15 minutes, or until heated through. Serve with additional sour cream and salsa.

Yield: 4–5 servings.

Optional Suggestions: Leftover chicken is fine in this recipe.

CAESAR CHICKEN ROLL-UPS

flour tortillas
grilled chicken breasts (or leftover chicken, warmed)
bacon, cooked until crisp,
drained, then crumbled
shredded Romaine lettuce
Mock Caesar Dressing (p .27)

Warm the tortillas according to package directions. Place some chicken, bacon, and Romaine lettuce on each tortilla. Drizzle the dressing over, roll up, and serve.

SLOPPY JOES

Definitely Cowboy Food. Serve with paper towels.

1 tbsp. olive oil
1 onion, chopped
1 clove garlic, minced
½ green pepper, chopped
1½ lbs. lean ground beef
1 cup ketchup
2 tbsp. apple cider vinegar
1 tbsp. fresh lemon juice
1 tbsp. Dijon mustard
1½ tsp. paprika
1½ tbsp. brown sugar
1 tsp. salt, or to taste
2 tbsp. Worcestershire sauce
4–6 hamburger buns

In a large skillet in the olive oil sauté the onion, garlic, and green pepper for a few minutes. Add the beef and sauté, breaking the meat up with a fork and stirring until no longer pink, about 10 minutes.

Stir in the ketchup, apple cider vinegar, lemon juice, Dijon mustard, paprika, and brown sugar. Turn down the heat until it is at a low simmer. Cook, uncovered, for about 10 more minutes. Stir in the salt and Worcestershire sauce.

Split the hamburger buns and pile the sloppy joe mixture on each bottom half. Cover with top half. Serve with lots of napkins.

Yield: 4–6 sloppy joes.

BEEF-MUSHROOM DIP

Great way to use leftover roast beef.

2 tbsp. olive oil
1 shallot, minced
½ lb. mushrooms, washed and
sliced
1 cup red wine
⅓ cup water
2 tbsp. butter
1 tsp. Worcestershire sauce
1 tsp. brown sugar
1 tsp. red wine vinegar
salt and pepper, to taste
1 lb. or more leftover roast
beef, sliced thin
hamburger buns

In a large skillet heat the olive oil and sauté the shallot for a few minutes. Add the mushrooms and continue sautéing and stirring until cooked through, 3–4 minutes. Add the red wine and water and simmer until reduced by at least half.

Add the butter, Worcestershire sauce, brown sugar, red wine vinegar, and salt and pepper, to taste. Simmer a few more minutes. Add the roast beef slices and heat through. To serve, place some of the roast beef and mushrooms on each bun. Dip each bun top (cut-side down) in the pan juices, top the sandwich, and serve with extra sauce for dipping.

Yield: 4–6 servings (depending on amount of roast beef)

NOTES

PASTAS

PESTO

Pesto is one of the most important basic recipes in this book. It is heavenly on fresh pasta and essential in many other recipes. Add a few tablespoonfuls to soup, stew, omelette, risotto, spaghetti sauce, etc., for amazing flavour. It can be frozen (without the cheese), and used throughout the winter to remind you of summer. But it is best fresh.

It is essential to have fresh basil. If you haven't a source of fresh basil, you can't make pesto.

Traditionally, pesto is made with pine nuts. I usually use **almonds** because they cost a lot less and seem just about as good. I have also used **pecans** with great success.

The amount of olive oil used is very flexible. The maximum amount (⅔ cup) is traditional. However, if you want a low-fat pesto, several tablespoons of olive oil is enough. The result is different, and definitely healthier. I usually use about ⅓ cup—with great results.

⅛–¼ cup almonds, or 3 tbsp. pine nuts
2–3 cloves garlic cut in chunks, or more to taste
pinch of salt
freshly ground pepper, to taste
2 cups gently packed shredded fresh basil leaves
2 tbsp.–⅔ cup olive oil—extra virgin, if possible
½–⅔ cup grated Parmesan cheese—freshly grated, if possible

In a food processor put the nuts, garlic, salt, and pepper. Buzz for a few seconds until the nuts are ground. Put in the basil leaves and pulse on and off until the leaves are minced and blended into the nut mixture. (Do not over-process, since this makes the pesto mushy.) With food processor on low, slowly add olive oil in a steady stream until it is incorporated. Scrape every bit into a bowl and stir in the cheese (unless you are freezing your pesto or your recipe specifies pesto without cheese).

Yield: 4 servings.

Variation:
Coriander Pesto: 8 large pecan halves, 1 clove garlic, 1 cup packed fresh coriander, 1 tbsp. lemon juice, salt and pepper, to taste, ⅛ cup olive oil.

To Freeze Pesto: Proceed as in basic recipe. **Do not add cheese.** Freeze in small plastic bags. You may want to freeze some in the amount needed for pasta, and some in smaller amounts to be added to soups or other recipes. (Ice cube trays are great for this.) To use, bring to room temperature, add cheese, and use as you would fresh pesto.

PESTO ON NOODLES

The simplest manner in which to eat pesto. This is of course best with freshly made pesto and homemade noodles.

1 recipe pesto (above)
375 g/12 oz. packaged pasta (spaghettini or linguini are best), or ½ lb. fresh pasta
pasta cooking water

Cook noodles as directed. When cooked al dente, remove ½ cup pasta cooking water. Drain noodles, place in a large warm pasta bowl, and keep warm. Add ¼–½ cup of the cooking liquid to the pesto a few tablespoons at a time and mix thoroughly until desired consistency is reached. Add pesto to the noodles and toss gently but thoroughly. Serve immediately, with more Parmesan cheese on the side. Pass the pepper mill.

Yield: 4 servings.

Variations:
Pesto-Vegetable Toss (our favourite pesto pasta in the summer): In a skillet sauté about **1 lb. fresh vegetables** in olive oil gently until tender-crisp and toss with the pesto and noodles. **Fresh green beans** and **snow peas** and **young zucchini,** halved and sliced, are a good combination. **Tomatoes,** quartered and sautéed a few minutes, add colour and flavour.

Pesto-Artichoke Heart Toss: Drain **1 jar marinated artichoke hearts**, reserving marinade. Quarter the hearts and add them, along with **2–3 tbsp. reserved marinade**, with the pesto. (Omit the ¼ cup noodle cooking liquid.) Toss and serve.

Lizzie's Creamy Pesto Sauce: Make pesto, or thaw frozen. In a double boiler whisk until slightly thick: **1 cup milk, 1 tbsp. Parmesan cheese, 1 egg yolk,** and **3 tbsp. butter.** Add pesto to taste and toss with noodles. Serve with more Parmesan cheese.

Winter Pesto Sauce: In mid-winter when your frozen pesto loses its "pizzazz" try adding any or all of the following: ⅓ **cup pitted Kalamata olives** (sliced), **2 tbsp.** capers (with a bit of juice), **2 scallions** (minced), ⅓ **cup roasted red peppers** (chopped), **8 dried tomato halves** (soaked 10 minutes in hot water, drained, and sliced), or **1 cup frozen peas** (cooked and drained).

Grilled Chicken with Pesto Pasta: Grill **2–3 chicken breasts** on the barbecue. Cut them up and toss with the pesto. Veggies (peas, tomatoes, peppers, etc.) may also be tossed in, if desired. Leftover chicken, diced and sautéed in olive oil with garlic, is good as well.

CREAMY PESTO-TOMATO-CHICKEN SAUCE

This is one of our favourite recipes.

1 whole chicken breast (from a free-range chicken), or 2 commercial chicken breasts (4 breast halves) (see p. 190-1, on homegrown birds)
2 tbsp. butter
1 tbsp. olive oil
2 cloves garlic, minced

Mrs. Corsi's Marinara Sauce (p. 157), or 3 cups good purchased tomato or tomato-pesto sauce
½–1 batch *Pesto* (p. 152-3), minus the cheese, or good purchased pesto, to taste
½ cup or less white wine (optional)
salt and pepper, to taste
dried or fresh oregano and basil to taste (if needed)

½ cup bottled roasted red pepper, diced (optional)
3 tbsp. butter
3 tbsp. flour
1½ cups milk
grating fresh nutmeg
¼ cup Parmesan cheese
500 g dried pasta
grated Parmesan cheese

Remove the skin from the chicken breast and remove the meat from the bone. Cut the chicken meat in ½" dice. In a large saucepan, heat the butter and olive oil until sizzling. Add the chicken meat and sauté over high heat, stirring often, for about 5 minutes, adding the minced garlic about halfway through. Add the tomato sauce, pesto, and white wine, if desired. Adjust the seasonings to taste and add the roasted red pepper, if desired. (If you are preparing this ahead, cool and refrigerate at this point. Bring to a simmer again before you proceed.)

Have the chicken-tomato sauce just below simmer. In a separate saucepan melt the butter. Add the flour, stirring, and slowly add the milk, blending with a whisk, until mixture is smooth and bubbly. Add the nutmeg and Parmesan cheese and slowly add mixture to the tomato sauce.

Cook noodles according to directions. Drain, toss sauce with noodles, and serve with additional Parmesan cheese on the side.

Yield: 4 servings.

Optional Suggestion: Add to the tomato sauce ½ **lb. fresh mushrooms**, cleaned, sliced, and sautéed in butter, and/or **1 small zucchini**, sliced and sautéed in olive oil. **Leftover chicken** may replace the chicken breasts.

BASIC SKILLET FRESH TOMATO SAUCE

This is the basic sauce to make in the summer when you have an abundance of fresh tomatoes. It is better if you peel and seed the tomatoes, especially if you freeze the sauce, but it is not necessary. You may serve this by itself on pasta—please pass the Parmesan cheese—or you may use it as a base for many other sauces.

2–2½ lbs. fresh ripe tomatoes
1–2 tbsp. olive oil
1 onion, chopped
2 cloves garlic, minced
1 jalapeño pepper (optional)
½ cup white wine
pinch of sugar
salt and pepper, to taste
dried oregano and Italian herbs, to taste
fresh basil, if available

Peel and seed tomatoes: Place tomatoes in a pot of boiling hot water for about 30 seconds. Remove tomatoes with a slotted spoon and place in a colander under cold running water. Slip skins off tomatoes and discard. Cut each tomato in half crosswise and squeeze seeds out over a colander placed over a bowl. Coarsely

chop tomatoes and place in a bowl. Press out any pulp left with the tomato seeds and add to the tomatoes.

In a large non-reactive skillet, heat the olive oil and in it briefly sauté the onion, garlic, and jalapeño pepper, if desired. Add the reserved tomatoes and juices along with the white wine, sugar, salt, pepper, fresh basil, oregano, and Italian herbs, to taste. Cook over high heat, stirring often, for about 5 minutes. Lower heat to a simmer and cook until desired thickness. Stir in fresh basil, if available, and serve.

Yield: 3–4 servings.

LATE SUMMER CHICKEN (OR PORK) RAGU SAUCE

Use the previous recipe as a base, but add some lean ground chicken (or pork) and fresh vegetables for a light and satisfying pasta sauce. Best over a chunkier pasta such as fusilli or rotini.

1 recipe **Basic Skillet Tomato Sauce** (above)
1 lb. lean ground chicken or pork
1 tbsp. olive oil
1 small onion, chopped
1 clove garlic, minced
½ red or green pepper, chopped
½ lb. mushrooms, chopped
1 small zucchini, chopped
2–3 tbsp. white wine
fresh basil, if available
375 g/12 oz. pasta, cooked and drained

Prepare **Basic Skillet Tomato Sauce**. Set aside and keep warm.

In a small cast-iron skillet sauté the ground chicken or pork over medium-high heat, stirring and breaking it up with a fork, until meat is cooked through. Remove with a slotted spoon and add to the tomato sauce.

Clean out skillet, if necessary. Add the olive oil and in it sauté the onion, garlic, and green pepper for a few minutes, stirring often. Add the mushroom and zucchini and sauté a few more minutes. Add the white wine, cover, and "steam" vegetables until just tender, 1–2 minutes. Add the vegetables to the tomato sauce, stir, and heat through. Add the basil, if needed, and serve over cooked and drained noodles.

Yield: 4 servings.

MRS. CORSI'S MARINARA SAUCE

I got this recipe from Phil (The Salad King). Being of Italian descent, and knowing that his Mother was a great cook, I of course went to him when I needed a good basic marinara sauce. He was kind enough to give me his mother's recipe.

1 large can (796 ml/28 oz.) ground tomatoes (Pastene brand tomatoes are very good)
a little onion, garlic, and celery, sautéed in olive oil
salt and pepper, to taste
pinch of sugar

Combine ingredients in a small saucepan and cook, stirring often, until nicely thickened. Serve over noodles as a side dish, or in any recipe that calls for marinara sauce.

Yield: Approx. 3 cups.

BASIC WINTER MARINARA SAUCE AND POSSIBILITIES

This is a good basic tomato sauce that can be used whenever a recipe calls for tomato sauce. I like to have some on hand in the freezer—in 1 cup and 2 cup amounts. If you have this on hand, you can add meat or veggies or both and have an excellent quick pasta dinner.

2 tbsp. olive oil
1 large onion, chopped
3–4 cloves garlic, minced
1 stalk celery, chopped (optional)
½ green or red pepper, chopped, or bottled roasted red pepper, chopped (optional)
1 large can (796 ml/28 oz.) diced tomatoes
1 small can (796 ml/28 oz.) tomato paste, plus 1 can water
½ cup white or red wine (optional)
salt and pepper, to taste
1 tbsp. dried oregano, or more to taste
1 tbsp. Italian herbs
1 tsp. sugar
1 tsp. Worcestershire sauce (optional)

In a large saucepan heat the olive oil. Add the onion, garlic, celery, and pepper (if desired) and sauté about 5 minutes, or until soft. Add the tomatoes. (If you don't have diced tomatoes, then put them in a large bowl and squish them up with your hands.) Add tomato paste, wine, salt, pepper, oregano, Italian herbs, sugar, and Worcestershire sauce, if desired. Bring to a simmer, lower heat, and cook over low heat until nice and thick, about 45 minutes–1 hour.

Yield: 4 servings.

Optional Suggestions: Fresh basil is always a welcome addition, or other herbs that suit the other ingredients (for instance, **fresh tarragon** complements added **seafood).** Try a tablespoon of **red wine vinegar** for added piquancy. **Leftover chicken or turkey** is a good addition, as well as cooked, drained **chick peas.**

Variations:
Pesto Marinara Sauce: To recipe, add ½ **recipe (½ cup) fresh or frozen** *Pesto* (p. 152-3), without cheese.

Meat Sauce: Add **1 lb. hamburger** and ½ **lb. Italian sausage**, sautéed until cooked through and drained.

Veggie Sauce: Add **2–3 small zucchini** and ½ **lb. mushrooms**, sliced and sautéed together in a little olive oil, and/ or ½ **cup Kalamata olives**, pitted and sliced.

MIDDLE EASTERN PASTA SAUCE WITH LAMB, CHICK PEAS, AND SPINACH

1 recipe *Mrs. Corsi's Marinara* (p. 157), or *Basic Winter Marinara Sauce* (p. 157-8), omitting the celery, red or green pepper, and Italian herbs and using the white wine plus:
1 tsp. cinnamon
1 tsp. dried oregano
½ tsp. ground coriander
1 tsp. ground cumin
1 tbsp. red wine vinegar

Lamb Meatballs and Assembly:
1 lb. ground lamb
1 shallot, minced
1 clove garlic, minced
salt and pepper, to taste
1 tsp. ground cumin
1 tbsp. olive oil
2 cups cooked chick peas (garbanzo beans), or 1 540 ml/19 oz. can, drained

500 g pasta (chunky, such as bow-ties, fusilli, or rotini, if possible—wholewheat pasta is good)
8–10 oz. fresh spinach, cleaned and torn into pieces
½ cup fresh parsley, minced
½ cup Kalamata olives, pitted and sliced (optional)
½ cup crumbled feta cheese (optional)

In a large, non-reactive frypan make the sauce adding the cinnamon, coriander, cumin, and red wine vinegar. Simmer until nicely thickened. While sauce is cooking make the meatballs.

In a medium bowl mix well the ground lamb, shallot, garlic, salt, pepper, and cumin and form the mixture into small meatballs. (Wet your hands with cold water when forming meatballs.)

Brown the meatballs in the olive oil in a medium cast-iron frypan. Continue cooking and turning until they are cooked through and evenly browned. Add to the tomato sauce along with the cooked chick peas. Simmer about 20 minutes. (If you are going to serve this later, cool and refrigerate now. Then reheat and proceed.)

In the meantime, cook the pasta according to package directions and drain well.

Add the spinach to the sauce, a third at a time, and cook just until the spinach is wilted. Serve over the noodles garnished with the fresh parsley, olives, and feta cheese, if desired.

Yield: 4–6 servings.

BOW-TIES WITH LAMB MEATBALLS AND ARTICHOKE HEARTS

Sauce:
2 tbsp. olive oil
1 large onion, chopped
½ red or green pepper, sliced, or ⅔ cup **Roasted Red Pepper** (p. 56), chopped
2 cloves garlic, minced
1 large can (796 ml/28 oz.) tomatoes, with juice
1 small can (156 ml/5.5 oz.) tomato paste
½ cup white wine
1 tsp. dried oregano
½ tsp. allspice or cinnamon, or both
salt and pepper, to taste

Meatballs and Assembly:
1 lb. ground lamb
1 clove garlic, minced
1 tsp. herbes de Provence
½ tsp. cinnamon
salt and pepper, to taste
1 tbsp. olive oil
½ cup Kalamata olives, pitted and sliced (optional)
1 can artichoke hearts, drained and quartered
2 tbsp. fresh parsley, minced
500 g/1 lb. bow-ties, or other chunky pasta

In a large saucepan heat the olive oil and in it sauté the onion, pepper (if desired), and garlic over medium-high heat for a few minutes, stirring often. Add the tomatoes, tomato paste, white wine, oregano, allspice and/or cinnamon, salt, and pepper. Cook, stirring occasionally, until sauce is thickened, about 30 minutes.

In the meantime, make the meatballs: In a bowl combine the lamb, garlic, herbes de Provence, cinnamon, and salt and pepper, to taste, and form the meat into small meatballs.

Heat the olive oil in a medium cast-iron skillet, and sauté the meatballs, turning often until they are browned and cooked through. Remove with a slotted spoon to a paper towel-lined plate to drain excess fat.

Add the meatballs to the sauce along with the Kalamata olives and artichoke hearts and simmer about 10 minutes longer. Stir in parsley.

Cook noodles according to package directions. Drain, rinse under hot water, and drain well again.
Serve with the sauce.

Yield: 4–6 servings.

PASTA WITH SCALLOPS, MUSHROOMS, AND GREENS

A spring favourite with new greens! Use different greens for different results: Some arugula, sorrel, or watercress will add a burst of flavour, whereas spinach or radicchio will make a homier sauce.

1 tbsp. olive oil and 1 tbsp. butter
2 cloves garlic, minced
1 shallot, minced
½ lb. mushrooms, sliced
½ cup dry white wine
salt and pepper, to taste
2 tbsp. butter
1 lb. scallops
1 *Roasted Red Pepper* (p. 56), chopped, or equivalent bottled (optional)
2 scallions, minced
½ cup fresh cilantro, minced, or ½ cup parsley and 1 tsp. fines herbes
1 cup coffee cream, warmed to just below simmering
4 cups fresh greens, thinly sliced (spinach, arugula, sorrel, watercress, or radicchio)
340 g/12 oz. dried noodles (a thinner noodle such as linguini is preferable)
grated Parmesan or Romano cheese

In a medium-sized saucepan sauté the garlic and shallot in the olive oil and butter for 1 minute. Add the mushrooms and sauté for a few more minutes, stirring constantly. Add the wine and cook about 5 minutes longer, or until liquid is reduced by half. Season to taste with salt and pepper.

In a separate skillet melt remaining 2 tbsp. butter. When it is frothy add scallops and sauté, stirring constantly, for about 5 minutes or until they are cooked through. Remove the scallops with a slotted spoon and add any remaining "juice" to the mushroom sauce. Reduce the liquid until ⅓ cup remains. Add the red pepper, scallions, herbs, and reserved scallops. Simmer 1 minute. Add cream and gently warm mixture until it is hot, but do not boil because the cream may curdle. Keep hot.

Cook noodles following directions on package. Drain thoroughly in a colander. In a large pasta bowl place the cooked noodles. Add half the sauce and half the greens, and gently toss. Add remaining sauce and greens and continue gently tossing until greens are slightly wilted and all is well mixed. Serve with grated Parmesan or Romano cheese on the side.

Yield: 3–4 servings.

ROASTED GARLIC, CLAM, AND MUSHROOM PASTA SAUCE

An old favourite with a few new twists. This sauce is quick and easy to prepare and surprisingly delicious for minimum effort. If you cannot obtain **canned bar clams**, a can of baby clams is an adequate substitute. I like to add a **zucchini** in the summer, but it is not necessary.

2 tbsp. olive oil, plus 1 tbsp. additional olive oil
2 cloves garlic, minced
225 g/8 oz. fresh mushrooms, washed, trimmed, and sliced
⅓ cup white wine
1 can (140 ml/5 oz. drained weight) bar clams
salt, to taste
½ tsp. red pepper flakes
1 tsp. fines herbes
1 tbsp. *Tarragon Vinegar* (p. 100-1)
½ cup bottled roasted red pepper, diced (optional)
1 small zucchini, sliced and sautéed in olive oil until tender (optional)
2 green onions, chopped
½ cup fresh parsley, minced
375 g/12 oz. dried linguini or spaghettini
Parmesan cheese

In a medium saucepan over low heat, sauté the garlic in 2 tbsp. olive oil for 3–4 minutes, stirring often, until the garlic is browned but not burnt. (It can burn easily if you are not careful.) Add the additional 1 tbsp. olive oil and the mushrooms and sauté a few minutes more, stirring occasionally. Add the wine and bring to a boil. Drain the clams, reserving liquid and cutting large pieces if needed. Add them to the sauce with ⅓ cup of the liquid. Taste before adding any salt, since the clams are a bit salted already, and you may not need additional salt. Add the red pepper flakes, fines herbes, and tarragon vinegar. Simmer a few minutes longer. Do not boil, as this can toughen the clams. Remove pot from heat and add the roasted red pepper and/or zucchini, along with the green onions and fresh parsley. Keep warm.

Cook noodles as directed. Drain well and toss with the sauce. Serve with Parmesan cheese, if desired.

Yield: 3–4 servings.

CREAMY CURRY SAUCE WITH SCALLOPS

Try this dish with a commercial curry paste. They are widely available, easy to use, and delicious! It is best to add less curry at first, taste the results, and add more if you want it hotter—you can add more, but once it is in, you can't take it out.

2 tbsp. butter
2 tbsp. flour
1 cup milk
½ tsp. salt
⅔ cup white wine
2 tbsp. curry paste, or 1 tbsp. curry powder, or to taste
2 tbsp. olive oil, or more as needed
1 large onion, chopped
½ red pepper, chopped, or ½ cup bottled roasted red peppers, chopped (optional)
2 cloves garlic, minced
1 tbsp. fresh ginger, minced
1 lb. scallops, fresh or frozen (thawed), large ones quartered
3 green onion, minced
¼ cup fresh coriander, minced (optional)
375 g/12 oz. dried pasta, prepared according to package directions

In a medium saucepan over medium heat melt the butter. Stir in the flour, slowly add the milk, and whisk until the mixture is smooth. Cook over medium heat, stirring constantly, until mixture is smooth and thick. Whisk in the salt, white wine, and curry. Taste and adjust seasoning to your liking. Heat the olive oil in a skillet over medium-high heat and cook the onion (and pepper, if used), until soft, about 5 minutes. Add the garlic (and ginger, if used) and sauté a few minutes more. Add to the curry sauce. Heat 1 more tbsp. olive oil in skillet and quickly sauté the scallops, stirring constantly, until they are cooked through. Depending on the size of scallops, this could take 3–5 minutes. Add scallops to curry sauce. Sauce can be cooled and refrigerated at this point. Reheat to simmering before proceeding.

Cook noodles as directed. Drain them and place them in a large pasta bowl. Pour sauce over noodles and add the green onions and coriander, if used. Toss gently but thoroughly and serve.

Yield: 3–4 servings.

LUTHER AND LINDA'S FRENCH RIVER BAR CLAMS AND PASTA

Luther and Linda are great fans of canned New London Bar Clams. With them, we go to the French River Cannery where they purchase a case to take back to New York State with them every year. Over one winter they developed this recipe. Luther thinks this should be served with Scotch whisky—I would prefer a good bottle of red wine myself!

250 g/8 oz. wholewheat pasta, such as Japanese udon noodles
1 bottle (250 ml/8 oz.) clam juice
1 can bar clams, drained and liquid reserved
1 tbsp. olive oil
6 cloves garlic, minced
1 onion, or 4 scallions, chopped
1 red pepper, chopped
1 yellow pepper, chopped
1 cup broccoli florets, or any other vegetable you have
3 plum tomatoes, chopped
¼ cup fresh basil leaves, minced, or more to taste

Drain clams, reserving liquid.

Cook pasta in a pot of boiling water until firm but not done. Drain well and return to the pot. Add the clam juice and all of the liquid from the New London bar clams. Simmer until most of the clam juice has been absorbed, 2–4 minutes.

While pasta is cooking, heat the olive oil in a large frypan. Add the garlic and onions and stir-fry 1–2 minutes. Add the red and yellow peppers and broccoli (or other veggies) and cook until semisoft. Add the clams and tomatoes and cook just until they are heated through. Add the vegetable/clam mixture to the pasta, sprinkle with the fresh basil leaves, and toss until well mixed. Serve.

Yield: 2–3 servings.

SZECHUAN NOODLES WITH GROUND CHICKEN, TURKEY, OR PORK AND VEGETABLES

An economical, healthy, and delicious combination which is a complete meal and is easy to make from scratch in under one hour. All of the vegetables used are readily available any time of year. I have used lean ground chicken, turkey, and pork with equally yummy results. One of the optional ingredients is **Thai sweet chili sauce.** It adds zest, if that is what you like, but is not necessary.

1 head broccoli, cleaned and cut into bite-sized pieces
1 carrot, cut into thin rounds
1 stalk celery, cut into thin slices
½ green pepper, slivered
⅔ cup chicken stock (unsalted if possible)
3 tbsp. tamari soy sauce
1 tbsp. sugar
1 tbsp. rice wine vinegar
250 g/8 oz. spaghettini, or a thicker pasta
2 scallions, chopped
2 tbsp. canola or safflower oil
2 large cloves garlic, minced
3 tbsp. fresh ginger, minced
1 large onion, halved and thinly sliced
1 lb. lean ground chicken, turkey, or pork
2 tbsp. hoisin sauce
2–3 tsp. sesame oil
2–3 tbsp. Thai sweet chili sauce (red or green) (optional)
additional tamari soy sauce, to serve (optional)
Thai sweet chili sauce, to serve (optional)

Prepare the broccoli, carrot, celery, and green pepper and set the vegetables aside in a bowl.

Combine the chicken stock, tamari soy sauce, sugar, and vinegar in a bowl and set aside.

Cook the noodles according to package directions. Drain, rinse well with hot water, drain very well again, and set aside.

Prepare the scallions and set them aside.

Set out on your stove a large frypan (with a lid) and a wok. In the frypan place 1 tbsp. of the oil. In the wok, place remaining 1 tbsp. oil. Place half of the garlic and ginger in each of the pans.

Heat the frypan. Add the onion and stir-fry a minute or two. Add the vegetables from

the bowl and stir-fry a few minutes longer. Add half the chicken stock mixture, cover, and "steam" until vegetables are just tender, stir-frying a few times while they are cooking.

Heat the wok and add the ground chicken, turkey, or pork to the garlic and ginger and cook over high heat, stirring the meat constantly and breaking it apart until meat is browned and cooked through. Add the hoisin sauce, sesame oil, and sweet chili sauce to the remaining chicken stock mixture, and add this to the meat in the wok. Bring to a boil and cook about 2 minutes. Check the noodles, and if they are sticking, rinse them quickly under hot water and drain again very well. Add the noodles, tossing them into the meat mixture, and heat them through. Add the vegetables and the prepared scallions and toss until blended. Serve with additional tamari and/or Thai sweet chili sauce.

Yield: 4 servings.

CREAMY SUN-DRIED TOMATO SAUCE WITH WINTER VEGGIES AND CHICKEN

A very hearty and satisfying dish that is good for a crowd. If serving to children you may want to omit the pickled jalapeño peppers.

10 sun-dried tomato halves
1 cup chicken broth
½ cup white wine
3 tbsp. olive oil
2 medium onion, chopped
4 cloves garlic, minced
2 shallots, minced
2 carrots, peeled and thinly sliced
1 cup parsley
⅔ cup bottled roasted red peppers, chopped
⅓–½ cup pickled jalapeño peppers, minced (optional)
salt and pepper, to taste

Cream Sauce:
1½ tbsp. butter
1½ tbsp. flour
1½ cups light cream (or milk)
1 small can (156 ml/5.5 oz.) tomato paste
⅓ cup Parmesan cheese

2 tbsp. olive oil, or more if needed

1½ lbs. boneless chicken thighs, trimmed of skin and excess fat then cubed
1 head broccoli, washed and cut into bite-sized pieces
2 tbsp. white wine
500 g/1 lb. pasta, cooked according to package directions and drained

In a small saucepan simmer the sun-dried tomatoes in the chicken broth and white wine for 15 minutes. Set aside.

In a large saucepan, in the olive oil, sauté the onion, garlic, shallots, carrots, and parsley for about 5 minutes, stirring often, until vegetables are soft. Strain the broth mixture into the veggies, cover, and cook 15–20 minutes. In the meantime, using scissors, cut the simmered sun-dried tomato halves into slivers. Add these, along with the roasted red peppers and jalapeño peppers, if desired, to the veggie mixture and simmer. Taste and add salt and pepper, if desired. (It is important to taste first since some sun-dried tomatoes are quite salty.)

Make cream sauce: In a small saucepan melt the butter. Stir in the flour and add the light cream or milk slowly, whisking all the time. Cook over medium heat, whisking often, until the mixture is thickened and smooth. Whisk in the tomato paste and cook until heated through. Remove from heat and add the Parmesan cheese. Slowly add this mixture to the veggie mixture. Blend gently but thoroughly and keep warm over low heat.

In a wok over high heat add 1 tbsp. olive oil. Wait until it is smoking, then add the chicken pieces and stir-fry for about 3 minutes. Cover and cook 2–3 more minutes to ensure the chicken is cooked through. Add chicken and any juices to the pasta sauce.

Return wok to high heat, add remaining 1 tbsp. olive oil, and stir-fry the broccoli for 30 seconds. Add the white wine, lower heat slightly, cover, and "steam" until desired tenderness is reached. You may need to add additional white wine (or water). When done, add to pasta sauce and keep sauce warm.

Cook pasta according to package directions, drain well, and place in a large serving bowl. Pour sauce over and mix all together well. Serve with additional Parmesan cheese, if desired.

Yield: 8–10 servings.

CREAMY MACARONI AND CHEESE

Macaroni and cheese is a humble and comforting dish. Made "from scratch" it can be quite special. The sauce can be prepared ahead of time, making it good for a busy day. Just be careful warming up the sauce, since it burns quite easily. You may need to add a bit more milk. We like this served with *Piquant Tomatoes* (p. 28) on the side.

2 tbsp. butter
4 tbsp. flour
3 cups milk
1 tsp. dry mustard
salt and pepper, to taste
½ lb. (or more, to taste) sharp Cheddar cheese, grated, or a combination of Cheddar and mozzarella
1 tsp. Worcestershire sauce
½ small onion, grated (optional)
250 g/½ lb. dry elbow macaroni (or fusilli, or any smaller pasta), cooked and drained

In a saucepan, melt the butter. Stir in the flour and gradually add 3 cups milk, stirring constantly with a whisk, until well blended. Cook over a medium-low heat, whisking often, until mixture is smooth, thickened, and just bubbling. Remove from heat and add cheese, Worcestershire sauce, and onion, if desired. Stir until cheese melts. Add to cooked noodles and serve.

Yield: 4 servings.

Variation:
Creamy Noodles and Cheese with Ham: This is our favourite variation. Add 1–2 cups **leftover ham**, cut into small pieces. Or use a **ham slice** (half a slice, if it is large) that has been sautéed in butter until cooked through, then cooled and cut into small pieces.

OUT-OF-THE-GARDEN-AND-INTO-THE-PAN PASTA

As the title indicates, this is an impromptu guide to a delicious vegetable sauce in late summer.

2 tbsp. olive oil
1–2 onions, chopped
1 garlic shallot, chopped
1 clove garlic, minced
1 pepper, chopped
6–8 cups fresh tomatoes, peeled and chopped
¼ cup white wine
½ cup tomato paste
1 tsp. red wine vinegar
salt and pepper, to taste
1 tsp. Italian herbs
1 tbsp. dried oregano
1 small zucchini, diced
kernels from 1 large corn cob, or 2 cups fresh green beans, stemmed and sliced
1 cup sliced chanterelle mushrooms (optional)
375 g/12 oz. pasta, cooked according to package directions and drained
Parmesan cheese

In a large frypan heat the olive oil and in it sauté the onions, shallot, garlic, and pepper about 5 minutes, stirring often, or until vegetables are soft. Add the tomatoes, white wine, tomato paste, red wine vinegar, salt, pepper, Italian herbs, and oregano. Turn up the heat and cook, stirring often, until the tomatoes are soft and enough of the liquid has evaporated so you have the consistency you desire, 20 minutes or more. Add the zucchini, corn (or beans), and chanterelles, if available. Cover and cook until vegetables are tender-crisp—about 5 more minutes, or until desired tenderness is reached. Serve over pasta and pass the Parmesan cheese.

Yield: 4 servings.

Optional Suggestion: This sauce is good as a vegetable side dish with grilled chicken or fish. Any leftovers make a good filling for omelets.

FUSILLI WITH TOMATOES AND ARUGULA

An incredibly easy sauce to make. It is robust and looks so Italian!

375 g/12 oz. fusilli (corkscrew) or rotini pasta
2 tbsp. olive oil
4 cloves garlic, minced
pinch red pepper flakes
1 large can (796 ml/28 oz.) Italian plum tomatoes
salt, to taste
1 tsp. sugar
4 tightly packed cups arugula
½ cup Kalamata olives, pitted and slivered
Parmesan or Romano cheese

Cook pasta according to package directions.

In a large skillet heat the olive oil and sauté the garlic and red pepper flakes for 1 minute. Drain the tomatoes and cut them up in the can. (Do not drain again after you cut them up.) Add the tomatoes, salt, and sugar and cook for 5 minutes. Add the arugula and olives and heat until the arugula is just wilted. Serve with Parmesan or Romano cheese.

Yield: 3–4 servings.

Optional Suggestion: If you don't have that much arugula, use **fresh spinach** for some of it. **Fresh tomatoes** (2 lbs.), peeled and seeded, may be used for the canned—cook 5–10 minutes longer.

Variation:
Fusilli with Tomatoes and Spinach: Substitute **fresh spinach** for the arugula and top with crumbled **Feta cheese** instead of Parmesan.

CREAMY MELANZA (EGGPLANT) PASTA

I first made this for a fall potluck cook-out in the woods—and it is a perfect dish for such an occasion—filling and full of the good autumn flavours.

2 tbsp. olive oil
1 large clove garlic, minced
2 large (or 3–4 small) tomatoes
1 small can (156 ml/5.5 oz.) tomato paste
1 tomato-paste can water
½ cup white wine
1 tsp. sugar
4 tbsp. olive oil
2 large cloves garlic, minced
1 medium green pepper, chopped
2 medium eggplants, cut into ½" dice
salt and pepper, to taste
½ tsp. red pepper flakes, or to taste
½ cup Kalamata olives, pitted and sliced
Cream Sauce:
2 tbsp. butter
2 tbsp. flour
1 cup milk
½ cup Parmesan cheese

375 g/12 oz. fusilli or rotini, cooked according to package directions and drained

In a small saucepan heat 2 tbsp. olive oil. Add the garlic and cook, stirring, about 1 minute. Add the diced tomatoes and cook, stirring, an additional 5 minutes. Add the tomato paste, 1 can of water, white wine, and sugar. Cook, stirring, until sauce is slightly thickened, about 10 minutes.

In the meantime heat the 4 tbsp. olive oil in a large non-reactive frypan. When it is hot add the garlic and green pepper and sauté, stirring, about 1 minute. Add the eggplant and cook, stirring constantly, about five minutes. Add the tomato sauce, salt, pepper, red pepper flakes, and olives. Cover and cook for about 10 minutes or until the eggplant is tender. You may need to add a bit more water or wine if the sauce seems too thick. While the sauce is cooking make the cream sauce: In a small saucepan melt the butter. Blend in the flour and slowly add the milk, stirring and whisking until sauce is thick and bubbling. Remove from heat and stir in Parmesan cheese. When the eggplant is tender, remove tomato/veggie sauce from heat, add the cream sauce and blend thoroughly. Pour over the cooked and drained noodles, stirring until it is thoroughly mixed. Serve.

Yield: 6 servings. More as part of a potluck.

GRILLED CHICKEN-ASPARAGUS PASTA À L'ESTRAGON

Marinade:

1 whole chicken breast (from a free-range chicken) or 2 whole commercial breasts (4 breast halves) (see p. 190-1 on home-grown birds)

½ cup *Tarragon Vinegar* (p. 100-1)

¼ cup white wine

salt and pepper, to taste

3 tbsp. fresh tarragon, minced

3 tbsp. fresh chives, minced

In the morning prepare the chicken: Remove the chicken meat from the bone, separate it into pieces, and gently flatten the thicker sections with your hands until the chicken pieces are of uniform thickness.

In a medium-large flat glass container mix the tarragon vinegar, white wine, salt, pepper, tarragon, and chives with a fork. Gently lay the chicken pieces in the marinade and carefully turn them, spooning the marinade over, until they are evenly covered. Cover container with plastic wrap and refrigerate. If you can, after several hours, gently turn the chicken pieces in the marinade.

Pasta Sauce:

chicken and marinade (above)

1 cup chicken broth

½ cup white wine

¼ cup *Tarragon Vinegar* (p. 100-1)

1 cup drained and chopped canned tomatoes

1 lb. fresh asparagus, washed and cut into 2" lengths, keeping tips separate

salt and pepper, to taste

1 tbsp. cornstarch, dissolved in 2 tbsp. water

1 lb. dried pasta, cooked according to package directions

3 tbsp. fresh tarragon, minced

2 green onions, chopped

Remove chicken from marinade and grill on outdoor barbecue, basting frequently, until chicken is thoroughly done. Cut into the thickest part—if pink juice runs out it needs more cooking. When chicken is done, cut it into slivers and keep warm.

In a medium skillet place the chicken broth, white wine, and tarragon vinegar and bring to a boil. Lower to a simmer, add the tomatoes and cook 2 minutes. Add the asparagus spears and cook 2 minutes, then add the asparagus tips and cook 2 more minutes. Add salt and pepper to taste, then slowly add the dissolved cornstarch, simmering a minute or two more until sauce thickens slightly.

Cook pasta according to package directions. Drain well and place in a large bowl. Add the asparagus sauce and toss well. Add the reserved chicken, fresh tarragon, and green onions, and toss again. Serve.

Yield: 4–6 servings.

PASTA WITH FRESH HERBS

Nothing could be simpler or yummier in the summer. I often serve this. Best with chunky pasta.

375 g/12 oz. pasta of your choice
3 tbsp. olive oil
2 tbsp. soft butter
salt and pepper, to taste
1 clove garlic, minced
⅓ cup fresh chives, minced
⅓ cup fresh parsley, minced
½ cup fresh tarragon, minced
2 tbsp. fresh thyme, minced
½ cup Parmesan cheese, grated

Cook pasta according to package directions. In the meantime place the olive oil and butter in a pasta serving bowl. Add the salt, pepper, and garlic and blend well. Add the chives, parsley, tarragon, and thyme and stir well to blend.

When the noodles are al dente drain them well and immediately place them in the bowl with the herbed mixture and toss. Serve, sprinkled with Parmesan.

Yield: 3–4 servings.

Optional Suggestion: Replace the tarragon with **fresh basil**. In winter use **fines herbes** to taste instead of the fresh herbs.

MUSSEL-ZUCCHINI PASTA

This is good in late summer when the fresh zucchini and tomatoes are abundant. Paired with steamed mussels, the veggies make a delicious pasta sauce.

To Steam Mussels:
1 tbsp. olive oil
1 large shallot, minced
1 clove garlic, minced
½ cup white wine
3 lb. fresh mussels, scrubbed and debearded if necessary

Sauce:
3 tbsp. olive oil
1 large onion, chopped
2 cloves garlic, minced
1 medium zucchini (⅔ lb.), or 2 small zucchini, diced into ¼" cubes
1½ lbs. small ripe tomatoes, diced
½–⅔ cup mussel broth (reserved from above)
salt, to taste
red pepper flakes, to taste (optional)
½ cup each fresh basil and parsley, minced
375 g/12 oz. noodles, cooked according to package directions, drained
Parmesan cheese, for serving

In a large stockpot sauté the shallot and garlic in the olive oil for a few minutes. Add the white wine and bring to a boil. Add the mussels, cover, and steam until mussels are open. Remove from heat and drain, saving the liquid. Set mussels aside to cool. When they are cool, remove from shells, discarding any that do not open. Set mussels aside.

In a large skillet sauté the onion and garlic in olive oil for about 5 minutes, stirring often. Add the zucchini, tomatoes, and reserved mussel broth. Cook about 10 minutes. Taste and add salt and red pepper flakes, to taste. Stir in the reserved mussels and cook, stirring, until heated through. Remove from heat and stir in the fresh basil and parsley. Toss with the cooked noodles, and serve with Parmesan cheese on the side.

Yield: 3–4 servings.

FILLED AND BAKED PASTA DISHES

CREAMY SPICY LASAGNA

A creamy, spicy lasagna—perfect on a cold day with a green salad, French bread, and a good bottle of red wine. You may substitute your favourite sauce if you wish. You'll need 5–6 cups.

Sauce:
1 lb. hamburger
½ lb. hot Italian sausage, casings removed
2 tbsp. olive oil
1 medium onion, chopped
2 cloves garlic, minced (or more to taste)
½ green pepper, seeded and chopped, or ½ cup bottled roasted red pepper, chopped
1 large can (796 ml/28 oz.) tomatoes, with juice, chopped
1 small can (156 ml/5.5 oz.) tomato paste
1 tomato paste-can full red wine
1 tsp. salt (or to taste)
pepper, to taste
2 tsp. dried oregano
2 tsp. Italian herbs
1 tsp. sugar

In a skillet sauté the hamburger and sausage, breaking it up with a fork, and stirring often to brown meat evenly. When it is thoroughly cooked (no longer pink), remove with a slotted spoon, drain on paper towel, and set aside.

In a large saucepan in the olive oil sauté the onion and garlic about 5 minutes or until soft. Add the green pepper and sauté 5 minutes more. (If using bottled roasted red peppers they do not have to be sautéed.) Add the red peppers, if used, along with the tomatoes, tomato paste, red wine, salt, pepper, oregano, Italian herbs, and sugar. Simmer over low heat about 1 hour, or until it thickens up a bit.

Cream Sauce:
4 tbsp. butter
4 tbsp. white flour
1½ cups milk
salt and pepper, to taste
grating of whole nutmeg

While the meat sauce cooks, make the cream sauce. In a medium saucepan over medium heat, melt the butter and stir in the flour. Slowly add milk, mixing constantly with a whisk, until mixture is smooth and just bubbling. Add salt, pepper, and freshly grated nutmeg, and set aside.

Assemble and Bake:
tomato-meat sauce (above)
cream sauce (above)
9 lasagna noodles, cooked according to package directions, rinsed, and drained
⅔–¾ lb. grated mozzarella cheese
½ cup Parmesan cheese

Preheat oven to 375°F. Have both sauces and remaining ingredients lined up and ready to use.
In a 9" x 13" x 2" pan spread just enough of the tomato-meat sauce on the bottom to barely cover it (less than 1 cup). Layer three noodles over sauce. Spread ⅓ of the meat sauce over noodles. Drizzle ½ the cream sauce over it and spread with a spoon to even it out. Top with ⅓ of the mozzarella cheese. Place another layer of noodles on top, spread with ⅓ of the meat sauce, then the remaining cream sauce, again smoothing with a spoon. Sprinkle on another ⅓ of the mozzarella cheese. Place remaining noodles on top. Cover with remaining meat sauce. Sprinkle remaining mozzarella and Parmesan cheese on top. (Lasagna may be prepared to this point and kept covered in refrigerator for up to one day. Remove from refrigerator 1 hour before baking.)

Bake in preheated oven 35–40 minutes, or until baked through and bubbling. (If cheese browns too quickly, cover with aluminum foil.) Serve.

Yield: 6–8 servings.

Variation:
Spicy Pasta Sauce: The spicy sauce above is good as a sauce on noodles as well. The recipe is enough for 1 lb. of dried pasta.

BAKED MOUSSAKA-PASTA CASSEROLE

This is much better made in the morning of the day it is to be served—it gives the flavours a chance to mellow and the extra juice to be absorbed.

Tomato-Lamb Sauce:
2 tbsp. olive oil
2 onions, chopped
1 large red pepper, seeded and chopped
3 cloves garlic, minced
1 large can (796 ml/28 oz.) diced tomatoes, or 3 cups fresh

tomatoes
½ cup white wine
3 tbsp. tomato paste
1 tsp. cinnamon
½ tsp. allspice
salt and pepper, to taste
1 tsp. sugar
1 tsp. dried oregano
1 lb. ground lamb
½ cup fresh parsley, minced

In a large saucepan heat the olive oil and in it sauté the onion, peppers, and garlic for about 5 minutes, stirring often. Add the tomatoes, white wine, tomato paste, cinnamon, allspice, salt, pepper, sugar, and oregano. Bring to a simmer, lower heat, and simmer sauce while you sauté the lamb.

In a separate, smaller skillet, over medium-high heat, quickly sauté the ground lamb, breaking meat up with a fork and stirring until meat is just cooked through. Remove meat with a slotted spoon and add to the tomato sauce. Continue simmering sauce for about 30 more minutes. Add parsley and simmer 5 minutes more. Set aside.

Eggplant, Cream Sauce, and Assembly:
1 large eggplant
4 tbsp. olive oil, plus more if needed
2 tbsp. butter
2 tbsp. flour

1½ cups milk
grating fresh nutmeg
½ tsp. salt
1 egg yolk
250 g/½ lb. fusilli (or macaroni) noodles
½ cup Parmesan cheese

Peel the eggplant. Slice it lengthwise into slices ¼"–⅓" thick, sprinkle lightly with salt, and allow to stand 20–30 minutes. Press out excess moisture between paper towels.

Heat the olive oil in a large cast-iron frypan over medium-high heat. Add the eggplant slices in one layer and quickly cook them, turning once, until soft, adding more oil when needed. Remove slices to a paper towel-lined plate. Repeat with remaining slices until they are all cooked. Set aside.

In a small saucepan over medium heat melt the butter. Stir in the flour and slowly add the milk, stirring constantly with a whisk until the mixture is smooth, thickened, and just bubbling. Add the nutmeg and salt and remove from heat. In a small bowl beat the egg yolk. Add a small amount of the cream sauce and blend in quickly. Return the saucepan to the heat, add the egg yolk mixture and cook, stirring constantly, until sauce again comes to a bubble. Remove from heat and set aside.

Cook the fusilli (or macaroni) according to package directions. Drain and spread out in an oiled 9" x 13" x 2" baking dish. Pour half of the tomato-meat sauce over the noodles. Place the eggplant slices over the sauce, cover with remaining tomato-meat sauce, then spread the cream sauce over all. Sprinkle with Parmesan cheese, cover and refrigerate until 1 hour before baking time. Then remove from refrigerator and bring back to room temperature.

Bake in 375°F oven for 45 minutes. Serve.

Yield: 4–6 servings.

CHEESE AND PESTO-STUFFED MANICOTTI

Filling:
2 cups ricotta cheese (1-lb. carton)
1 recipe **Pesto** (p. 152-3), without cheese
⅔ cup Parmesan cheese, grated
1–2 garlic shallots or green onions, minced
1 garlic glove, minced
1 egg

Combine all ingredients in a bowl and mix together thoroughly. Set aside.

Assembly and Baking:
1 recipe (4 cups) **Basic Marinara Sauce** (p. 157), or **Mrs. Corsi's Marinara** (p. 157), or **Basic Skillet Tomato Sauce** (p. 155-6)

12 manicotti noodles, cooked according to package directions, rinsed, and drained
½ lb. mozzarella cheese, grated
2–3 tbsp. Parmesan cheese
Preheat oven to 350°F. Lightly oil an 8" x 11" baking dish. Spread some sauce lightly over the bottom of a baking dish.

Fill each cooked manicotti noodle with some of the filling. (This can be tricky, since the noodles are slippery!) Place them side by side in the baking dish. Pour the sauce over the noodles, getting some in between each pair of manicotti. Sprinkle with mozzarella and Parmesan cheese. Cover with aluminum foil and bake in preheated oven for about 40–45 minutes, or until manicotti are heated through and sauce is bubbling. Serve.

Yield: 4–6 servings.

FISH AND
SHELLFISH

SPANISH POACHED FISH

Extremely easy to make and delicious to eat! I love it over plain brown rice.

brown or basmati rice, cooked
2 tbsp. olive oil
½ cup onions, chopped
½ cup green pepper, chopped
1–2 cloves garlic, minced.
3 large or 4 medium tomatoes, coarsely chopped, or 1 small can (398 ml/14 oz.)
⅔ cup white wine (use ½ cup with frozen fish)
salt and pepper, to taste
2–3 tsp. fresh tarragon, minced (or 1–2 tsp. fines herbes)

1 tsp. *Tarragon Vinegar* (p. 100-1)
1½ lb. fresh white fish (cod, haddock, etc.)

In a large skillet in the olive oil sauté onion, green pepper, and garlic until soft. Add tomatoes and sauté 5 minutes longer.

Add the white wine, salt, pepper, tarragon, and tarragon vinegar. Cover and simmer 5 minutes.

Lay fish, cut into serving pieces, on top of vegetables. Replace lid and let fish "poach" until it is done. This will take about 10 minutes. Serve over brown or basmati rice.

Yield: 3–4 servings.

BAKED HADDOCK WITH HERBED WHOLEWHEAT BREADCRUMBS

An easy dish to make that is delicious enough to serve to company. This has been one of our favourite fish dishes for years. We love haddock. It is inexpensive and readily available.

1 lb. fresh haddock fillets (or cod)
4 tbsp. butter (or more, if desired)
1½–2 cups wholewheat breadcrumbs (from approx. 2 slices bread)
½ tsp. salt
pepper, to taste
1 tsp. fines herbes
½–1 tsp. dried dill

Preheat oven to 375°F.
Wipe fish with paper towels and lay in one layer in a buttered baking pan.

Melt butter. In the meantime, mix breadcrumbs, salt, pepper, fines herbes, and dill in a small bowl. Toss gently with a fork. Pour butter over crumbs and toss again. Distribute buttered crumbs over the fish fillets and bake in preheated oven for 15–20 minutes, depending on thickness of fish. The fish should flake easily when touched with a fork. Serve.

Yield: 2–3 servings. This recipe may easily be doubled.

Optional Suggestions: Other herb blends may be used—**herbes de Provence** or **Italian herbs.**

CURRIED HADDOCK

Another recipe for our favourite fish: a nice light fish curry. Excellent with a nutty, spicy pilaf and steamed peas.

2 lbs. fresh haddock fillets, cut into serving pieces
1 cup white wine
1 carrot, chopped
1 stalk celery, chopped (or ½ tsp. celery seed)
3–4 garlic shallots, minced (or 1 small onion, minced)
1 large clove garlic, sliced
1 bay leaf

¼ salt, or to taste
pepper, to taste
an additional ¼ cup white
wine

Sauce:
3 tbsp. butter
2–3 garlic shallots, minced
½ small red (or green) pepper, minced (or ½ cup bottled roasted red peppers, chopped)
1 tbsp. fresh ginger (optional)
3 tbsp. flour
1 tsp. good quality curry powder
reserved liquid (above)
¼ cup fresh coriander, minced (not absolutely necessary, but really good!)

Wash and dry haddock fillets and set aside. Pour the wine into the skillet and slowly bring to a boil while you add the carrot, celery, garlic shallot, garlic, bay leaf, salt, and pepper. Place the haddock fillets evenly over the veggies. Bring back to a simmer, lower heat a bit, cover, and "poach" the fillets gently for 10 minutes. Set pan aside, remove lid, and let fish cool in stock for 5–10 minutes at least. Remove fish with a slotted spoon and set aside. Reserve stock.

Butter a shallow medium-sized casserole and gently arrange the fish in one layer. Cover and keep fish warm. Strain stock into a large measuring cup and add the ¼ cup wine, and water to make 1⅔ cup. Set aside.

Sauce: In a small saucepan melt the butter and in it sauté the garlic shallots, pepper, and ginger, if desired, for about 5 minutes over a medium heat, stirring occasionally. (If you are using the bottled roasted red pepper, add later.)

Preheat oven to 350°F.
Add the flour and curry powder and sauté, stirring constantly for another minute. Gradually add the reserved stock, stirring and blending. Bring it to a simmer. (If you are using the bottled roasted red pepper, add it now.) Simmer for 10–15 minutes, stirring occasionally, until sauce is slightly thickened. Pour over fish, sprinkle fresh coriander over (if available), and bake in preheated oven for 10 minutes, just to heat it through. Serve.

Yield: 4 servings

Optional Suggestion: Replace the haddock with **halibut steaks** for special occasions.

LIGHTLY FRIED CATFISH WITH CORIANDER PESTO

Farm-raised catfish is becoming widely available and is absolutely delicious. The fish has a sweetness to it and is firmer than many others. Topped with **Coriander Pesto**, it is a feast.

**Coriander Pesto
(or use recipe on p. 152-3):**
8 large pecan halves
1 clove garlic
1 cup packed fresh coriander
(or a combination of coriander and parsley)
1 tbsp. lemon juice
salt and pepper, to taste (pepper is good in this)
⅛ cup olive oil

Place the pecan halves and garlic clove in a food processor and process on high for a few seconds until the mixture is ground. Add the coriander, lemon juice, salt, and pepper and process again until mixture is smooth. Slowly add olive oil until it is blended in. Scrape all of the pesto into a small serving bowl and set aside.

Catfish:
¾ cup unbleached white flour
¾ cornmeal
1 tsp. dried thyme
1 tsp. chili powder, or to taste
salt and pepper, to taste
¼ cup olive oil
¼ cup butter
1 cup milk
4 catfish fillets, or portions
1 recipe **Coriander Pesto** (p. 152-3)

In a flat bowl mix together the flour, cornmeal, thyme, chili powder, salt, and pepper. In another flat bowl place the catfish.

In a medium-large cast-iron skillet heat the olive oil and butter until sizzling. Dip each catfish portion first into the milk then into the flour mixture. Sauté in the skillet until fish is golden on both sides—about 5 minutes per side. Drain quickly on a paper towel-lined plate and serve, topped with the pesto.

Yield: 4 servings.

MUSSELS STEAMED WITH FRESH HERBS

A very simple but elegant preparation for fresh mussels. Fresh herbs are essential. Excellent for part of a summertime potluck.

1 cup white wine
1 medium onion, chopped
1 clove garlic, minced
8–10 sprigs of fresh tarragon (a "sprig" is a 4–5" piece of the branch, with leaves)
6–8 sprigs of fresh thyme
5 lbs. fresh mussels, rinsed and debearded if necessary
butter, melted
In a large stockpot bring the white wine, onion, garlic, and half the fresh herbs to a boil. Add the mussels, top with remaining fresh herbs, cover, and "steam" until mussels are opened and cooked through, 8–10 minutes.

Drain mussels, reserving some cooking liquid for dipping, and serve with hot melted butter.

Yield: 4 servings.

GRILLED MARINATED SEAFOOD

This marinade is good for a variety of fish and seafood. Scallops, shrimp, and most fresh fish can benefit from a few hours in this marinade. Different herbs will give different results, all of which are delicious.

4 tbsp. olive oil
2 tbsp. white wine
1 tbsp. lemon juice
1 tbsp. fresh herbs, minced (try dill, tarragon, or thyme)
1 tbsp. fresh chives, minced
salt and pepper, to taste
1–2 cloves garlic, minced
¼ tsp. red pepper flakes, optional
1–1½ lbs. fresh fish, scallops, or shrimp (or a combination)
Combine olive oil, wine, lemon juice, fresh herbs, fresh chives, salt, pepper, garlic, and red pepper flakes, if desired, in a small dish. Arrange your seafood on a glass or ceramic plate and pour marinade over. Carefully lift fish to allow marinade to seep under, or mix smaller seafood so all is evenly coated. Cover and refrigerate for 1–2 hours. Prepare your grill. Remove seafood and reserve marinade. Arrange fish on a lightly oiled barbecue rack or place scal-

lops or shrimp on skewers. Grill about 5 minutes on each side, basting with the reserved marinade, or until done. Remove from rack or skewers and serve.

Yield: 4 servings.

Variations:
Scallop (or Shrimp) and Vegetable Kebabs: After marinating, arrange scallops (or shrimp) alternately with fresh chunks of **tomato, onion, green or red pepper, zucchini,** or **mushroom.** Brush vegetables with marinade and proceed as above.

GRILLED TERIYAKI SEAFOOD

This is a basic recipe with some options. I prefer sherry in the marinade, although white wine will do in a pinch. **Sake** is the traditional wine used. This is excellent served with *Thai Noodle Salad* (p. 45). For 1 lb. seafood, halve the marinade recipe (except garlic—use a whole clove.)

½ cup tamari soy sauce
½ cup sherry (or white wine)
⅓ cup sugar
1 clove garlic, minced
1 tbsp. fresh ginger, minced, or
½ tsp. dried (optional)
2 lbs. fresh firm fish, shrimp, or scallops

Combine soy sauce, sherry, sugar, garlic, and ginger, if desired. If you have a very firm fish such as halibut, you may cut it into cubes before marinating. If you use cod or haddock, it is best to keep the pieces whole. Marinate for 2–3 hours. To grill the fish, use an oiled wire basket—or grill halibut, scallops, or shrimp on skewers.

Grill, turning a few times and basting often until fish (or seafood) is done. Serve.

Yield: 4–6 servings.

Variations:
Chicken or Beef Teriyaki: Although this recipe specifies seafood, the marinade can also be used for **chicken** or **beef.** Increase the marinating time and proceed as in this recipe. Beef can be marinated overnight. For chicken, cut the skinned and boned white meat into cubes, marinate it, and grill on skewers like kebabs. You may alternate veggies with the meat.

GRILLED SALMON FILLETS OR STEAKS

This is one of the simplest and most delicious recipes! It is hard to believe that something this easy can be so delicious. It works well with trout fillets, arctic char fillets, or swordfish steaks, and it is easily doubled or tripled.

3 tbsp. butter
1 tbsp. olive oil
1 tsp. fines herbes
¼ tsp. salt
1 lb. salmon fillets or steaks

In a small dish melt the butter and mix in the herbs. Use this mixture to baste the fish while grilling it on an outdoor grill. Serve.

Yield: 2 servings.

SESAME-GRILLED SALMON

Another simple and delicious grilled salmon recipe. This one benefits from an hour or two of marinating.

Marinade:
1 lb. salmon fillets or steaks
juice of 1 lime
1 tbsp. canola or safflower oil
1 tbsp. tamari soy sauce
Place salmon in a large flat-bottomed ceramic or glass container. Mix together the lime juice, oil, and tamari soy sauce. Pour over fish. Leave to marinate for an hour or two, turning the fish a few times and spooning the marinade over the fish occasionally.

Basting Sauce and Grilling:
3 tbsp. butter, melted
1 tsp. sesame oil
1 tsp. soy sauce

1 green onion, minced
Remove salmon from marinade and discard marinade. Prepare basting sauce: Mix together in a small bowl the butter, sesame oil, soy sauce, and green onion.

Grill salmon, basting frequently with the sauce, until cooked through. Serve.

Yield: 2–3 servings.

Optional suggestion: If you don't have a barbecue, broil the salmon, basting often and turning once.

KEDGEREE

An old dish the English developed when they first went to India and came into contact with curry powder. It is simple and quite delicious. We like it best with salmon but have enjoyed haddock as well. If you don't have any leftover fish, salmon (or other fish) may be poached in a little white wine and shallot to prepare it for the recipe.

2 tbsp. butter
1 shallot or small onion, minced
1 cup brown rice
1 tsp. salt (or to taste)
2 cups water
1lb. or more leftover salmon, haddock, cod, or halibut
2 tbsp. white wine (or water)
5 tbsp. butter
5 tbsp. flour
3 cups milk
1 tsp. salt, or to taste
1 tbsp. curry powder
2 hard-boiled eggs

In a small saucepan, melt the butter and gently sauté the shallot for a few minutes, until soft and lightly browned. Add the brown rice and sauté a few minutes more. Add the salt and the 2 cups water. Cover, bring to a boil, lower heat to a simmer, and gently cook rice until tender and all water is absorbed, about 40–45 minutes. Fluff with a fork and set aside.

In a medium frypan place the salmon and white wine (or 2 tbsp. water). Cover and simmer until fish is heated through and liquid has evaporated. Set aside to cool, then flake fish, discarding any skin or bones.

In a saucepan, melt the 5 tbsp. butter, stir in the flour, and blend together well. Slowly add the milk, using the whisk to blend the mixture. Bring to a simmer, whisking, until mixture is smooth and creamy. Remove from heat. Add the salt and curry powder and blend together well. Gently fold in the fish and the hard-boiled eggs.

In a buttered 3-quart serving dish layer half the rice, half the fish mixture, the remaining rice, and the remaining fish. Serve.

Yield: 4 servings.

NOTES

CHICKEN

HOMEGROWN CHICKENS (BIG BIRDS!)

If you want to be more self-sufficient in food production, you might consider raising chickens for meat. Besides having the most delicious chicken you can imagine, you will have a compost machine for your garden refuse, and your own fertilizer for next year! Anyone who has used chicken manure knows it is dynamite, although it must be used with caution because it can "burn" plants if it is too new, or if you use too much. Properly used (as side dressing for corn, tomatoes, and other heavy feeders), it is invaluable in an organic garden.

Using the chickens to clean up your garden scraps is the best way to compost the scraps. There are few exceptions—you shouldn't feed them potato tops or tomato plants. Chickens are great to eat up any parts of the broccoli, cabbage, kohlrabi, etc., that you don't eat. But if your zucchinis turn into baseball bats, you can cut them in half and feed the chickens. Any harmful worms (like the corn borer) will get devoured by them also.

The resulting bird, if raised to maturity, can be the size of a small turkey (if male) or have quite a bit of excess fat (if female). We usually raise about half of our chickens for about 8 weeks, when they average 4–6 lbs. These are then good for sautéing, grilling, etc. The rest we keep until our garden is all cleaned up, and then we use them for roasting, stews, etc.

If you can't or don't want to raise your own birds, homegrown birds are available at farmers' markets, or through health food stores. They do cost more, but once you find out how different they taste, you might not mind.

I learned over the years that these chickens are not like the ones called for in most recipes, and you can't use them as the recipes often indicate. (For instance, one whole chicken breast from a homegrown bird is equal to four, or even more, of the commercial chicken breast halves!) With much trial and some error I have developed several methods of dealing with these big birds.

The first thing we always do is trim it of any and all excess fat. If it is a hen (they can accumulate quite a bit of fat), we even skin the pieces. This doesn't seem to affect most recipes, unless you want to roast the bird—then you should keep the skin on.

Smaller birds are great barbecued, oven-fried, or in any recipe that calls for broilers. Be sure to allow more cooking time since even these smaller birds are quite a bit larger than the commercial broiler. To test for doneness, you can always pierce a meaty thick piece with a sharp, small knife, and if any blood runs out it needs more cooking. Keep note of the time changes and you'll gradually make the proper time allowances. It is always important to thoroughly cook chicken. When we barbecue a chicken, we always prebake the pieces, and just finish it off, basting with sauce, on the grill. And I have also found that it is difficult to follow recipes for any "fried" chicken and have it turn out right. By the time the chicken is properly done, the crust is getting quite overdone. Perhaps this is just as well since fried chicken is not the healthiest use of a good chicken.

If you have a large bird and you don't want to roast it, you can cut it up and use the pieces in a variety of ways. The breasts are great stir-fried, kebabbed, sauced, and served over pasta, or poached and used in many of your favourite recipes. Then the rest of the chicken can be oven-fried, cacciatoried, fricasseed, stewed, etc. Or use the bony pieces (back, wings, neck) for chicken soup, and the remaining pieces oven-fried, etc. Be sure to quarter the breasts—into serving sizes.

There are so many different ways of cooking chicken that you could eat it a lot (as we do) and never, ever get tired of it.

CHICKEN CACCIATORE

One of our favourite chicken dishes! It seems to have a taste of summer to it that is always delicious. Better made ahead and reheated.

3–4 lbs. chicken pieces
1 cup white flour
2 tsp. herbes de Provence
1 tsp. dried oregano
salt and pepper, to taste
3 tbsp. olive oil, plus additional if needed
1 large onion, chopped
2 cloves garlic, minced
½–1 red or green pepper, chopped
2 cups chopped fresh tomatoes, or 1 can (398 ml/14 oz.) diced or stewed tomatoes, with juice
½ cup white wine
2 tsp. red wine vinegar
1 tsp. dried oregano and/or herbes de Provence, or to taste
salt and pepper, to taste
2 tbsp. fresh basil, slivered, if available
cooked brown rice, to serve

Trim the chicken pieces of excess fat and skin. In a flat bowl mix the flour, herbes de Provence, oregano, salt, and pepper. Dredge the chicken pieces in the flour mixture and shake off excess flour. In a large skillet, heat the olive oil until smoking. Sauté the chicken pieces in the skillet until they are well browned, adding more olive oil if needed. Remove to a large casserole with a lid.

Preheat oven to 350°F.

Drain any remaining fat from the skillet. Add 1 tbsp. olive oil and sauté the onion and garlic about 5 minutes. Add the pepper and sauté a few minutes longer. Add the tomatoes, wine, red wine vinegar, oregano, herbes de Provence, and salt and pepper, to taste. Cook over medium-high heat, stirring, for about 5 minutes. Sprinkle with basil, if available. Pour over the chicken. Cover and bake in preheated oven for 45 minutes, or until chicken is tender. Serve with brown rice.

Yield: 4 servings.

ORANGE GLACÉ CHICKEN

3 tbsp. butter
3–4 lbs. chicken pieces
½ cup flour
salt and pepper, to taste
1 tsp. dried tarragon (or 1 tbsp. fresh, minced)

4 tbsp. frozen orange concentrate, thawed
1 tbsp. fresh ginger, minced (or 1 tsp. ground ginger)
water if needed

Trim chicken pieces of excess fat and skin. Mix the flour, salt, pepper, and tarragon on a large plate. Lightly dredge the chicken pieces in this and sauté in a large skillet in 3 tbsp. butter until lightly browned. Place pieces in baking dish and set aside.

Preheat oven to 350°F

Sauce:
1 tbsp. Dijon mustard
1 tbsp. honey
2 tbsp. butter, melted
1–2 tbsp. vinegar (white wine or tarragon)
1 tbsp. cornstarch

In a small saucepan, mix the Dijon mustard, honey, 2 tbsp. butter, vinegar, cornstarch, orange concentrate, and ginger. Bring to a simmer, stirring constantly.

Brush chicken pieces with half the sauce. Bake in the preheated oven for 30 minutes, basting occasionally. Brush remaining sauce on chicken and continue baking for 10 more minutes, or until the chicken is cooked through. Serve with rice.

Yield: 4 servings.

ISLAND PAELLA

The following recipe is a deluxe version of paella which includes a wide variety of meats and seafood. It is a beautiful sight to place in the centre of a table of hungry people. However, paella doesn't always have to be so elaborate. Simpler versions are excellent as well. Although basmati rice is Indian in origin, it is the perfect rice for paella.

Shrimp Marinade:
¾ lb. fresh (or frozen raw) shrimp, peeled and deveined
3 tbsp. olive oil
1 large clove garlic, minced

Prepare the shrimp in the morning: After peeling and deveining, gently mix shrimp with olive oil and garlic. Cover and refrigerate until later.

Paella:
1 bottle clam juice
1 can (284 ml/10 oz.) condensed chicken stock
water to make 4½ cups
½ tsp. Spanish saffron
1 tsp. salt, or to taste
pepper, to taste
1 frying chicken (about 3 lbs.), cut into serving pieces (save back and neck for another use)
¼ cup olive oil, plus more if needed
1 lb. centre-cut pork chops, cubed
2–3 hot Italian sausages, cut into ½" slices
2 cloves garlic, minced
1 large onion, chopped
1 red or green pepper, sliced
2 tomatoes, chopped
2 cups white basmati rice
marinated shrimp (above)
¾–1 lb. large scallops
1 cup frozen peas
1 can artichoke hearts, drained and halved (optional)
2 dozen fresh mussels, rinsed

Heat the clam juice, chicken stock, and water (to have 6½ cups liquid in all) in a saucepan until it just simmers. Taste and add salt and pepper, if desired. Remove from heat, sprinkle the saffron over the surface, and keep warm.

In a large skillet heat the olive oil and sauté the chicken pieces until they are lightly browned. Remove from skillet and keep warm. Likewise sauté the pork and then the sausage pieces until lightly browned. Remove and keep warm.

Preheat oven to 400°F.

Drain excess fat from skillet. Add 1–2 tbsp. more olive oil (if needed) and sauté the garlic, onion, and green peppers until lightly browned. Add the tomatoes and sauté a few more minutes, stirring, until most of the liquid has been absorbed.

Add the rice and the warm stock and bring mixture to a boil. Transfer to a large casserole with a lid. Mix in the pork and sausage, and arrange the chicken pieces on top. Cover and bake in preheated oven for 20 minutes.

Remove from oven and remove chicken from the top. Add the reserved shrimp, scallops, peas, and artichoke hearts, if desired, and gently stir them in. Return chicken pieces and scatter the mussels on top. Cover and return to oven for an additional 15–20 minutes, or until rice is cooked. Serve. **Yield:** 6 hearty servings. (8 normal servings.)

RITA SAHAJPAL'S CHICKEN CURRY

I worked five years with Rita, who is an excellent East Indian cook. We spent quite a bit of time over those years talking about food, and flowers. Rita brought me many taste treats, too—I wasn't always sure what I was eating, but it was always delicious. Rita was kind enough to give me the following recipe.

1 medium onion
1–2 tbsp. fresh ginger
8 cloves garlic
1 cup tomatoes, fresh or canned (drain if using canned)
⅓–½ cup butter (Rita always uses ghee)
2 tbsp. curry powder
1 tbsp. water, if needed
1½ lb. chicken, cut into 1" cubes
1 tsp. salt
1 tsp. *Garam Masala* (recipe follows), plus additional for garnish
¾ cup yogurt (or sour cream)
½ cup water
1 tbsp. fresh coriander, minced

Grind together the onion, ginger, garlic, and tomatoes to a fine paste in a food processor.

In a large heavy pot, heat the butter to sizzling. Add the vegetable paste along with the curry powder. Fry spice-paste mixture on low heat, stirring gently and adding 1 tbsp. of water, or more if needed, so the paste doesn't burn or stick to the pan. Continue until the paste is fried well and the butter separates. Add the chicken, salt, and 1 tsp. garam masala. Continue frying for 5 minutes.

Add the yogurt or sour cream, a little at a time, stirring gently, and fry till the "whole of it is consumed."

Add the ½ cup water, cover, and let simmer at medium-low heat for ½ hour, or until the meat is cooked.

Remove, transfer to a serving dish, sprinkle with fresh coriander, and sprinkle with about ½ tsp. garam masala. Serve with boiled rice or chapatti/pita bread.

Yield: 4 servings.

Variation:
Lamb Curry: Substitute **1½ lbs. fresh lamb**, cut into 1" cubes, for the chicken. **Leftover roast leg of lamb**, cubed and added after the yogurt, is good also. This recipe is easily doubled.

GARAM MASALA

A sprinkle of this spice blend is great on any curry, rice pilaf, etc.

1½ tbsp. brown cardamom seeds
1½ tbsp. cinnamon
½ tbsp. whole clove seeds (remove from stems)
½ tbsp. black cumin seeds
2 tbsp. whole coriander
1 tbsp. black peppercorns
good-sized pinch mace
good-sized pinch nutmeg

Place all ingredients in a spice grinder or clean electric coffee-grinder. (Your coffee will have some added zing the next day!) Grind for 30–40 seconds, or until the spices are finely ground. Store in small jar with a tight-fitting lid. Keep away from heat and sunlight.

FRENCH CASSEROLED CHICKEN— "SMOTHERED" CHICKEN

A delicious wintertime chicken dish, good enough for company. Another winter favourite. We prefer it served over brown rice, although it is also good over egg noodles or with mashed potatoes.

1 cup unbleached white flour
2 tsp. beau monde seasoning
2 tsp. fines herbes, or herbes de Provence

salt and pepper, to taste
3 tbsp. olive oil
1 3–4 lb. chicken, cut into pieces and trimmed of excess

skin and fat
1 tbsp. olive oil
1 large onion, chopped
2 cloves garlic, minced
2 stalks celery, diced
1 carrot, peeled and diced
1 cup chicken stock
½ cup white wine

On a dinner plate combine the flour, beau monde seasoning, fines herbes, salt, and pepper. Heat the 3 tbsp. olive oil in a large cast-iron frypan and, after dredging the chicken pieces in the flour mixture, sauté them in batches in the olive oil, turning, to brown all sides. Place them in a large, oven-proof casserole. Add more olive oil to the frypan if needed and continue browning batches of chicken.

Preheat oven to 350°F.

Drain the remaining fat from the skillet. Add 1 tbsp. olive oil and in it sauté the onion, garlic, celery, and carrot for a few minutes until the veggies are beginning to brown. Distribute vegetables over the chicken pieces. Combine the chicken stock and white wine and pour the mixture over the chicken and veggies. Cover and bake in preheated oven for 1½ hours. (If you have a lot of fat you may drain the stock from the casserole into a pot and let it set a few minutes so the fat rises to the surface. You can then skim and discard the fat, reheat the sauce, and pour over the chicken.) Serve over brown rice, noodles, or mashed potatoes. (We prefer brown rice.)

Yield: 4–6 servings.

OVEN-FRIED CHICKEN

Yet another of our favourite recipes. This is healthier than the traditional fried, or even oven-fried, chicken. Great family fare—and delicious cold for a picnic.

1 chicken, cut into serving pieces and trimmed of excess fat and skin
1 cup milk
1 cup unbleached white flour
2 tsp. dried Italian herbs or herbes de Provence

1 tsp. beau monde seasoning
1 tsp. salt (or to taste)
pepper, to taste
3 tbsp. butter
¼ cup olive oil

Place milk in a flat dish. In another flat dish mix the flour, herbs, beau monde, salt, and pepper.

Preheat oven to 350°F.

Heat the butter and olive oil in a large frypan. Dip the chicken pieces first in the milk, then in the flour mixture. Brown them in batches, turning until both sides are nicely browned. Place them on a rack, in one layer, in a baking dish. Add ½" hot water to baking dish.

Bake the chicken in the preheated oven for 35 to 45 minutes, or until the chicken is cooked through. (The juices will run clear when pierced with a sharp knife.) Serve.

Yield: 4–6 servings.

QUICK AND YUMMY CHICKEN BREASTS

Extremely quick and easy, and always delicious. You may use other dried herbs of your liking.

boneless, skinless chicken breasts, trimmed of excess fat if necessary
flour
herbes de Provence
salt and pepper, to taste
olive oil
fresh garlic, minced
white wine

Combine the flour, herbes de Provence, salt, and pepper in a flat bowl. Heat a skillet, add the olive oil, and heat until just beginning to smoke. Lightly dredge the chicken breasts in the flour mixture, shaking off excess flour. Add to the pan and sauté until the bottom is browned, 4–5 minutes.

Turn pieces over, add the garlic, and sauté another 4–5 minutes. Add white wine to cover the bottom of the pan, cover, and "steam" through, 5 minutes or more, depending on thickness.

Serve.

ROAST CHICKEN AND GRAVY

One of the best ways to use a good-sized homegrown chicken is to roast it and serve it with **mashed potatoes and gravy.** The following is one of our favourite recipes and is good enough for your best Sunday Dinner. If you're lucky, you'll have some leftovers. Then you can try some of the recipes for leftover chicken!

1 large (6–8 lb.) chicken (or larger)
1 small onion, or garlic chives, minced
1 tsp. fines herbes, or herbes de Provence, or thyme, or more to taste
1 tsp. salt, or to taste
pepper, to taste
1 cup water, or chicken broth
1 cup white wine, or more water or broth
2–3 tbsp. white flour (more for a thicker gravy), mixed with ½ cup cold water
additional liquid (from veggies, or more wine, stock, or water)

Preheat oven to 425°F.

Trim chicken and place, breast-side up, on a rack in a large roasting pan. Place in preheated oven for 15 minutes. Turn the heat down to 350°F. After 15 more minutes baste the chicken then flip it over. Sprinkle the onion (or garlic chives), fines herbes, salt, and pepper over the chicken and pour the wine and water into the pan. Baste chicken again and return to the oven. Continue roasting and basting every 20 minutes or so until the chicken is done—20 minutes per pound from the first time you put it in the oven. With 1 hour baking time left, turn bird over to brown the top.

Remove bird to carving platter and strain all the pan juice into a saucepan. Let it settle a few minutes and the fat will rise to the top so you can skim off all except about 2 tbsp. In a small jar mix the flour into the water and shake it until it is smooth. Place saucepan over medium heat, whisk in the flour mixture, and cook, whisking until mixture is thickened. Add the potato cooking water and the vegetable cooking water, if desired, and keep whisking until smooth. (We always add the vegetable water from mild veggies such as peas, beans, corn, etc., but not from the stronger-tasting veggies such as broccoli, cabbage, etc.) If gravy is still too thick, add additional water. Serve.

Yield: Varies, depending on the size of the chicken.

MASHED (OR WHIPPED) POTATOES

Some people call them mashed, others call them whipped. I am including this recipe to remind you that mashed potatoes are one of the yummiest ways to serve potatoes—especially with well-grown organic potatoes.

potatoes, washed, peeled, and cubed
milk
butter
salt and pepper

Cook potatoes over medium to medium-high heat. We usually cook them in a small amount of water, 1–2" in the pot. Bring to a boil, then turn down heat until it is at a gentle boil. Cook, mixing and stirring a few times so potatoes cook evenly, until potatoes are soft. This usually takes about 20 minutes. Check your water during cooking and add more if needed. When the potatoes are tender remove from heat and drain any excess water to use in gravies, etc. Add butter, milk, and salt and pepper, to taste. Mash until smooth and blended together well. Serve. (The amount of milk used will depend upon the type of potato used. Mix in a bit, then more, and keep beating with the masher and then a spoon, until desired consistency is reached.)

Leftover Mashed Potato Cakes: If you have any leftover potatoes, they are good formed into little cakes and sautéed in butter and/or olive oil. (If they are too moist, they will not stick together.) You may add a bit of green onion or dill, etc., if you like.

OUR FAVOURITE STUFFING

Over the years this recipe has evolved into our favourite for stuffing our Christmas turkey.

½ cup butter
2 large onions, chopped
2 stalks celery, chopped
½ red pepper, chopped (optional)

1½ cups pecans, chopped
½ lb. hot Italian sausage
1 recipe *Cowboy Cornbread* (p. 256)

½ loaf homemade **White or Wholewheat Bread** (p. 237-9)
2 tbsp. fines herbes (or more to taste)
1 tbsp. herbes de Provence
1 tsp. salt, or to taste
pepper, to taste
1 cup fresh parsley, minced
½ cup pickled jalapeños, minced

In a large saucepan heat the butter over medium-high heat and sauté the onion, celery, and red pepper, if used, until soft. Add the pecans and sauté a few minutes longer. Remove from heat.

In a small frypan sauté the sausage, breaking it up with a fork, until cooked through. Add to the stuffing mixture.

Remove the side crusts from the cornbread and crumble the loaf by hand. Add ½ to the veggies. Cube the white or wholewheat bread, either by hand or in a food processor. Add to the mixture along with the fines herbes, herbes de Provence, salt, pepper, fresh parsley, and pickled jalapeños. Add the remaining cornbread.

I prefer to make this stuffing the day before, cool it down, and keep it in the fridge overnight. Then I bring it back to room temperature before carefully stuffing the bird.

Yield: Enough for 1 large (20–25 lb.) turkey.

LEFTOVER POULTRY POSSIBILITIES

BOLIVIAN CHICKEN PIE

3 medium sweet potatoes
3 tbsp. olive oil

1 large onion, chopped
½ red pepper, chopped (optional)
2 cloves garlic, minced
3 medium tomatoes, chopped
salt and pepper, to taste
½ tsp. cinnamon
1 tsp. dried oregano

1 tsp. thyme
⅓ cup raisins, plumped in hot water
4 cups or more leftover chicken, cubed (some dark meat, please)
½–1 cup chicken stock
1 hard-boiled egg, chopped
Kalamata olives (enough pitted and chopped to make ¼ cup)
Steam sweet potatoes. Cool, peel, and cube. Set aside.

Oil a large ovenproof casserole and set aside.

In a large ovenproof skillet, gently sauté the onion, peppers, and garlic in the olive oil for about 5 minutes, or until soft. Add the tomatoes and cook, stirring often, about 10 minutes more. Add the salt, pepper, cinnamon, oregano, thyme, raisins, chicken, and reserved sweet potatoes, hard-boiled egg, and olives and gently fold mixture together. Add ½ cup of the stock (more if mixture seems dry). Pour into the oiled casserole.

Crust:
4 cups corn kernels (fresh or frozen, thawed)
¼ cup butter, melted
1 tbsp. sugar
1 tsp. salt
3 eggs
Purée corn kernels in a food processor. Pour into a saucepan. Stir in melted butter, sugar, and salt. Over very low eat, keep beating mixture while you add the eggs, one at a time, and keep beating, with a wooden spoon, while mixture thickens. Cool slightly.

Preheat oven to 350°F.

Spread topping over chicken mixture in the large skillet and bake in preheated oven for 50 minutes, or until crust is set and lightly browned. Serve.

Yield: 4–6 servings.

CHICKEN (OR TURKEY) HASH

A great way to use up leftover chicken or turkey. Especially good on a cold winter day! It can be mixed up the day before and kept in the fridge. The hash cooks up in a short time and is an almost "instant" meal on a busy day.

6–8 medium potatoes, scrubbed and left whole
1 tbsp. olive oil
1 medium-large onion, chopped
2 cloves garlic, minced
1 stalk celery, diced
½ red or green pepper, diced, or equivalent **Roasted Red Pepper** (p. 56)
½ cup milk
2 eggs
1 tsp. Worcestershire sauce
salt and pepper, to taste
1 tsp. chili powder
1 tsp. dried oregano
3 cups (or more) cooked chicken (or turkey), diced
2 tbsp. olive oil
leftover **Gravy** (p. 199), if available

Steam (or boil) the potatoes until tender. Drain and set aside to cool.

In a small skillet, heat the olive oil and sauté the onion, garlic, celery, and pepper until soft. Covering the skillet for a few minutes will hasten this process. Set aside to cool.

In a large mixing bowl beat the milk, eggs, Worcestershire sauce, salt, pepper, chili powder, and oregano. Add the chicken. When the potatoes are cool enough to handle, peel and cut them into ½" dice, then add to hash mixture along with the cooked vegetables. Stir together gently, cover, and refrigerate for at least 1 hour, or as long as overnight.

Heat the 2 tbsp. olive oil over medium-high heat in a large cast-iron skillet. Add hash and press it down into the skillet with a spatula or large spoon. Cover and cook gently until the bottom is lightly browned and the hash is heated through. This will take between 5 and 10 minutes. Turn gently, using a spatula, and brown the other side. Serve immediately, with warmed leftover gravy, if available.
Yield: 4–6 servings.

Optional Suggestions: If you have leftover **baked or garlic-roasted potatoes**, you may use them in place of the cooked potatoes.

Variation:
Roast Beef Hash: Leftover roast beef may be used as well for an excellent beef hash.

LEFTOVER CHICKEN PAELLA

Here is a simple paella for everyday supper.

2 hot Italian sausages, casings removed
1 can (284 ml/10 oz.) chicken broth
1 can clams, drained and liquid reserved
water to make 3½ cups liquid
1 tsp. saffron
salt and pepper, to taste
2 tbsp. olive oil
1 medium onion, chopped
2 cloves garlic, minced
½ red or green pepper, diced (optional)
1½ cups white basmati rice
1 cup chopped fresh or canned tomatoes, drained
2 cups or more leftover chicken, cut in bite-sized pieces
2 cups peas
1 dozen fresh mussels, rinsed well

In a skillet over medium-high heat, sauté the sausage, breaking it up with a fork, until it is cooked through. Drain on a paper towel and set aside.

In a small saucepan heat the chicken broth, reserved clam juice, water, and saffron until hot. Add salt and pepper if needed.

In a very large skillet (cast-iron preferred) with a lid, sauté the onion, garlic, and pepper in the olive oil for a few minutes. Add the rice and sauté 1–2 minutes more. Add the hot liquid and the tomatoes. Cover and let mixture simmer for about 15 minutes, stirring occasionally.

Preheat oven to 350°F.

Add the reserved sausage, clams, chicken, and peas. Taste and add salt, if needed. Bake, with the lid on, for 15 minutes. Add the mussels, cover again, and return to oven for another 10 minutes, or until liquid is absorbed and all the mussels are open. Discard any that are not. Serve.

Yield: 4 servings.

CAJUN CHICKEN (OR TURKEY) BURGERS

Another great way to use up leftover turkey or chicken. Serve on wholewheat buns.

2 slices wholewheat bread
⅓ cup milk
3 cups cooked chicken or turkey meat, white and/or dark, coarsely chopped
1 shallot (or small onion), minced
1 stalk celery, minced
1 tsp. Italian herbs or fine herbes
salt and pepper, to taste
1 egg
3 tbsp. sour cream
3 tbsp. fresh chives and/or parsley, minced (optional)
1 cup flour
3 tbsp. Cajun spice (or to taste)
2 tbsp. olive oil, plus more if needed

Soak the bread slices in milk for 10 minutes. Remove bread, squeeze out excess milk, and shred. Set aside.

In a large mixing bowl, using a fork, toss the chicken, shallot or onion, celery, thyme, salt, and pepper until well blended. Add the bread and toss again. In a small bowl beat together the egg and sour cream and mix into the chicken mixture with the chives or parsley, if used. In two batches, process the mixture in a food processor, just until blended. Do not over-process—you still want some chunks remaining. Cover and refrigerate for 1 hour.

Combine the flour and the Cajun spice mixture on a plate. Form the meat mixture into eight patties and place each one in the breadcrumb mixture to coat both sides. Heat a medium-sized cast-iron skillet until hot. Add the olive oil and quickly sauté the patties, four at a time, until they are golden-brown on both sides (about 5 minutes per side). Add more olive oil if necessary. Serve.

Yield: 8 patties.

MEXICAN CHICKEN CASSEROLE

2 cups water
1 tsp. salt
1 cup brown rice
¼ cup butter
1 onion, chopped
1 clove garlic, minced
¼ cup unbleached white flour
2½ cups hot milk
½ cup sour cream
1½ cups Cheddar cheese
¾ cup salsa
1 tsp. chili powder
1 tsp. dried oregano
3 green onions, chopped
¼ cup fresh coriander, minced (optional)
¼ cup pickled jalapeño pepper, minced (optional)
salt and pepper, to taste
3–4 cups diced cooked chicken
1 cup coarsely crushed tortilla chips
¼ cup additional salsa
1 cup additional Cheddar cheese

Cook rice in the boiling salted water until tender, about 30 minutes. Set aside.

Melt butter in a large saucepan and in it sauté the onion and garlic for about 5 minutes. Add the flour and continue cooking for another minute. Slowly add the milk, using a whisk to blend, and cook over medium heat, stirring often, until mixture is thick and starting to bubble. Add the sour cream and heat through, then add the cheese and stir until melted. Add the salsa, chili powder, oregano, green onions, coriander, and jalapeño peppers, if desired. Add salt and pepper, to taste, and stir together until blended. Remove from heat.

Preheat oven to 375°F.

Oil a 2-quart casserole with a lid. Spread the rice evenly on the bottom. Cover with half the sauce, all of the chicken, and the remaining sauce. Cover and bake in preheated oven for 30 minutes. Remove lid, sprinkle on the tortilla chips, drizzle on the additional salsa, and top with the Cheddar cheese. Return to oven and bake an additional 15 minutes. Serve.

Yield: 4–6 servings.

LEFTOVER CHICKEN "TETRAZZINIED"

Simple, economical, and very delicious. This leftover chicken dish is good enough for company. We prefer it with the sausage.

2 tbsp. olive oil
1 tbsp. butter
2 shallots, or 1 small onion, chopped
¼–½ red pepper, finely chopped (optional)
½ lb. mushrooms, washed, trimmed, and sliced
3 tbsp. unbleached white flour
2½ cups chicken broth (including pan juices from roast chicken, strained and skimmed of all fat)
3 tbsp. sherry
3–4 cups leftover chicken, diced
2–3 hot Italian sausage, removed from casings, cooked, and drained on paper towel (optional)
salt and pepper, to taste
1 tsp. herbes de Provence
⅓–½ cup **Roasted Red Pepper** (p. 56), chopped (optional)

Melt the olive oil and butter in a medium-large saucepan. Sauté the shallots or onions and red pepper, if used, a few minutes until soft. Add the mushrooms and sauté, stirring often, until the mushrooms are cooked. Stir in the flour and slowly add the chicken broth, stirring and blending. Keep stirring often as it comes to a simmer. Add the sherry, chicken, sausage (if used), salt, pepper, herbes de Provence, and roasted red pepper, if desired. Return mixture to a simmer, and simmer until chicken is heated through. Remove from heat and set aside.

Cream Sauce, Noodles, and Assembly:
1½ tbsp. butter
1½ tbsp. unbleached white flour
1 cup milk
salt and pepper, to taste
a grating of fresh nutmeg
250 g/8 oz. pasta or egg noodles, cooked according to package directions, rinsed, and drained well
½ cup Parmesan cheese

Preheat oven to 350°F. Oil a large ovenproof casserole and set aside.

In a small saucepan melt the butter. Stir in the flour until blended and slowly add the milk, using a whisk to blend. Slowly bring to a simmer, whisking all the while. Add the salt, pepper, and nutmeg. Slowly add this (or the leftover gravy) to the chicken mixture and blend thoroughly.

Place the noodles in one layer in the oiled casserole. Cover with the chicken tetrazzini mixture and sprinkle the Parmesan cheese over the top. Bake in preheated oven for 20–25 minutes, or until the mixture is bubbling and the top is lightly browned. Serve.

Yield: 4–6 servings.

CANADIAN CHICKEN-FRIED RICE

Quickly put together if your rice is ready—great to use up some leftover chicken.

2 cups cooked long-grain brown rice, chilled (1 cup raw rice, cooked)
3 slices bacon, chopped
2 tbsp. canola or safflower oil
1 shallot or small onion, minced
2 cloves garlic, minced
1 stalk celery, sliced thin
1 tbsp. fresh ginger, minced (optional)
3 cups cooked chicken, cubed
3 eggs
3 tbsp. tamari soy sauce
2 green onions, chopped (optional)

In a large skillet cook the bacon until crisp. Remove bacon with a slotted spoon and set aside on paper towels to drain. Drain excess fat from skillet. Add the oil and sauté the onion, garlic, celery, and ginger, if used, a few minutes. Add the chicken and continue sautéing until heated through. Add the rice and continue to stir-fry until rice is heated through.

Beat together the eggs and tamari soy sauce and stir this mixture into the rice, stirring constantly, until the egg is cooked and the mixture is hot. Add the reserved bacon and green onions, if used, and serve.

Yield: 4 servings.

COWBOY FOOD

HERE'S THE BEEF

COWBOY CHILI

Definitely a cowboy meal. Full of meat and heat. Better if made ahead and refrigerated so all the flavours blend. It reheats very well. The chili also freezes very well. We like it best on brown rice, topped with grated Cheddar cheese, fresh cilantro, and green onions for garnish. We always serve it with **Cowboy Cornbread** (p. 256).

3 tbsp. olive oil
2 large onions, chopped
4–6 cloves garlic, minced
¼–½ cup good chili powder, according to taste
1 tbsp. ground cumin
½ tsp. cayenne pepper (optional)
1 tsp. cinnamon
4 lbs. beef stew, trimmed of excess fat
1 can (284 ml/10 oz.) beef consommé, plus water to make 3 cups liquid in all
1 large can (796 ml/28 oz.) ground tomatoes (tomato purée)
1 tsp. salt, or to taste
1 whole fresh or pickled jalapeño chili, minced, or to taste
1 can (540 ml/19 oz.) kidney beans, rinsed and drained
cooked brown rice, to serve
Cheddar cheese, grated, for serving
fresh cilantro, minced, for serving
green onions, minced, for serving

In a large heavy pot sauté the onion and garlic in the olive oil, stirring often, for about 5 minutes, or until onions are soft. Add the chili powder, cumin, cayenne (if used), and cinnamon. Keep cooking and stirring for another minute. Add the beef, consommé and water, tomatoes, and salt. Simmer the mixture, uncovered, for about 1½ hours, stirring occasionally. Add the jalapeño and simmer another 30 minutes. Stir in the beans and simmer another 5 minutes, or until beans are heated through.

You may cool the chili down now, and refrigerate until needed, then gently reheat, stirring often, or you may serve in large bowls over brown rice. Place the Cheddar cheese, cilantro, and green onions in separate bowls for garnish.

Yield: 6–8 servings.

COZY WINTER BEEF STEW

This is an excellent dish to prepare ahead for a busy winter day. It is even better reheated.

1½ tbsp. olive oil
1 onion, chopped
1–2 stalks celery, chopped
½ a red or green pepper, chopped (optional)
1 can (340 ml) tomato or V-8 juice, plus ½ can water
½ cup red or white wine
1–2 tbsp. Worcestershire sauce
1 tbsp. brown sugar
1 tsp. salt
freshly ground pepper, to taste
2 tsp. dried herbs—Italian blend, oregano, thyme, herbes de Provence, etc.
1 tsp. beau monde seasoning (or Spike, etc.)
½ tsp. cinnamon
1½ tbsp. olive oil
2 lbs. beef stew meat, trimmed of excess fat and gristle
2 cloves garlic, minced
2–3 carrots, peeled and cut into chunks
2 lbs. potatoes, peeled and cut into chunks

In a large saucepan over medium-high heat add the olive oil and sauté the onion, celery, and pepper, if desired, until soft. Add the tomato juice, water, wine, Worcestershire sauce, brown sugar, salt, pepper, dried herbs, beau monde seasoning, and cinnamon, stirring and blending the mixture together well. Cover and lower heat to a simmer.

In a separate skillet heat the additional 1½ tbsp. olive oil, and over medium-high to high heat brown the meat and garlic for about 5 minutes, stirring often. Add mixture to the saucepan, cover, and cook about 1 hour. Add carrots and keep stew barely at a simmer for about 30 minutes more.

Add the potatoes and cook until potatoes are done, about 20–25 minutes. Be careful not to overcook the potatoes. Adjust seasoning and serve.

Yield: 4–6 servings.

Optional Suggestions: Other vegetables may be added to your liking. Try adding a bit of **turnip** with the carrots (add more water if needed), or ½ **lb. fresh mushroom,** added 10 minutes before stew is done, or **about 1 cup peas**, added during the last five minutes.

Variation:
Beer Beef Stew: Replace the ½ cup water and ½ cup wine with **1 cup beer.**

WINTER POT ROAST

Definitely a "comfort food"—the kind you want on a cold, blustery winter day. Use the leftovers in the next recipe, *Pot Roast Pasta in a Bowl.*

1 large pot roast (5–6 lbs.)
4 tbsp. olive oil
⅔ cup unbleached white flour
salt and pepper, to taste
1–2 tsp. Italian herbs
½ tsp. beau monde seasoning
2 cloves garlic, minced
1 can (340 ml) tomato juice
2 tbsp. red wine vinegar
1 tbsp. brown sugar
1 tbsp. Worcestershire sauce
½–1 cup red or white wine, or beer, or stout, or beef broth (optional)
2 tbsp. unbleached white flour

Trim the pot roast of any excess fat and gristle.

In a large cast-iron frypan with a lid, heat the olive oil until smoking. Combine the flour, salt, pepper, Italian herbs, and beau monde seasoning on a plate. Dredge the pot roast in this on both sides. You may need to pat it on with your hands. Shake off the excess and brown both sides in the frypan. After you flip it scatter the garlic on top. In a bowl mix together the tomato juice, vinegar, brown sugar, Worces-

tershire sauce, and wine, if used. Pour over the pot roast, cover, and simmer over medium-low to low heat—just enough to keep it simmering gently—covered, for 2–2½ hour. Turn the pot roast over once halfway through. (When done, the pot roast should be very tender. The cooking time varies with the age of the meat, etc.) Remove from liquid and keep warm. Strain liquid into a small saucepan. Let it set a few minutes for the fat to rise, and skim in with a spoon to remove any excess. You want about 1 tbsp. left in the saucepan. (If you make this ahead of time you can chill down the liquid. It is much easier to remove the fat once it is chilled.)

Return saucepan to a simmer. In a small jar shake together the flour and about ⅓ cup water. Add this to the saucepan and whisk it in well. Bring to a boil, whisking a bit, until mixture is smooth. Serve in a gravy boat with the pot roast.

Yield: 4–6 servings.

POT ROAST PASTA IN A BOWL

Almost better than the pot roast itself. This is a juicy dish that is between a soup and a pasta dish, so serve with both a spoon and a fork and enjoy!

leftover pot roast (above)
2 tbsp. olive oil
1 onion, chopped
1 stalk celery, chopped
1 carrot, chopped
1 clove garlic, minced
1–1½ cup leftover gravy
1 large can (796 ml/28 oz.) tomatoes, crushed
1 tsp. dried oregano
1 tsp. Italian herbs
salt and pepper
250 g/8 oz. bow-ties (more if you have a lot of leftovers), cooked according to package directions and drained.

Remove pot roast from bone and trim any excess fat and gristle. Cut into slices and strips. Set aside.

In a large saucepan heat the olive oil and in it sauté the onion, celery, carrot, and garlic for about 5 minutes. Add the reserved pot roast, leftover gravy, tomatoes, oregano, Italian herbs, and salt and pepper, to taste. Bring to a boil, lower heat, and simmer 30–45 minutes.

Cook bow-ties (or other chunky pasta) according to package directions. Drain well and place some pasta in each serving bowl. Top with the pot roast medley and serve.

Yield: 2–4 servings.

Optional Suggestion: If you have no leftover gravy, you may make some using 1 cup canned beef broth, or beef bouillon. You may want to cook the sauce down a bit to thicken.

BARBECUE BEEF SANDWICHES

This is a great way to use leftover roast beef.

1 recipe *Texas Barbecue Sauce* (p. 223-4)
leftover roast beef, thinly sliced
Make the sauce in a saucepan, then add the thinly sliced roast beef and bring to a simmer, mixing gently until beef is heated through. Serve on hamburger buns or focaccia sandwich bread.

BEEF-VEGGIE STIR-FRY

This is another basic recipe with many variations and is good with many different combinations of veggies—use whatever you have. We have this often, summer and winter, and find that it is best served with brown rice.

Marinade and Meat:
1 tbsp. white wine
1 tbsp. soy sauce
1 tbsp. fresh ginger, finely minced (or 1 tsp. ground ginger)
1–2 cloves garlic, minced
freshly ground pepper, to taste
1 lb. steak, thinly sliced across the grain

At least 30 minutes before cooking, combine the wine, soy sauce, ginger, garlic, and ground pepper in a small bowl and add the steak. Set aside to marinate. (For 1½–2 lbs. of meat, double the amount of white wine and soy sauce and proceed as above.)

Sauce:
⅔ cup chicken broth
3 tbsp. soy sauce
1 tbsp. white wine
1 tsp. sugar
1½ tbsp. hoisin sauce
1 tsp. sesame oil, or more to taste
2–3 tbsp. Thai sweet chili sauce (optional)

In a small bowl combine the chicken broth, soy sauce, white wine, sugar, hoisin sauce, sesame oil, and Thai sweet chili sauce, if desired. Set aside.

The Stir-fry:
2 tbsp. Canola or other vegetable oil—2 tbsp. more when needed
marinated meat, drained, marinade reserved (above)
1 medium onion, sliced
1 tbsp. fresh ginger, minced (optional)
2 cups broccoli, washed and cut into bite-sized pieces
2 carrots, thinly sliced
1 stalk celery, sliced
½–1 green or red pepper, sliced
1 cup snow peas, cut into ½" pieces (optional)
1 cup kohlrabi, peeled and cut into chestnut-like pieces (optional)
1 tbsp. cornstarch mixed with 2 tbsp. water (or more cornstarch for a thicker sauce)
1–2 green onions, minced (optional)

In a wok over high heat add the oil. When it is very hot (about 10 seconds) add half the meat and stir-fry, stirring constantly, until the meat is no longer pink. This should take about 1–1½ minutes. Remove beef from wok and clean out the wok with a paper towel. Repeat process with remaining meat. (If you have doubled the recipe, you may need to repeat this step again.)

Wipe out wok again and return to heat. Add 2 tbsp. more oil, and when it is very hot, add the onion and ginger and stir-fry about 1 minute. Add the broccoli, carrot, celery, pepper, snow peas, and kohlrabi, if desired, and stir-fry about 30 seconds. Add the sauce, bring to a boil, lower heat slightly, cover, and let steam until veggies are crisp-tender, about 3–4 minutes. Return beef to wok and mix well. Cover and let steam about 1 minute. Add any reserved marinade. Bring to a boil, add the cornstarch mixed with water, bring to a boil again, and cook, stirring gently, until the sauce is thickened. Add green onions, if desired, and serve over brown rice.

Yield: 3–4 servings.

Optional Suggestions: You may use substitute other vegetable to taste: **zucchini, fresh green beans, Chinese cabbage, mung bean sprouts,** etc. are excellent. Add mung bean sprouts with 1 minute left to "steam" veggies.

Variations:
Chicken-Vegetable Stir-fry: Substitute for the beef **1 lb. raw chicken breast**, cut into bite-sized pieces. Proceed as above. Be sure chicken is cooked through. Chicken is especially good with snow peas and red peppers.

Seafood-Vegetable Stir-fry: Substitute **1 lb. raw shrimp**, shelled and deveined, or **scallops.**
You may use **½ cup bottled clam juice** instead of the chicken broth, although it is not necessary. Proceed as above.

Pork-Vegetable Stir-fry: Substitute **1 lb. pork chops,** trimmed of excess fat and cut into bite-sized pieces, for the beef.

STUFFED MEATLOAF

This is delicious left over and sliced for sandwiches.

2 lbs. lean ground beef
½ lb. garlic sausage, casings removed
1 cup breadcrumbs
1 egg, lightly beaten
2 cloves garlic, minced
½ onion, finely chopped
¼ green pepper, finely chopped (optional)
1 tsp. salt
freshly ground pepper, to taste
½ tsp. freshly grated nutmeg

Preheat oven to 350°F. In a large mixing bowl thoroughly combine the beef, sausage, 1 cup breadcrumbs, egg, garlic, onion, green pepper (if desired), salt, pepper, and nutmeg.

Stuffing:
3 slices bacon, cooked crisp, drained, and crumbled
1½ cups grated Cheddar cheese
2 cups fresh breadcrumbs
½ cup fresh parsley, minced

In another bowl combine the bacon, cheese, 2 cups breadcrumbs, and parsley.

On the counter, place two sheets of wax paper overlapped to make a 2' square. Place meat mixture on wax paper and pat it out into a rectangle about 20" long by 16" wide. Distribute the stuffing mixture to within 1½" of the edge of the meat. Pat it down a bit. Use the wax paper to roll the meat up, trying to keep the filling inside. (This is the tricky part.) Pat the meatloaf smooth and mould it into a good shape.

Roll the meatloaf onto a rack in your roasting pan. Bake in preheated oven for 1 hour. Remove meatloaf from oven, let it set about 15 minutes, slice, and serve.

Yield: 8–10 servings.

Variation:
Pesto-Stuffed Meatloaf:
Replace bacon and Cheddar cheese with **½ recipe *Pesto*** (p. 152-3), with cheese.

MEATLOAF À LA BLEU

Good the first day, and great in sandwiches.

2 lbs. lean ground beef
½ cup small rolled oats
1 tsp. salt
pepper, to taste
1 egg, lightly beaten
¼ cup milk
1½ cups coarse breadcrumbs (2 slices)
½ cup bleu cheese, crumbled
2 tbsp. chopped fresh parsley
1 tbsp. Dijon mustard

Preheat oven to 350°F.

Mix together the ground beef, rolled oats, salt, pepper, egg, and milk. In another bowl mix together the breadcrumbs, crumbled bleu cheese, parsley, and Dijon mustard.

On a sheet of wax paper, shape the meat into a rectangle, about 11" square. Put the breadcrumb mixture on centre ⅓ of the meat. Overlap the two sides of the meat to form a roll, 11" x 4". Push the meat together on the top to seal. Seal ends as well and gently transfer the roll to a rack in a 9" x 13" pan.

Bake in preheated oven for 1 hour.

Yield: 4–6 servings.

SWEET AND SOUR MEATBALLS

Meatballs:

1 lb. hamburger
½ lb. sausage, casings removed (garlic sausage is good)
2 cloves garlic, minced
salt and pepper, to taste.
½ tsp. ginger
1 tbsp. oil

Mix all ingredients together well and form into meatballs. Heat oil in a medium-large heavy skillet over high heat. Sauté meatballs until they are evenly browned. Lower heat to medium and continue cooking until they are done through— about 20 minutes. Keep shaking pan to keep them from sticking and to keep them turning. Remove with a slotted spoon and let them drain on paper towel.

Sauce:

1–2 tbsp. canola oil
1 medium onion, minced
½–1 green or red pepper, sliced thin, and cut into 2" lengths (or some of each, red and green)
1 carrot, thinly sliced
2 cloves garlic, minced
1 tbsp. fresh ginger, minced (or 1 tsp. ground)
1 medium can (398 ml/14 oz.) pineapple chunks
½ cup apple cider vinegar
¼ cup water
3 tbsp. soy sauce (tamari is best)
2 tbsp. sherry or white wine pepper, to taste
⅓ cup sugar
3 tbsp. cornstarch
¼ cup water

In a large saucepan heat the oil. Add the onion and sauté over high heat for about 2 minutes. Add green pepper, carrot, garlic, and fresh or ground ginger. Lower heat and sauté another 3 minutes, stirring constantly. Add the pineapple and juice, vinegar, ¼ cup water, soy sauce, sherry or white wine, pepper, and sugar. Bring the sauce to a boil, add the meatballs, and return to a simmer for 10 minutes. Add the 3 tbsp. of cornstarch mixed with the ¼ cup cold water. Let it simmer until it thickens slightly, about 5 minutes. This is better made ahead and reheated. Serve with brown rice.

Yield: 4–6 servings.

Optional Suggestion: Use 1½ lbs. hamburger and omit the sausage.

Variations:
Sweet and Sour Chicken Balls: Substitute **1½ cups ground chicken** for the ground beef and sausage. Proceed as in above recipe.

Sweet and Sour Ribs: Pre-bake **pork ribs or riblets** until they are cooked through, 45 minutes at 375°F. Drain excess fat, baste generously with the sauce, and continue baking for 10 minutes. Turn ribs, baste again, and continue baking 10 minutes. Serve with extra sauce on the side.

STUFFED RED OR GREEN PEPPERS

Two summers past we had an unusual glut of peppers which inspired this dish. It quickly became a favourite. These smell delicious when they are baking and are excellent left over.

2 tbsp. olive oil
2 medium onions, chopped
2 cloves garlic, minced
1 lb. lean ground beef
⅔ cup basmati rice
2 cups **Smooth Piquant Tomato Sauce** (below)—or another spicy tomato sauce, homemade or bought
½ cup red wine or beef broth
salt and pepper, to taste
½ tsp. cinnamon
1 tsp. dried oregano
6–8 medium red or green peppers, or 4 very large, halved
1 additional cup spicy tomato sauce
½ additional cup red wine

In a medium frypan heat the olive oil and in it sauté the onions and garlic for about 5 minutes. Add the beef and sauté it, breaking the meat up with a fork, until it is no longer pink. Drain any excess fat. Add the basmati rice, tomato sauce, red wine, salt, pepper, cinnamon, and oregano. Cover and simmer for 10 minutes. Turn off heat and let set another 15 minutes.

Preheat oven to 350°F.

Prepare the peppers: Oil a baking pan or casserole. Depending on the size and shape of the peppers, either cut off the top and scoop out the seeds and membranes, or cut in half, leaving the top on, and remove the seeds and membranes. Fill each pepper, or half, with some of the filling and arrange them in the casserole.

Mix together the 1 cup tomato sauce and the ½ cup red wine or beef broth. Spoon some of the sauce on each pepper and pour the rest around them. Cover with aluminum foil and bake in preheated oven for 1 hour. Baste the stuffed peppers occasionally with the juices. Serve.

Yield: 6–8 servings.

SMOOTH PIQUANT TOMATO SAUCE

1 onion, chopped
2 cloves garlic, minced
½ red or green pepper, chopped
5–6 cups fresh tomatoes, chopped
1 tbsp. red wine vinegar
1 tbsp. sugar
salt and pepper, to taste
1 tsp. dried oregano

Place all ingredients in a large pot. Bring to a boil, lower heat, and simmer until vegetables are tender and sauce is slightly thickened. Cool and put through a food mill, or process in a food processor, in batches, until smooth.

WHERE'S THE PORK?

Right here! Island pork is getting better all the time. An increasing awareness in the industry of the consumers' demands for lower-fat alternatives has led to leaner pork. And it is delicious! Following are some of our favourite pork recipes. As well, throughout the book I have used lean ground pork in many recipes that called for ground beef. I find it excellent as well.

RONALD'S BARBECUE SAUCE AND BARBECUED RIBS

The best barbecued ribs I've ever had!

Sauce:
1 small can (156 ml/5.5 oz.) tomato paste
⅔ cup water
1 bottle (341 ml/12 oz.) beer
1½ cup brown sugar
juice ½ lemon
1/6 cup white vinegar

Place all ingredients in a large pot and simmer, stirring often, for about 1 hour, or until mixture is thick.

Marinating and Barbecuing Ribs:
3–4 lbs. ribs, trimmed of excess fat

Cut ribs into serving portions. Place them in a non-reactive dish, in one layer if possible. Cover with sauce. Cover and refrigerate until needed. (Overnight is best.)

Preheat oven to 375°F. Scrape off excess sauce. Bake in preheated oven for 35–45 minutes, or until cooked through.

Prepare the barbecue. Baste the ribs with the sauce, place on the barbecue, cover, and cook 3 minutes. Turn, cover, and cook an additional 3 minutes. Repeat this process 3 more times. Ribs should be cooked through and delicious! Serve with cornbread, greens, potato salad, and lots of napkins.

Yield: 4 servings.

Variations:
Barbecued Chicken: Precook the chicken until it is cooked through. Proceed as you would for the ribs, but only dip the pieces twice.

Hickory-Smoked Ribs: Ronald always uses hickory chips when making ribs. Smoke the ribs, following directions with your smoker. Then dip and grill as above. You do not have to prebake the ribs if you smoke them. Hickory-smoked ribs are quite unbelievable.

TEXAS BARBECUED RIBS

Cowboy food without a doubt! This sauce is great on chicken as well!

Barbecue Sauce:
2 tbsp. olive oil
1 small onion, minced
1 clove garlic, minced
1 cup ketchup
¼ cup apple cider vinegar
¼ cup Worcestershire sauce
3 tbsp. honey or brown sugar
1 tbsp. prepared mustard
2 tsp. paprika
1 tsp.–1 tbsp. chili powder, depending on "heat" desired
½ tsp. salt

In a small saucepan cook the onion and garlic in the olive oil for a few minutes, stirring constantly so the veggies don't burn. Add the ketchup, cider vinegar, Worcestershire sauce, honey or brown sugar, mustard, paprika, chili powder, and salt. Cook, stirring occasionally, over low heat for about 10 minutes, or longer for a thicker sauce.

Marinating and Barbecuing Ribs:

3–4 lbs. ribs, trimmed of excess fat

In the morning (if possible), cut ribs into serving portions and place them in a non-reactive dish where they fit in one layer. Pour the sauce over them, cover, and refrigerate.

Preheat oven to 375°F. Remove ribs from fridge and scrape the sauce off them. Place them in one layer in a roasting pan and bake in preheated oven for 35–45 minutes, or until cooked through.

Prepare the barbecue. Grill the ribs, basting often, until they are browned and cooked through. Serve.

Yield: 4 servings.

Variation:
Texas Barbecued Chicken: Substitute chicken for ribs. Prebake and proceed as above.

GRILLED MUSHU PORK CHOPS

This uses the marinade from *MuShu Pork Fajitas* (p. 144-5) for pork chops that are delicious on their own or with the *Thai Noodle Salad* (p. 45) for an Oriental-flavoured summer barbecue.

Pork Marinade:
1 lb. centre-cut pork tenderloin cut ½" thick (4 chops)
2 tbsp. hoisin sauce
1 tbsp. soy sauce
1 tbsp. white wine vinegar
1 tbsp. ketchup
1 tsp. sesame oil
1 tsp. sugar
1–2 cloves garlic, minced

Trim the pork of all fat. Combine remaining ingredients in a small bowl. Add the pork chops and turn until pork is well coated. Cover and place in fridge until needed.

Grill pork chops slowly over medium coals, basting frequently, until cooked through. Serve with the *Thai Noodle Salad* (p. 45).

Yield: 4 servings.

QUICK AND YUMMY PORK CHOPS

Extremely quick and easy, and always delicious.

pork chops—centre-cut boneless are best, trimmed of excess fat if necessary
flour
herbes de Provence
salt and pepper, to taste
olive oil
fresh garlic, minced
white wine

Combine the flour, herbes de Provence, salt, and pepper in a flat bowl. Heat a skillet, add the olive oil, and heat until just beginning to smoke. Lightly dredge the pork chops in the flour mixture, shaking off excess flour. Add to the pan and sauté until the bottom is browned, 4–5 minutes.

Turn chops over, add the garlic, and sauté another 4–5 minutes. Add white wine to cover the bottom of the pan, cover, and "steam" through, 5 minutes or more, depending on thickness of chops.

Serve.

Optional Suggestions: Use **apple cider** for the white wine, and **sautéed onion** or **shallot** for the garlic.

CASSUELA (PORK STEW)

Another yummy winter dish to serve your family and friends. One of our favourites—especially with the great sausages available at the farmers' market.

2 tbsp. olive oil
1½ lbs. lean pork chops, trimmed of excess fat and cut into chunks
½ lb. hot Italian sausage, cut into chunks
1 tbsp. olive oil
1 large onion, chopped
1–2 stalks celery, chopped
1 clove garlic, minced
3–4 carrots, cut into chunks
4–5 large potatoes, peeled and cubed
2 tbsp. flour
1½ cups chicken broth
1 cup white wine, or additional broth
1 bay leaf

salt and pepper, to taste
1 tsp. herbes de Provence
1 tsp. Cajun seasoning, or to
taste (optional)

Preheat oven to 375°F.

Heat the olive oil in a large
heavy pan and sauté the pork
chops, stirring and browning the pieces. Place them in
a large casserole with a lid.
In the same pan, brown the
sausage and add it to the pork.
Drain any excess fat. Add the
additional 1 tbsp. olive oil and
in it sauté the onion, celery,
and garlic, stirring until vegetables are beginning to brown.
Distribute the vegetables over
the meat and mix in the prepared carrots and potatoes.

Add the flour to the skillet and
blend in with a fork, scraping
up any bits. Add the chicken
broth and white wine. Stir and
cook until slightly thickened.
Season with the bay leaf, salt,
pepper, herbes de Provence,
and Cajun seasoning, if desired. Pour over the meat and
veggies, cover, and bake in preheated oven for 1½ hours. Discard bay leaf before serving.

Yield: 4–6 servings.

Optional Suggestion: The Cajun seasoning gives this dish a
bite if you want one. You may
prefer a milder version without
the Cajun spice.

SPICY BLACK BEANS AND RICE

Great on a cold winter day—with cornbread for dipping and mopping!

1 lb. (about 2 cups) dried black beans
7 cups water
pinch baking soda
1 lb. kielbasa, diced
1 lb. ham, diced (1 meaty ham bone is even better)
1 tbsp. chili powder
½ tsp. red pepper flakes, or to taste
1 bay leaf
2 tsp. dried oregano
2 tbsp. olive oil
3 cups onions, coarsely chopped
2 large cloves garlic, minced
½–1 red or green pepper, diced
1 large can (796 ml/28 oz.) diced tomatoes, drained
1–2 tsp. cumin
salt and pepper, to taste
2 tbsp. red wine vinegar
⅓ cup fresh coriander, minced (optional)
red onion, chopped, for garnish (optional)
1½ cups raw brown rice, cooked (3 cups cooked)

Soak beans in water overnight.

Drain very well and place beans in a large soup pot with 7 cups fresh water, pinch of baking soda, kielbasa, ham, chili powder, red pepper flakes, bay leaf, and oregano. In a medium skillet, sauté the onion, garlic, and pepper in the olive oil for about 5 minutes, stirring constantly, until lightly browned. Add to the stew, cover, bring to a boil, and simmer for 1½ hours, or longer (until beans are tender). Remove the lid for some of the cooking time if you want your dish to be thicker.

Remove the ham bone, if used. Let it cool, remove the meat, and return meat to pot. Discard bone. Discard bay leaf.

Add the tomatoes, well-drained, and the cumin. Simmer 15–20 minutes longer. Taste and add salt and pepper, to taste. Stir in the red wine vinegar and simmer a few more minutes. Serve over cooked rice with fresh coriander and red onion for garnish, if desired.

Yield: 6 servings or more.

Optional Suggestion: You may add **2–3 spicy sausages**, cut and sautéed, instead of the kielbasa.

LOVELY LAMB

Not everyone loves lamb, but I think if you have well-raised lamb that is properly cooked, it is most delicious! Island lamb is a real treat for us, that's for sure. It lends itself well to stews and exotic spices. What better way to warm yourself on a cold winter day!

MEDITERRANEAN LAMB STEW

Great on a chilly day. This recipe is better if it is made ahead—in the morning, or one or two days in advance. If possible, it should be served with a simple risotto flavoured with fresh thyme and tarragon.

2 tbsp. olive oil
2½–3 lbs. boneless lamb
(a rolled shoulder is good),
trimmed of excess fat and cut
into large chunks
1 large can (796 ml/28 oz.)
whole tomatoes, drained of
excess juice
4–5 cloves garlic, minced
4–5 tbsp. (½ frozen batch) basil
Pesto (p. 152-3), without the
Parmesan
1 tsp. salt, or to taste
pepper, to taste

Heat the olive oil in a large saucepan and sauté the lamb over high heat, stirring often, for about 10 minutes. Remove from heat and drain the excess fat. Return to heat, lower to medium. Add the tomatoes,

garlic, pesto, salt, and pepper. Simmer, uncovered, for about 1½ hours. Check every 15 minutes and cover when stew reaches desired consistency. Let it cool and place in the refrigerator until 45 minutes before serving time. Before you reheat it, skim any excess fat from the surface. Heat and serve.

Yield: 4 servings.

Optional Suggestions: If you have no frozen pesto, an adequate substitute would be ½ package (14 g.) **pesto sauce mix** or **½ cup fresh basil**, minced, and **¼ cup ground almonds.**

STEWED LAMB SHANKS

We like this best with noodles (rotini or fusilli), but it is also good with risotto, rice pilaf, or a white bean side dish. Like most stews it is better if made ahead and reheated.

4 meaty lamb shanks
2 tbsp. olive oil
salt and pepper, to taste
1 large onion, chopped
1 stalk celery, chopped (optional)
225 g/8 oz. mushrooms, sliced (optional)
2 cloves garlic, minced
1 large can (796 ml/28 oz.) tomatoes, with juice
½ cup red wine
1 tsp. red wine vinegar
1 tsp. sugar
1 tsp. herbes de Provence
1 large bay leaf
½ tsp. allspice, or cinnamon, or both
salt and pepper, if desired
2 tbsp. fresh parsley, minced (optional)

Trim the lamb shanks of any excess fat. In a large cast-iron skillet with a lid, brown the meat in the olive oil, sprinkling each side with salt and pepper. Remove and set aside. In the same pan sauté the onion, celery, mushrooms (if used), and garlic until vegetables are soft. Add the tomatoes and juice, red wine, red wine vinegar, sugar, herbes de Provence, bay leaf, and allspice and bring to a simmer. Add the reserved lamb shanks, cover, and simmer for 1½ hours. Remove lid and cook down sauce, if desired. Discard bay leaf. Before serving, taste and add more salt and pepper, if desired, and sprinkle with the parsley. Serve.

Yield: 4 servings.

Variation:
Lamb and White Bean Stew: Add **1 can (540 ml/19 oz.) white beans**, drained, or **1 cup dried baby lima beans** (soaked and cooked). With 15 minutes cooking time remaining, add **½ cup Kalamata olives** and serve with French bread.

LAMB CHOPS BAKED IN WHITE WINE SAUCE

A simple yet elegant presentation for lamb chops.

8 lamb chops, trimmed of all
excess fat
2 tbsp. olive oil
salt and pepper, if desired
1 garlic shallot, minced
1 clove garlic, minced
1½ tbsp. white flour
½ cup white wine
½ cup chicken broth
1 sprig of fresh rosemary (or ½
tsp. dried, or 1 tsp. herbes de
Provence)

Preheat oven to 400°F.

Trim the chops of all excess fat
that you can. Heat the olive oil
in a large cast-iron skillet until it is hot and in it sauté the
chops for 3–4 minutes on each
side, or until lightly browned.
Lightly sprinkle with salt and
pepper after you turn them.

Remove chops to a casserole
where they can all fit in one
layer. Keep warm. Drain any
excess fat from the pan. (You
want about 1–1½ tbsp. left in
the pan.) In it sauté the shallot
and garlic for a few minutes, or
until they are lightly browned.
Stir in the flour and blend well.
Add the white wine, chicken
broth, and rosemary or herbes
de Provence. Cook, stirring
constantly, until smooth and
slightly reduced. Pour sauce
over the lamb chops, cover
with a lid, and place in the
preheated oven for 15 minutes.
Remove lid and bake 10 more
minutes. Remove rosemary
sprig and serve.

Yield: 4 servings.

EAST INDIAN LAMB CHOPS AND RICE

I developed this recipe during one wild April snowstorm when
we were storm-stayed without power for a few days. I used what
I had in the house, and the result was a wonderful surprise!

6–8 (2 per person) lamb chops,
trimmed of all excess fat
1 tbsp. olive oil
1 can (284 ml/10 oz.) chicken

broth
½ cup white wine
water
juice from ½ a lemon

1 tbsp. olive oil
1 onion, chopped
1 clove garlic, minced
1 tbsp. fresh ginger, minced
1 cup basmati rice
⅓ cup dried apricots, chopped
⅓ cup roasted unsalted peanuts
1 tsp. salt
1 tsp. *Garam Masala* (p. 196), plus additional to sprinkle on top

In a large heavy skillet heat 1 tbsp. olive oil and in it brown the lamb chops on both sides. Remove chops and drain any excess fat. While the chops are sautéing, combine the chicken broth, white wine, and water to make 3 cups liquid, and add the lemon juice. Set aside.

Add 1 tbsp. olive oil to the skillet and in it sauté the onion, garlic and fresh ginger for a few minutes. Add the basmati rice, reserved liquid, apricots, peanuts, salt, and 1 tsp. garam masala. Arrange chops on top, cover, and simmer for 30–40 minutes, or until rice is tender. Gently stir a few times to prevent rice from sticking to the bottom. Serve.

Yield: 3–4 servings.

Variation:
Leftover Lamb and East Indian Rice: Instead of lamb chops, use **2–3 cups leftover lamb from a roast**, cubed and added with the rice and broth.

SPICY STUFFED WINTER SQUASH

3–4 acorn squash

Preheat oven to 350°F.

Halve squash. Scoop out seeds and membranes and discard. Place halves upside-down on a rack in a large casserole. Pour boiling water to 1". Bake in preheated oven 45 minutes to 1 hour, or until squash is tender. Remove, let cool slightly, turn halves over, and return to casserole.

While squash is baking prepare the filling.

Filling:
1 lb. ground lamb
1 onion, chopped
1 clove garlic, minced
1 small can (398 ml/14 oz.) tomatoes, drained, reserving ½ cup juice
¼ cup red wine
1 tbsp. apple cider vinegar
½ cup raisins
1 tbsp. Worcestershire sauce

salt and pepper, to taste
½ tsp. cinnamon
1 tsp. dried oregano
1 tsp. cumin

In a large skillet sauté the lamb, breaking it up with a fork and stirring, until meat is no longer pink. Drain any excess fat. Add the onion and garlic and sauté about 5 minutes longer, stirring occasionally. Add the tomatoes, reserved juice, red wine, apple cider vinegar, rai-sins, Worcestershire sauce, salt, pepper, cinnamon, oregano, and cumin. Cook over medium heat, stirring often, for an additional 10 minutes.

Spoon the mixture in the pre-baked squash halves, return them to the oven, and bake 15–20 minutes longer. Serve.

Yield: 4–6 servings, depending on size of squash.

SHEPHERD'S PIE

Definite comfort food. Make this in the morning (or previous evening) to reheat for dinner. Good with *Tzatziki* (p. 16) or *Piquant Tomatoes* (p. 28) on the side.

Potatoes:
1½–2 lbs. potatoes (4–5 medium potatoes), cubed
1 tbsp. butter
1 tbsp. olive oil
1 clove garlic, mashed
salt and pepper, to taste
¼ cup sour cream (or plain yogurt)
1–3 tbsp. milk

Cook potatoes in a medium-small saucepan until tender. Drain very well. Mash the potatoes, adding the butter, olive oil, garlic, salt, pepper, and sour cream, mashing all the ingredients together. Add the milk and beat in with a spoon until smooth. Use 1–3 tablespoons, depending on how dry your potatoes are. (You want them to spread fairly easily.) Set aside.

Filling and Assembly:
1–2 tbsp. olive oil
1 large onion, chopped
1 stalk celery, chopped
1 carrot, chopped
1 clove garlic, minced
115–170 g/4–6 oz. mushrooms, cleaned and diced
1 tbsp. flour

¾ cup white wine (or half red wine, half water)
1 lb. ground lamb
⅓ cup **Roasted Red Pepper** (p. 56) (optional)
salt and pepper, to taste
2 tsp. herbes de Provence
a grating of nutmeg
1 tbsp. butter

Preheat oven to 400°F.

Heat the olive oil in a medium-large skillet and sauté the onion, celery, carrot, and garlic until vegetables are soft and beginning to brown, about 5 minutes. Add the mushrooms and sauté a few minutes longer. Stir in the flour and then slowly stir in the white wine and continue to simmer. In a separate skillet sauté the lamb, breaking it up with a fork until no longer pink. Remove to paper towel-lined plate with and drain excess fat. Add to the vegetable mixture with the roasted red pepper (if used), salt, pepper, herbes de Provence, and nutmeg. Simmer a few more minutes.

Pour meat mixture into a 10" pie plate with 2" sides, or a casserole. Spread the potatoes on top. Using a butter knife, spread 1 tbsp. butter over the top of the potatoes.

Bake in preheated oven for 25–30 minutes or until potatoes are nicely browned. Serve.

Yield: 4 servings.

RUSSIAN-STYLE LAMB AND CHICK PEA CASSEROLE

This is based on an Azerbaijani dish, but is here made with meatballs, which makes it both quicker to prepare and less fatty. It is quite different, full of the tastes of autumn, and surprisingly delicious.

1 lb. ground lamb
1 clove garlic, minced
1 shallot, minced
salt and pepper, to taste
½ tsp. cinnamon
½ tsp. ground coriander
2 tbsp. olive oil
2 large onions, chopped

½ cup white wine
½ cup water
1 can (540 ml/19 oz.) chick peas, rinsed and drained
salt and pepper, to taste
5 damson plums, pitted and quartered, or 4–5 tbsp. plum butter

2 large or 3 medium fresh tomatoes, chopped
1 tsp. sugar
2 tsp. red wine vinegar
3 medium potatoes, cubed
2 tbsp. fresh coriander, minced
2 tbsp. fresh parsley
1 tbsp. fresh thyme

In a bowl combine the ground lamb, garlic, shallot, salt, pepper, cinnamon, and ground coriander. Form into small meatballs and quickly brown in a large skillet in 1 tbsp. olive oil. Remove meatballs and drain excess fat. Add remaining 1 tbsp. olive oil to skillet, add the onions, and gently sauté for about 5 minutes. Add the meatballs and sauté 5 more minutes. Add the white wine, water, drained chick peas, and salt and pepper, to taste. Cover and simmer about 15 minutes.

Add the plums, cover, and again simmer for 15 minutes. Add the tomatoes, sugar, and red wine vinegar. Simmer without cover 15 more minutes. Add the potatoes, cover again, and simmer for 30 minutes longer. Turn the heat off and add the fresh coriander, parsley, and thyme. Cover and let sit for 5 minutes. Serve.

Yield: 4 servings.

Optional Suggestion: If fresh plums are unavailable, you may substitute **dried prunes**, added with the chick peas. I have also used **canned plums,** added with the tomatoes

BREADS

BAKING BREAD

Bread baking is one of those basic chores women used to do all the time, and for some it was a labour of love. It's a chore everyone should attempt at some point, and enjoy more often. Why? Because it is such a good thing to do! Because it is fun. Because your house will smell so good. And because everyone who enters your house, or otherwise partakes of your bread, will love you. Try baking bread with your kids. I'd always get a batch of bread going when school was cancelled and the kids were getting cabin fever. When it was time to knead the dough I'd let them at it (after washing their hands with hot, soapy water of course), and we'd always have the best results. Everyone can have a turn since you cannot over-knead. How do you know when you've kneaded enough? When you pat it and it feels like a "baby's bum." (A wise friend once told me that, and she is right!)

Bread chemistry is quite interesting. In a nutshell, dough rises with three components working together: the yeast, the liquids, and the flour.

The yeast: It is essential to have good fresh yeast. If it has been sitting in the store for a while, you may not have the best results. Once you get it home, store it in the fridge. The yeast feeds on sugars in the flour to produce CO_2 and alcohol. The CO_2 is what makes the bubbles in your dough, once the dough becomes elastic through kneading. The alcohol evaporates.

The liquids: Usually the liquids include oil or melted butter, water or milk, and sometimes liquid honey. The liquid must be the right temperature. Yeast grows in temperatures between 105°F and 115°F (40 and 25°C), so if you can hold your finger in the liquids for 10 seconds without it getting uncomfortably hot, that is the right temperature.

The flour: Gluten, a part of hard wheat, is the stretchy stuff in your dough that works along with the yeast to make your bread rise. Kneading develops the gluten. If you want a really light bread, be sure to use a flour with high gluten content, like durum wheat flour. Many other flours, such as rye, rice, or others have little or no gluten, and making a light yeasted bread with them is difficult. (The reverse is true as well. Wheat with high gluten content does not make good pie crust, muffins, cakes, or pastries. The gluten gets in the way.) For general purposes, though, unbleached white flour is my standby in all kinds of cooking and baking. It smells and tastes much better than the bleached kind.

A few more hints I have discovered in my bread-baking experience: When you are baking your bread, if you want a crustier crust, give it a "steaming": Place your bread in the oven and close the oven door. Get a tablespoon of water ready, open the oven door, throw the water on the oven floor, and shut the oven door quickly. This is especially good for French or Italian loaves.

When your bread is rising, cover it with plastic wrap instead of the traditional towel. It seems to give a better seal and yields fewer dirty towels.

If you are following a recipe that calls for the old-fashioned yeast that needs proofing, you can still use it with a few minor changes: Mix all your liquids together, including the amount used to proof the yeast, usually ½ cup. Add the yeast with the first of the flour. I'll usually add about ¼ of the flour with the yeast and beat this for a few minutes with a whisk. Then set aside your whisk, which gets really gooey once more flour is added, and continue on with a spoon for beating.

And if you have any leftovers—don't waste a bit. Try making some *Homemade Croutons* (p. 23) or bread pudding or French toast or *Crostini* (p. 14)—the list goes on.

YEASTED BREADS

HONEY-WHOLEWHEAT BREAD

If you've never made bread before, this is the recipe to follow. Over the years, this bread has been our favourite bread, without a doubt. It was included both in my first and second cookbooks. However, this version is a bit different. It is made with instant yeast and includes really explicit directions on bread making and baking.

2½ cups water—1½ cups hot, plus 1 cup cold
½ cup honey
2 tsp. salt
3 tbsp. oil (canola or olive)
4 cups wholewheat flour

1 tbsp. yeast
½ tsp. ground ginger (optional)
3½–4 cups unbleached white flour

In a large bowl put the honey,

salt, and oil. Add 1½ cups hot water and stir until honey is dissolved. Add the remaining 1 cup cold water. The mixture should be the proper temperature for proofing yeast and making bread. (105–115° F). (A quick test: If you can hold your finger in for ten seconds comfortably, then it is okay to proceed. If it is still too hot, you can place the bowl in a sink of cold water and stir for a few minutes. Then test again. When it is the proper temperature, you may proceed.)

Add the wholewheat flour, yeast, and ginger and beat well for a few minutes. If you have a whisk, use this to beat—this helps break up the gluten in the wheat so the bread will rise better. With a large spoon beat in 3 cups of the white flour. Sprinkle ½ cup of the flour on a flat surface. Turn out the bread dough and knead it until it is smooth and elastic, at least 10 minutes. Add additional flour if needed. You should be able to knead the dough easily without it sticking too much. (Flours are different, and even the atmospheric conditions can affect flour. It is better to have your dough moister—you can always add more flour. Too much flour and your dough will be very stiff and hard to knead.)

When dough is smooth and elastic, place in a large, oiled bowl. Turn so dough is covered with oil. Cover tightly with plastic wrap and set in a warm place to rise. Allow to rise about 1½ hours.

Oil two loaf pans. Punch dough down. Divide in half and shape into loaves. Set dough in oiled pans and let rise again, about 45 minutes.

Preheat oven to 350°F.

Bake loaves in preheated oven for approximately 45 minutes. When it is done, the bread should be very crusty and should sound hollow when you tap it.

When they are finished baking, remove loaves from pans and let cool a while before slicing and eating.

Yield: 2 loaves.

Variations:
Heartier Wholewheat Bread: Use **6 cups wholewheat flour** and **2 cups white flour.**
Heartiest Wholewheat Bread: Use **8 cups wholewheat flour**. Kneading will be harder.
Rye Bread: Substitute **3 cups rye flour** for 3 cups wholewheat flour.

Oatmeal Bread: Add 1½ **cups rolled oats** to honey and hot water mixture. Let cool. Use 1 cup less wholewheat flour and 1 cup less white flour.

Molasses Wholewheat Bread: Substitute ½ **cup molasses** for the honey.

Chick Pea Flour and Wholewheat Bread: Substitute 1 **cup chick pea flour** for 1 cup wholewheat.

BUTTERMILK-RYE BREAD

I grew up eating buttermilk rye bread fresh every week from a Polish bakery. Lucky me!

¼ cup hot water
½ cup molasses
1 tbsp. caraway seed
1 tsp. salt
2 cups buttermilk, at room temperature
3 cups rye flour (or 2 cups rye flour and 1 cup wholewheat flour)
1 tbsp. instant yeast
3 cups unbleached white flour, plus additional for kneading
cornmeal, for the baking sheet
2 tbsp. hot water
1 tbsp. molasses

In a small bowl mix together the hot water, molasses, caraway seed, and salt. Stir until molasses is dissolved and stir mixture into the buttermilk.

Mix the rye flour and yeast. Add the mixture to the buttermilk mixture and beat with a spoon for a few minutes. Add the unbleached white flour and blend it in well with a spoon. Cover and set it in a warm place for about 15 minutes.

On a clean surface sprinkled with additional white flour, turn the dough out and knead it for about 5 minutes, or until it is smooth and elastic. Add additional flour if needed. Place in a clean, lightly oiled bowl, turn oiled side up, cover, and let rise in a warm place for about 1 hour, or until double in bulk.

Sprinkle a cookie sheet with cornmeal. Punch dough down and divide in half. Shape each half into a loaf about 10–12" long. Place on a cookie sheet, cover, and set in a warm place

for about 45 minutes, or until double in bulk.
Preheat oven to 350°F.

Mix the 2 tbsp. hot water with the 1 tbsp. molasses and brush the loaves with a bit of this mixture before baking. Bake until lightly browned, 45–50 minutes. Brush again with the glaze while hot. Remove the loaves to a wire rack and let them cool.

Yield: 2 loaves.

Optional Suggestion: To "make" buttermilk: For each cup place **1 tbsp. apple cider vinegar** in a microwavable container. Add **milk** to make one cup. Microwave at medium for about 10 seconds—only enough to warm the mixture to room temperature. If you don't have a microwave, let the apple cider vinegar-milk mixture set for about 10–15 minutes.

OVERNIGHT COUNTRY BREAD

This recipe makes a large country-style loaf of bread. Delicious with soups, or for sandwiches. I find this great in the summer when you don't want to heat your house in midday. You can bake this first thing in the morning, and then let everything cool down.

4½ cups unbleached white flour, plus additional for kneading
½ cup rye flour
½ cup natural bran
2½ tsp. salt
1 tsp. instant yeast
2⅓ cups cool water (about 70°F)
3 tbsp. olive oil
additional flour, for forming the loaf and sprinkling on top
cornmeal, for the baking sheet

The night before: Place 4½ cups of the white flour along with the rye flour, bran, salt, and yeast in a large mixing bowl. In another bowl mix the water and olive oil. Add the liquid to the dry ingredients and beat well with a large spoon. Turn dough out onto a floured surface and knead briefly, using additional flour as needed. Place in a clean, oiled bowl, turn to coat the dough, cover with plastic wrap, and leave to rise at room temperature overnight. (12–14 hours).

In the morning: Prepare a cookie sheet by sprinkling the cornmeal generously over the surface, especially where the bread will be. Using a spoon, form the dough into a large ball in the bowl, scraping the sides down into the dough with a spatula. The dough will be sticky. Turn out onto a floured surface and knead slightly, adding a bit of flour if needed. Form the dough into a loaf about 10" long and place this on the prepared cookie sheet. Sprinkle additional flour on the surface of the bread. Cover with plastic wrap and let it rise in a warm place about 1 hour.

Preheat oven to 400°F.

Place the bread in the oven, shut the door, get 1 tbsp. of water, open the oven door, throw the water on the oven floor and immediately close the door again. This will create some steam to make your loaf crusty. Bake 15 minutes, then turn heat down to 375°F and bake an additional 30 minutes. Remove from oven.

Yield: 1 large loaf.

ITALIAN BREAD

A relatively quick and simple bread recipe that makes any meal special.

1½ cups lukewarm water
1½ tsp. salt
2 cups wholewheat flour
1 tbsp. instant yeast
1½ cups unbleached white flour, plus ½ cup for kneading
cornmeal, for the baking sheet

In a large bowl mix together the water and salt. Add the wholewheat flour and instant yeast and beat together well using a whisk. Set aside your whisk in favour of a large spoon, add 1½ cups unbleached white flour, and mix well. Turn out on a lightly floured surface and knead, adding the additional flour as needed. (You may not need the entire ½ cup.) Knead until the dough is elastic and doesn't stick to the surface.

Place in a clean, oiled bowl, cover with plastic wrap, and

set to rise in a warm place for 1 hour, or until double in bulk.

Punch dough down and set to rise again until double in bulk, 30–45 minutes. (This step is preferable but not necessary.)

Sprinkle cornmeal on a baking sheet the approximate size of your loaves, 9"–10" long. Divide dough in half, knead each piece lightly, then form each into a loaf 9"–10" long, by rolling and pulling it. Dust with flour, then cover with plastic wrap and set to rise in a warm place until double in bulk, 45 minutes to 1 hour.

Preheat oven to 400°F. Place the bread in the oven. Close the oven door. Have ready 1 tbsp. water. Open the oven door, throw the water on the oven floor and quickly shut the door again. Bake 15 minutes, then reduce the temperature to 350°F and bake 10–15 minutes longer.

Yield: 2 loaves.

MOCK SOURDOUGH MINI FRENCH BREADS

A delicious small French loaf which is great to have frozen. I'll make a batch of these when I have a quiet day, freeze them, and have them ready to thaw when company comes. They are great also for a rustic baguette sandwich. One loaf, split horizontally and filled with a good sandwich filling, will be adequate for two hearty servings.

2 cups wholewheat flour
1 tbsp. sugar
1 tsp. salt
½ tsp. ginger
1 tbsp. instant yeast
1 cup low-fat plain yogurt, or buttermilk, at room temperature
1 cup warm water
1 tbsp. apple cider vinegar
2½ cups unbleached white flour, plus additional for kneading

cornmeal, for sprinkling on the baking sheet
1 egg white plus 1 tbsp. water, lightly beaten
poppy seeds or sesame seeds, for garnish (optional)

In a large bowl mix together the wholewheat flour, sugar, salt, ginger, and instant yeast. In another bowl, whisk together the yogurt, warm water, and apple cider vinegar. You want this mixture to be quite warm, but not hot or it will kill the yeast.

Add the liquid ingredients to the dry ingredients. Blend in and beat with a rotary beater (or whisk) for about 3 minutes. Set aside your whisk. Add the 2½ cups of white flour and beat with a spoon until dough is smooth. Turn out onto a floured surface and knead, adding more flour if necessary, until the dough is smooth and elastic. Place in a clean, oiled bowl, cover with a clean cloth, and place in a warm place to rise until double in bulk, about 30–45 minutes.

Lightly oil a large cookie sheet and sprinkle it with cornmeal. Punch down the dough and knead a bit to remove all bubbles. Divide dough into four pieces. Shape each into a loaf about 10" long. Place the loaves on the cookie sheet so they do not touch and are well spaced from each other. Cover and let rise until double in bulk, about 30 minutes.

Preheat oven to 375°F.

Brush loaves gently with the egg white/water mixture, and sprinkle with poppy or sesame seeds if desired. Place loaves in the oven, quickly throw 1 tbsp. water on the oven floor, shut oven door quickly, and bake for 25 minutes, or until loaves are golden-brown. Cool on a wire rack.

Yield: 4 mini loaves.

Optional Suggestion: To reheat frozen loaves: Thaw completely. Place in a paper bag, wet the bag with wet hands, and place in a 350°F oven for about 10 minutes. This will warm and freshen the bread.

BRIAN'S BAGELS

Brian's are the best bagels East of Montreal! The fact that Brian bakes them in his wood stove is one reason they are special. You must have the potato water for this recipe. You can use the potatoes for a salad—or other recipes that call for boiled potatoes.

½ cup warm water
1 tbsp. yeast
½ tsp. sugar

1 quart potato cooking water
1 tbsp. salt
¼ cup sunflower oil (or canola

oil)
½ cup honey
6 cups unbleached flour
2 quarts water
2 tbsp. brown sugar

In the warm water in a warm place, proof the yeast with the sugar.

In a large bowl mix the warm potato cooking water, salt, sunflower oil, and honey. Stir until the honey is dissolved. The mixture should be warm, but not hot. Stir in the proofed yeast. Add 5 cups of the flour and beat with a large spoon until all the flour is incorporated. Sprinkle remaining 1 cup flour on your kneading surface and knead the dough until it is smooth and doesn't stick to the surface. Use additional flour if needed.

Place dough in a clean, oiled bowl, turn until all sides are coated with oil, and set dough to rise in a warm place for 2 hours.

Form the bagels: Punch down the dough. Take a piece the size of a lemon and form it into a cylinder about 8" long. Wrap it in a circle around your left thumb and with your right hand pinch the ends together. (Moisten your hands with cold water to make this process easier.) Lay the bagels on a clean surface that has been lightly dusted with flour to keep them from sticking. Cover and let them rise for 10–15 minutes.

Preheat oven to 425°F.

Bring to a boil in a large stockpot the 2 quarts water and the brown sugar. Add the bagels a few at a time and boil them for 1½ minutes. (Brian does 4 bagels at a time. He finds that he can get the next 4 ready while one batch is boiling.)

Drain very well. Place them on a cookie sheet and bake in preheated oven, near the top, for 15 minutes, or until they are nicely browned. (Brian likes his bagels very brown.)

Yield: 16–20 bagels.

A DILLY LOAF

Great right from the oven—and toasted for sandwiches.

1 cup low-fat cottage cheese
½ cup hot water
1 egg
1 tbsp. butter, melted
1 tbsp. sugar
1 tsp. salt
1 tsp. pepper, or to taste (optional)
1½ tbsp. instant yeast
2½ cups unbleached white flour
⅔ cup fresh dill, minced
½ cup fresh garlic chives, minced

In a large mixing bowl, place the cottage cheese, water, egg, butter, sugar, salt, and pepper, if desired, and beat well with a whisk or egg beater. Bring this mixture to a warm temperature before proceeding. (The top of a double boiler works well to warm the mixture.)

Add 1 cup of the white flour and the instant yeast and beat together vigorously. Add ½ cup of flour and beat well again. Add the dill and garlic chives and blend in well with a spoon.

Sprinkle additional flour on a clean surface, turn out the dough, and knead well for 5–10 minutes, or until dough is smooth and does not stick.

Oil a large bowl, place dough in bowl, turn to coat the dough with oil, cover with a clean towel, and leave to rise in a warm place until double in bulk, about 1–1½ hours.

Generously butter a bread pan. Punch down the dough, form it into a loaf, and place in the bread pan. Cover and leave it to rise until double in bulk, about 45 minutes.

Preheat oven to 350°F. Bake bread in preheated oven until loaf is nicely browned, about 45 minutes. (Smaller loaves will take less time—about 35–40 minutes.) Remove from oven, loosen sides, and turn out on a wire rack to cool slightly. Slice and serve.

Yield: 1 loaf.

CHRISTÖLLEN

I've made this for Christmas morning. Over the years I have substituted more natural fruits for the glacé variety called for in the traditional recipe, and I have added some almond paste. The result is too good to have just once a year. This bread keeps well and is a lovely Christmas present.

2 cups milk
2 tsp. salt
⅔ cup sugar
1 cup butter, cut in small pieces
2 cups unbleached white flour
2 tbsp. instant yeast
1½ cups raisins, softened in sherry or brandy to cover
1 cup dried cherries, softened in sherry or brandy to cover
4 eggs, beaten
2 tsp. vanilla
6 cups additional flour, more for kneading
1½ cups blanched slivered almonds
½ cup citron
½ cup dried pineapple, finely chopped
½ cup dried apricots, finely chopped
grated rind of 1 lemon
½ lb. almond paste

In a saucepan over medium-high heat scald the milk. Remove from heat and add the salt, sugar, and butter. Stir until butter is melted and the mixture cools to room temperature.

Place the milk mixture in a very large bowl. Add the 2 cups of flour and the yeast, and beat with a spoon (or whisk) until smooth. Cover with plastic wrap and set in a warm place until it is bubbly, about 1 hour.

In the meantime soften the raisins and dried cherries in warm sherry or brandy to cover, and keep them in a warm place until needed.

When the batter has risen, add the eggs and vanilla and 4 more cups of the flour. Beat well with a large wooden spoon until the mixture is smooth. Blend in 2 more cups of flour and continue to knead in the bowl, adding the drained raisins and cherries, almonds, citron, dried pineapple, dried apricot, and grated lemon rind. Turn out onto a clean, floured surface and continue kneading until the dough is smooth and elastic, adding more flour if the dough sticks. Turn into a clean, buttered bowl, cover, and let rise in a warm place until double in bulk, 1 to 1½ hours.

Punch down dough and divide into thirds. On a floured surface, roll out each piece of dough into a rectangle approximately 8" by 10". Take one third of the almond paste and roll it out between sheets of wax paper to make a sheet approximately 6" by 8" (to fit the dough with 1" edges all around). Carefully transfer the almond paste onto the dough and roll up into a loaf. Pinch together the seam and edges. Repeat process two more times with remaining dough and almond paste.

Place loaves on buttered baking sheets, cover with clean cloths, and let rise in a warm place for about 1 hour, or until double in bulk.

Preheat oven to 350°F.

Bake in preheated oven for 40–45 minutes, or until nicely browned and hollow-sounding when tapped. You may have to cover them with foil to prevent them from becoming too brown. Turn out onto a rack and cool completely before slicing.

Yield: 3 loaves.

HOMEMADE PITA BREAD

1¼ cups warm water
1 tbsp. olive oil
1 tsp. salt
4 cups unbleached white flour, plus additional for rolling (You may substitute ¼ cup gluten for ¼ cup flour, if desired—this gives the pitas more elasticity.)
1 tbsp. instant yeast

In a medium bowl combine the warm water, olive oil, and salt. Add 2 cups of the flour and the yeast. Beat well. Beat in an additional 1½ cups flour. Sprinkle remaining ½ cup of flour on a clean surface, turn the dough and knead for 5 minutes, or until dough is smooth and elastic. (Sprinkle additional flour on surface, if necessary.)

Place dough in a clean, oiled bowl, turn the dough to grease the top of it, cover with a clean towel, and place in a warm place for about 1½ hours, or until double in bulk.

Punch down dough and let it rise again for another 1 hour.

Preheat oven to 500°F. Place ungreased cookie sheet in oven to preheat also.

Punch down dough and divide into 12 equal pieces. Form each piece into a ball, flatten with your hand into a circle, and, on a generously floured surface, roll each into a circle 6" in diameter. Set aside on a clean, flat surface until all pitas are rolled out.

Remove cookie sheet from oven and quickly place as many pitas on it as comfortably fit without touching. Return to oven and bake 5 minutes. Remove to a cooling rack. Continue until all pitas are baked. When they are cooled down a bit, flatten each one gently with a spatula. These may be eaten immediately or cooled completely and stored in a plastic bag.

Yield: 12 pita rounds.

FOCACCIA SANDWICH BREAD

Focaccia is usually a pizza-like creation, used as a first course. For a delicious and different sandwich, try making a thick focaccia and filling it with grilled sausage or meat and sautéed vegetables. If you have leftover bread, it is good split, brushed with garlic butter, and baked until crunchy and golden.

Thick Focaccia:
1¾ cup warm water
1 tsp. sugar
1 tsp. salt
3 tbsp. olive oil
2 cups wholewheat flour
1 tbsp. instant yeast
3 cups unbleached white flour, plus additional for kneading
olive oil
sesame seeds or coarse salt (optional)

In a large bowl, mix the water, sugar, salt, and olive oil. Add the wholewheat flour with the instant yeast and beat it vigorously with a whisk for 2–3 minutes. Set aside your whisk. Add 3 cups of the white flour, 1 cup at a time, beating it in with a spoon until it is well blended. Turn out onto a lightly floured surface and knead for 5 minutes, adding more flour if necessary. The dough should be soft and slightly sticky. Place it into a lightly oiled bowl, turn it to coat the dough, cover with a clean towel or plastic wrap, and leave it to rise in a warm place for 1½ hours.

Lightly oil a cookie sheet (15½" x 10½"). First with a rolling pin and then using your hands, shape and pull the dough into the same size as the sheet. Lay it on and press it onto the cookie sheet, trying to get it evenly thick. Cut the dough into 12 pieces. Cover with a clean cloth and let rise for 1 hour.

About 15 minutes before baking, preheat the oven to 400°F.

When the dough is finished rising, brush the surface with about 2 tbsp. olive oil and sprinkle with sesame seeds or coarse salt, if desired. Bake in the bottom ⅓ of the oven for 20 minutes, or until focaccia is golden. If bottom is getting brown too quickly, move it to the top ⅓ of the oven. Remove from oven and remove the focaccia to a cooling rack. Break into serving pieces and serve.

Yield: 12 servings

GRILLED FLATBREAD

This is an unusual bread. I usually make it when I have a roast going in the oven and can't make a baked bread, so I make this, and grill it on top of the stove! It is like a sourdough bread, and takes a long time for the risings, so start it the night before, or in the morning.

2 tbsp. yogurt
2 tbsp. hot water
2 tsp. yeast
⅓ cup unbleached white flour
2 tsp. sugar

In a medium bowl place the yogurt and add the water, 1 tbsp. at a time. You want the mixture of yogurt and water to be at room temperature. Stir in the yeast, flour, and sugar and blend together well. Cover with plastic wrap and set to bubble in a warm place, over-

night or for at least 3 hours.

1 cup unbleached white flour
1 cup wholewheat flour
1 tsp. salt
1 cup lukewarm water
¾ cup additional unbleached white flour

In a large bowl combine the flours and salt. Add the yogurt starter and 1 cup lukewarm water. Beat well together with a spoon. Turn dough out on a lightly floured surface and

knead, using the additional flour as needed. Place dough in a clean, oiled bowl, cover with plastic wrap (or a clean towel), and let rise another 2 hours.

Divide dough in half and form each half into a circle about 8" in diameter. Heat a cast-iron griddle over medium-high heat and "grill" the breads, one at a time. First grill them over the higher heat on both sides to brown them (about 5 minutes total). Then reduce the heat, cover with a large lid and cook another 5 minutes. Remove lid, flip bread, and continue to cook another 5 minutes. Serve warm.

Yield: 2 rounds of flatbread.

APPLE KÜCHEN

A nice and simple apple cake. Not a great keeper, but it usually doesn't last long.

Dough:
½ cup milk
¼ cup butter, cut into pieces
¼ cup sugar
¼ tsp. salt
1 egg, beaten
1 tsp. vanilla
1 cup unbleached white flour, or wholewheat flour
1 tbsp. instant yeast
1¼ cup unbleached white flour, plus additional for kneading

Topping:
2 tbsp. melted butter
3–4 large apples, peeled, cored and sliced
½ cup + 2 tbsp. sugar
1 tsp. cinnamon

Scald the milk, remove from heat, and add the butter, sugar, and salt. Stir until butter is melted, then pour into a large mixing bowl. When the mixture has cooled a bit, whisk in the egg and vanilla, then add the 1 cup unbleached white flour and instant yeast, and whisk a few more minutes. Set aside your whisk and, with a large spoon, blend in the remaining 1¼ cups flour and beat until mixture holds together. Turn onto a clean surface that has been sprinkled with additional flour and knead, adding more flour if necessary, until mixture is smooth and not sticky. Turn into a clean buttered bowl, cover, and set in a warm place to rise about 1 hour, or until doubled in bulk.

Butter an 8" x 12" pan and set aside.

Punch down dough, roll out into a rectangle to fit the prepared pan, brush lightly with the melted butter, sprinkle with the 2 tbsp. sugar, and press the apple slices into the dough. Mix together the remaining ½ cup sugar with the cinnamon and sprinkle over the apples. Cover loosely and set in a warm place to rise for 45 minutes, or until doubled in bulk.

Preheat oven to 375°F.

Bake in preheated oven for 35–40 min., or until apple slices are tender. Cool slightly and serve.

Yield: 12 servings.

ORANGE FRENCH TOAST

A delicious recipe to use any leftover bread. You may make the batter up the night before and let the bread soak in it overnight, in the fridge. Recipe may be halved for 1–2 persons.

4 eggs
½ cup orange juice
⅓ cup milk
2 tbsp. sugar
½ tsp. vanilla
¼ tsp. salt
6 slices bread (approx.)
butter

In a bowl beat together the eggs, orange juice, milk, sugar, vanilla, and salt, using a whisk. If you are preparing this the night before, place the bread in a baking dish and pour the batter over, or if you are making it for immediate consumption, dip the bread in the batter one slice at a time and sauté: Heat a cast-iron griddle over medium heat. Melt butter until sizzling and sauté the French toast turning to brown evenly on both sides, until cooked through. Serve with maple syrup.

Yield: 2–3 servings.

QUICK BREADS, SWEET BREADS, AND COFFEE CAKES

❧

OATMEAL SCONES

These are delicious right out of the oven with homemade jam—or in the spring try drizzling some pure maple syrup over them! You may want to double the recipe.

¾ cup unbleached white flour
½ cup wholewheat flour
1 tsp. baking soda
½ tsp. baking powder
½ tsp. salt
1 tsp. cinnamon
¼ cup brown sugar
⅓ cup butter
1 cup rolled oats (small, if possible)
½ cup buttermilk, or yogurt thinned with a bit of milk

Preheat oven to 375°F.

In a medium bowl mix the white flour, wholewheat flour, baking soda, baking powder, salt, cinnamon, and brown sugar thoroughly. With a pastry cutter cut in the butter until mixture is "mealy." Stir in the oats. Add the buttermilk and gently mix just until mixture begins to hold together. In the bowl, with your hands, knead and form the dough into a ball. It will be quite stiff. Turn dough onto a lightly floured board and flatten the ball with your hands into an 8" circle. Cut the circle into 8 wedges. Place the wedges on an ungreased cookie sheet, being sure they are not touching each other. Bake in the preheated oven for 15 minutes, or until the scones are lightly browned.

Serve warm with butter and jam or maple syrup.

Yield: 8 scones.

CANADIAN BLUEBERRY COFFEE CAKE

Blueberries are so simple to freeze when they are abundant in the summer—just put them in a bag and freeze! In the winter they taste great in pancakes, muffins, and in this coffee cake.

Batter:
⅓ butter, softened
⅔ cup brown sugar
1 egg
¾ cup milk, warmed
1 tsp. vanilla
2 cups unbleached white flour
2 tsp. baking powder
1 tsp. cinnamon
½ tsp. salt
2 cups blueberries, thawed in a colander if frozen

Streusel:
¼ cup softened butter
⅓ cup brown sugar
¼ cup small-flaked rolled oats
¼ cup flour
½ cup slivered almonds, or unsweetened coconut
½ tsp. cinnamon
few gratings nutmeg

In a medium mixing bowl cream the butter and brown sugar a few minutes. Add the egg and mix in thoroughly. Add the milk and vanilla and stir until smooth. In a separate bowl combine the flour, baking powder, cinnamon, and salt and mix well. Add dry ingredients to the liquid mixture and blend thoroughly. Set aside.

Preheat oven to 350°F.

Make streusel: In a small bowl combine the butter, brown sugar, oats, flour slivered almonds, cinnamon, and nutmeg. Set aside.

Butter a 9" square baking pan. Spread about ⅔ of the batter evenly in the pan. Sprinkle blueberries over the batter. Drop remaining batter by spoonfuls evenly over the berries. Gently smooth the top as much as you can. Sprinkle with streusel and bake in preheated oven for 30–35 minutes or until golden-brown.

If you use frozen, unthawed berries, fold them into the batter, spread the crumble top on, and bake approximately 15 minutes longer.

Serve warm or cold. Good for breakfast, too.

JER'S PANCAKES

This recipe was in my first cookbook, and I have more people coming up and telling me that they often make it on Sunday mornings. We have the pancakes, or the following *Jer's Wholewheat Belgian Waffles* nearly every Sunday! They still are always delicious!

1½ cups wholewheat flour
1 cup unbleached white flour
4 tbsp. brown sugar
1 tsp. salt
4 tsp. baking powder
½ cup butter, melted
1¾ cups milk, or more
3 egg yolks
3 egg whites, stiffly beaten

In a large mixing bowl, combine the flours, brown sugar, salt, and baking powder.

In another bowl combine the melted butter, milk, and egg yolks. Beat together until blended. Add to dry ingredients and mix until blended.

Add the stiffly beaten egg whites and fold in gently. You may need to thin the batter with a bit of milk. Cook on griddle. Serve with maple or honey syrup.

Yield: 4 servings.

Optional Suggestion: You may vary the amounts of the flours—more wholewheat, less white, or vice versa. Just have the total flour amount at 2½ cups.

JER'S WHOLEWHEAT BELGIAN WAFFLES

The other Sunday morning staple. They are good with maple syrup, strawberries, raspberries, blueberries, etc. This is a large batch because they are great left over—just warm them up in the oven until they are heated through and crisped. We especially love them with applesauce and maple syrup.

2½ cups wholewheat flour
4 tbsp. brown sugar
1 tsp. salt
3 tsp. baking powder
5 egg yolks
½ cup butter, melted
1¾ cup milk, or more
1 tsp. vanilla
5 egg whites

In a large bowl combine the flour, sugar, salt, and baking powder. Set aside.

In a medium bowl beat the egg yolks with an egg beater until they are thick and lemon-coloured. Add the butter, milk, and vanilla and beat until well blended. Stir into the dry ingredients and mix in, using a spoon, until well blended. If the batter is too stiff, add more milk. (If you use small eggs, you will need additional milk.)

In a separate bowl beat the egg whites until they are stiff. Gently fold into the batter. Make waffles according to directions for your waffle maker.

Yield: 8 large hearty waffles.

Optional Suggestions: You can use unbleached white flour for some or all of the flour. We prefer them with 100% wholewheat flour—but you might not.

Variation:
Toasted Pecan Waffles: Toast **1 cup pecan halves:** Preheat oven to 350°F. Spread pecan halves in a pan or cookie sheet and bake for 5–7 minutes. Do not overbake—they burn quickly! Cool slightly then place in a small plastic bag and roll over bag with rolling pin to break the nuts into smaller pieces. Add to batter just before you begin to make the waffles.

COWBOY CORNBREAD

I make this often, to accompany Mexican or Tex-Mex meals and for potlucks as well. If you have any left over it is great warmed in the morning with maple syrup.

1 cup cornmeal
½ cup wholewheat flour
½ cup unbleached white flour
1 tsp. baking powder
¾ tsp. salt
½ tsp. baking soda
1 cup buttermilk (or ½ cup plain yogurt mixed with ½ cup milk)
2 eggs
2 tbsp. canola or vegetable oil
1 tbsp. light brown sugar
1 small can (240 ml/10 oz.) cream-style corn

Yield: 9 or 16 squares.

Optional Suggestion: You may add some **bacon,** cooked, drained, and crumbled, or **1 cup grated Cheddar cheese.**

Variation:
Hot Cornbread: If you are serving this for dinner, you may want to spice it up by adding **1 or 2 jalapeño peppers,** seeded and minced, or **1–2 tbsp. pickled jalapeño peppers**, minced.

Preheat oven to 400°F. Butter an 8" square baking pan.
In a medium bowl mix together the cornmeal, wholewheat flour, white flour, baking powder, salt, and baking soda.

In another medium bowl place the yogurt or sour cream, milk, eggs, canola oil, and sugar. Beat together well, using a whisk. Stir in the cream-style corn and add this to the flour mixture, combining well, using a large spoon or spatula. Pour into the prepared pan and bake for 25 minutes, or until top is nicely browned.

DESSERTS

HEARTY CHOCOLATE CHIP COOKIES

These cookies are a staple around our house. I've made thousands of them over the years!

¾ cup butter, softened
¾ cup brown sugar
½ cup white sugar
2 eggs, extra large
1 tbsp. vanilla
¾ cup wholewheat flour
1 tsp. salt
1 tsp. baking soda
1 cup white flour
1 cup rolled oats (small flakes, if available)
¾ cup desiccated coconut (finely grated)
1 pkg. (300 g) chocolate chips

Preheat oven to 375°F.

Place softened butter in a large mixing bowl and add the brown and white sugar. Beat the mixture vigorously until it is smooth and creamy. Add the eggs, one at a time, then add the vanilla, beating well after each addition. Add the whole-wheat flour, salt, and baking soda and beat well for a few more minutes. Add the white flour and blend well. Add the oats, coconut, and chocolate chips. Mix all together until well blended.

Drop by tablespoonfuls onto an ungreased cookie sheet. Bake 8–10 minutes or until cookies are nicely browned, turning the cookie sheet around midway through baking if necessary. Transfer to a cooling rack. Cool, eat, and enjoy.

Yield: Approx. 3 dozen cookies.

ALMOND-COCONUT WAFERS

A nice delicate cookie—good for tea time.

½ cup butter, softened
½ cup brown sugar
½ cup white sugar
¾ tsp. almond extract
1 egg, extra large
1 cup unbleached white flour
½ tsp. baking soda
½ tsp. baking powder
½ tsp. salt
1 cup natural almonds, finely ground
½ cup desiccated coconut

Preheat oven to 350°F.

Place softened butter in a medium-sized mixing bowl. Add the brown sugar, white sugar, almond extract, and egg, beating well after each addition. In a separate bowl mix together the flour, baking soda, baking powder, and salt. Add to the first mixture and beat well. Mix in the almonds and coconut.

Drop large tablespoonfuls of the dough onto an ungreased cookie sheet about 3–4" apart. Bake 10–12 minutes in preheated oven, or until a light golden-brown. Let them cool a few minutes on the cookie sheet, then remove to a wire rack for cooling.

Yield: 2½–3 dozen cookies.

Variation:
Pecan-Coconut Wafers: Substitute **1 cup pecans**, ground, for almonds and **1 tsp. vanilla** for almond extract.

MAIDA HEATTER'S OATMEAL-MOLASSES COOKIES

Maida Heatter is one of the best cookie and dessert cookbook writers ever. This particular recipe has become one of our favourites, especially in the winter, with a glass of cold milk for dunking.

½ lb. (2 sticks) butter, softened
½ cup molasses
1½ cups sugar
2 eggs, at room temperature
1½ tsp. vanilla
1 cup sifted wholewheat flour
2 cups sifted white flour
2 tsp. baking soda
1 tsp. salt
1 tsp. cinnamon
1 tsp. ginger
2 cups old-fashioned or quick-cooking rolled oats (small flakes, if possible)
1 cup desiccated coconut (finely grated)
1 cup pecans

Preheat oven to 375°F.

In a large bowl, cream the butter and blend in the molasses. (This can be done with an electric beater or by hand.) Add the sugar, ½ cup at a time, beating well after each addition. Add the eggs, one at a time, and the vanilla, and continue beating until mixture is smooth and thoroughly blended.

In a separate bowl sift together the wholewheat flour, white flour, baking soda, salt, cinnamon, and ginger. Stir the dry ingredients into the butter mixture and stir only until blended. Add the oats, coconut, and pecans, and again stir only until blended. The batter will be quite stiff. Use a well-rounded (but not heaping) teaspoonful of dough for each cookie. Place them 2" apart on an ungreased cookie sheet. Bake on the upper third of your oven for 12–13 minutes, or until cookies are lightly coloured. Reverse the cookie sheet front to back halfway through baking. When they are done, the cookies will still feel slightly soft and underdone, but do not overbake.

Remove from oven and let the cookies stand on the sheet for a minute or so and then, with a wide metal spatula, transfer them to racks to cool.

Yield: 72 cookies.

PEANUT BUTTER-CHOCOLATE CHIP BARS

These are quick and easy to make. Perfect for those lunch-boxes.

½ cup butter, softened
1 cup brown sugar

½ cup peanut butter
2 eggs
3 tbsp. maple syrup
2 tsp. vanilla
1 cup unbleached white flour
1 tsp. baking soda
1 tsp. salt
1 cup rolled oats
1 pkg. (300 g) chocolate chips

Preheat oven to 350°F. Butter a 9" x 13" pan.

Place the butter in a large mixing bowl. Butter must be soft. Using a spoon, mix in the brown sugar, peanut butter, eggs, maple syrup, and vanilla and beat together well.

In a smaller bowl mix together the white flour, baking soda, and salt and add this to first mixture. Stir in the rolled oats and chocolate chips and spread batter in the prepared pan. Bake in preheated oven for 25–30 minutes, or until light golden-brown and set (the centre should still be a bit wobbly when touched). Cover bars with foil if getting too dark before getting set. Cool slightly and serve—warm or cool.

Yield: 36–48 bars, depending on what size you cut them.

FRUIT JEWELS

Homemade fruit bars are a great energy boost. I wrap these individually and store them in the fridge.

4 cups dried fruit (include 1–2 cups dried cranberries, if possible)
¼ cup unbleached white flour
1 tsp. cinnamon
½ tsp. salt
4 eggs
½ cup brown sugar
1½ tsp. vanilla
¾ cup rolled oats
½ cup dried coconut
½ cup pecans (or omit coconut and use 1 cup pecans)

Preheat oven to 350°F.

Prepare an 11" tart pan. Oil, or spray with oil, and set aside.

Cut the dried fruit into small pieces. It is easier to snip some fruits with scissors (for instance, apples, pears, or peaches) and cut others with a sharp knife (for instance, prunes or apricots). In a bowl toss the fruit with the flour, cinnamon, and salt. Set aside.

In another bowl whisk together the eggs, brown sugar, and vanilla. Add the fruit and gently fold together. Add the oats, coconut, and pecans and, again, gently fold together. Pour the mixture into the prepared tart pan. Gently push the fruit mixture down and smooth the surface using a spatula.

Bake in preheated oven for 30–40 minutes, or until top is lightly browned. Cool and cut into wedges. Cool and serve or store.

Yield: 20–24 bars.

AWESOME CHOCOLATE-CREAM CHEESE BROWNIES

Cream Cheese:
1 large pkg. (250 g/8 oz.) cream cheese, softened
1 egg
⅓ cup sugar
1 tsp. vanilla

Place all ingredients in a small bowl and beat together well with a spoon until mixture is smooth and creamy. Set aside.

Chocolate Mixture:
1 oz. unsweetened chocolate
5 oz. semi-sweet chocolate (Callebaut if possible—this is the best chocolate!)
½ cup butter
1 cup sugar
4 eggs
2 tsp. vanilla
1 cup unbleached white flour
pinch salt

Melt the chocolates and the butter in a bowl or double boiler over (not in) boiling water. Stir often until all is melted. Remove and let cool a bit, but not longer than 10 minutes.

Preheat oven to 350°F. Butter and lightly dust with flour a 9" x 13" baking pan. Set aside.

Add the sugar to the chocolate mixture and beat well. Add the eggs, one at a time, beating well after each addition. Add the vanilla and mix it in well, then fold in the flour and salt, using a spatula, until well blended.

Pour half the chocolate mixture into the prepared pan—or enough to spread it until it covers the bottom. Drop the cream cheese mixture by spoonfuls over the chocolate batter, distributing it evenly. Pour remaining chocolate slowly over the batter, trying to cover most of the cream cheese mixture. Run the tip of a knife back and forth through the batter, starting in one corner, thereby swirling the cream cheese and chocolate mixtures. Bake in preheated oven for 23–28 minutes—being careful not to overbake. Cool in pan, cut, and serve. If you can keep these around for more than a day, place them in the refrigerator.

Yield: 16–24 bars, depending on how big you cut them.

RASPBERRY-CHEESECAKE BROWNIES

Some of the best brownies you'll ever have! The berries must be fresh for best results. I usually make these for parties, and they are even better made the day before.

Brownie Batter:
4 oz. bittersweet chocolate, chopped
2 oz. unsweetened chocolate, chopped
½ cup unsalted butter
1 cup sugar
3 large eggs
1 tsp. vanilla
½ tsp. almond extract
¾ tsp. salt
¾ cup unbleached white flour

Cheesecake Layer:
1 large pkg. (250 g/8 oz.) cream cheese, softened
⅔ cup sugar
1 large egg
1 tbsp. amaretto (or sherry)
1 tsp. vanilla
½ tsp. almond extract
¼ tsp. salt
2 tbsp. unbleached white flour

1½ cups fresh raspberries
1 tbsp. sugar

Preheat oven to 350°F. Butter and flour a 9" x 13" baking pan.

Make brownie layer: In a double boiler over, not in, boiling water place the bittersweet chocolate, unsweetened chocolate, and butter. Stir mixture until all is melted. Remove from heat and cool slightly. Blend in the sugar, using a whisk, then whisk in the eggs, one at a time. Add the vanilla, almond extract, and salt. Blend in the flour and spread batter evenly in the prepared pan.

Make cheesecake layer: In a medium bowl combine the cream cheese and sugar. Using an electric mixer, beat until mixture is light and fluffy. Add the egg, amaretto (or sherry), vanilla, almond extract, and salt, and continue to beat until mixture is smooth. Blend in the flour with a spatula and spread mixture evenly over the brownie layer.

Place raspberries in the cheesecake layer, poking each one into the batter a bit. Sprinkle with the sugar and bake in the middle of the preheated oven for 35–40 minutes, or until the top is puffed and pale golden.

Cool brownies in pan on a rack. Cover and chill completely before cutting. Serve at room temperature.

Yield: 24 brownies. You may cut them smaller for a larger crowd.

AUNT MITZ'S DECADENT CHOCOLATE CUPCAKES

Aunt Mitz is my aunt-in-law, with a well-deserved reputation as an awesome cook. When she visited quite a few years back, she brought the most delicious chocolate cupcakes I've ever had. Lucky for us, she gave me the recipe! They are not healthy, but I make them for special occasions, such as Valentine's Day, and they are always a hit! They are better aged a day or two.

4 oz. semi-sweet chocolate, coarsely chopped
1 cup butter
1 cup pecans, coarsely chopped
4 large eggs
1½ cups white sugar
1 tsp. vanilla
1 cup white flour

In the top of a double boiler over, not in, boiling water, melt chocolate and butter, stirring until melted. Add nuts and stir until nuts are well coated. Set aside to cool.

In a medium bowl beat the eggs, using a whisk, until they are lemony-coloured. Add the sugar and vanilla and continue whisking until the mixture is well blended. Add half the flour and blend, using a whisk; then add remaining flour, stir, using a spoon, until mixture is just blended. Do not beat. Add the chocolate mixture and stir until just blended.

The mixture is very runny at this point. Set it aside and let it cool until it stiffens. This will make it easier to fill muffin cups.

Preheat oven to 325°F. Using a heaping tablespoon for each cupcake, spoon batter into 18 mould lined muffin cups. Bake in preheated oven 25–30 minutes. Do not over-bake—the cupcakes should be set, but a toothpick should come out with a few crumbs still sticking to it. Let cool and do not frost.

Yield: 18 cupcakes.

BERRY GOOD SHORTCAKE

What could be better for dessert in the summertime than a fresh berry shortcake? I make this all summer and use whatever berries are in season. Our favourites are **raspberry** and the traditional **strawberry. Peach** shortcake is also great, as well as combinations like **peach and raspberry** or **raspberry and blueberry**.

Fruit:
3–4 cups fresh raspberries, strawberries, or other berries or fruit
⅓ cup white sugar (or less, to taste)

In the morning prepare the fruit: Clean berries well, discarding any that aren't sound. Sprinkle white sugar to taste over the berries, mix them gently, and let them sit at room temperature for about 30 minutes to allow the sugar to draw out some of the juice. Cover and place in fridge until needed.

Shortcake:
2 cups unbleached white flour
⅓ cup sugar
3 tsp. baking powder
½ tsp. salt
½ cup butter
2 eggs
¾ cup milk
1 tsp. vanilla and ½ tsp. almond extract

Preheat oven to 375°F. Butter and flour a 9" or 10" springform pan. Set aside. In a large bowl combine the flour, sugar, baking powder, and salt. Cut in the butter, using a pastry blender, until the mixture resembles coarse crumbs. In a separate bowl whisk together the eggs, milk, vanilla, and almond extract. Pour into the flour mixture, stirring just enough to blend. Spread the mixture evenly over the pan. Bake in preheated oven for 25–30 minutes.

Remove from oven, remove sides of pan, and let cake cool until you can remove the bottom of pan easily. Cool completely and set aside.

Whipped Cream and Assembly:
2 cups whipping cream
3 tbsp. sugar
1 tsp. vanilla
3–4 tbsp. sherry (optional)

In a small bowl whip the cream until it forms soft peaks. Sprinkle the white sugar over the cream and continue beating until stiff peaks form. Add the vanilla and beat just to blend.

Split the cake and place the bottom half on your serving plate. Sprinkle sherry over the cake, if desired. Cover with half the berries and half the juice, then spread the whip cream evenly over all. Place top half of cake carefully over berries, and gently spoon remaining berries and juice evenly over the cake. Serve.

Yield: 8 servings.

Optional Suggestion: If you are serving this to a larger crowd, cut it into smaller servings.

APPLE SNACKING CAKE WITH PRALINE TOPPING

The previous batter using butter for the oil, and topped with a richer praline topping.

cake batter from previous recipe, using ½ cup butter, softened, instead of oil

Praline Topping:
4 tbsp. butter, soft
½ cup brown sugar
¼ cup white flour
¼ cup small rolled oats
¼ cup desiccated coconut
½ cup pecan pieces
1 tsp. cinnamon

Preheat oven to 350°F. Butter a 9" square pan and set aside.

Prepare cake batter and spread into the prepared pan. Using a fork, mix together the butter, brown sugar, white flour, oats, coconut, pecans, and cinnamon. Spread over the cake, pressing the topping into the batter lightly with your fingertips.

Bake in preheated oven for 30–35 minutes, or until a toothpick comes out clean when poked into middle of cake. Cool slightly and serve.

Yield: 9–12 pieces.

CHOCOLATE-PECAN PIE

Truly delicious—the grated chocolate rises to the top and forms a creamy chocolatey layer. Try this on special occasions.

Crust:
1½ cups unbleached white flour
2 tsp. sugar
1 tsp. cinnamon
½ tsp. salt
8 tbsp. cold butter
¼ cup ice water

Combine the flour, sugar, cinnamon, and salt in a bowl. Cut in the butter using a pastry blender and slowly add the ice water, mixing with a fork, until mixture holds together. Form into a ball, wrap in wax paper, and put in the fridge until needed. (To use your food processor to make the dough, place dry ingredients in container, and buzz a few seconds. Add the butter and buzz until mixture is mealy. With the motor running, add the water and run until mixture holds together.)

Filling:
1¼ cup light corn syrup
½ cup sugar
1 tsp. vanilla
4 eggs
1½ cups (8 oz.) semi-sweet chocolate (Callebaut if possible), finely grated
2 cups pecan halves

Preheat oven to 325°F.

In a medium bowl whisk together the corn syrup, sugar, vanilla, and eggs. Stir in the grated chocolate. You can do this on a hand grater—it is a very messy job—or you can use a food processor. Roll out the dough to fit a 10" pie plate that is 2" high. Pour the filling into the prepared shell and place the pecan halves gently on top. Bake in preheated oven for 55–60 minutes, being careful not to burn the top. (You may need to cover the pie with foil toward the end of cooking.)

Topping:
1 cup whipping cream
¼ cup sugar (or less)
1 tsp. vanilla

Cool pie completely and serve with whipped cream: In a small bowl whip the cream until soft peaks form, then add the sugar and vanilla and continue beating a few seconds more. Serve.

Yield: 10–12 pieces (depends on who is the server!).

RHUBARB CUSTARD PIE

1 9" pie shell

Streusel:
3 tbsp. butter, softened
½ cup brown sugar
1½ cup unbleached white flour
½ cup ground almonds

Filling:
3 egg yolks
½ cup sour cream
1 tsp. vanilla
½ cup white sugar
4–5 cups rhubarb, cut into small cubes

Prepare your favourite pie shell and set aside.

Preheat oven to 350°F.

In a small bowl mix together with a fork the butter, brown sugar, flour, and almonds.

In a larger bowl, using a whisk, beat together the egg yolks, sour cream, vanilla, and white sugar. Fold in the rhubarb. Pour mixture into the prepared pie pan. Sprinkle the streusel mixture evenly over the top and bake in the preheated oven for 1 hour. Cool before serving.

Yield: 8 servings.

APPLE CRISP

Recently, I had a delicious apple crisp at a potluck dinner. Later I learned it was this recipe from my first cookbook! It was a nice surprise, and I decided to start making it again myself.

4 cups apples (5–6 apples), cored and sliced
⅓ cup butter, softened
½ cup unbleached white flour
¾ cup brown sugar
1 tsp. cinnamon
½ cup rolled oats
½ cup ground almonds (optional)
⅓ cup coconut (optional)
⅓ cup toasted wheat germ (optional)

Preheat oven to 350°F. Butter a deep baking dish. Put in the apples and about ¼ cup water. Cream the butter. Mix in the flour, brown sugar, cinnamon, and rolled oats. Add coconut, almonds, and/or wheat germ, if desired. Spread over the apples. Bake in preheated oven for about 35–40 minutes.

This is simple and delicious. Serve it hot out of the oven with whipped cream or ice cream.

Yield: 4–6 servings.

Variations:
Blueberry Crisp: Substitute about 2½ **cups blueberries** for the apples. Fresh or frozen are fine. Add ½ **cup water mixed with 1 tbsp. cornstarch**. Blueberry crisp is great with vanilla ice cream.
Peach Crisp: Substitute **peaches, fresh or frozen**, for the apples.

Apple-Cranberry Crisp: Substitute **1 cup cranberries** for 1 cup of the apples. This variation is very festive-looking.

Rhubarb Crisp: Instead of apples, use **4 cups rhubarb**, cut into 1" lengths, and add **½ cup sugar, ¼ cup orange juice,** and **1 tbsp. cornstarch**. Bake 5–10 minutes longer, covering, if necessary, with a bit of foil.

PEACH COBBLER

Cobblers are simple to make, and totally yummy!

6–8 fresh peaches
¼ cup sugar
1 tbsp. tapioca
1 cup unbleached white flour
1 tsp. baking soda
¼ tsp. salt
4 tbsp. butter, softened
⅓ cup sugar
1 egg
¼ cup buttermilk (or plain yogurt)
1 tsp. vanilla
½ tsp. almond extract

Peel and prepare peaches: Drop them into a pot filled with about 3" boiling water and let them cook about 1 minute. Remove with a slotted spoon to a colander and run them under cold water to cool them down. The skins will slip off easily. Then cut them in half, remove the pits and slice. Toss the slices with the sugar and tapioca and place in a fairly large baking dish. The baking dish must be at least 9" across and 2" high.

Preheat oven to 350°F.

In a medium bowl mix together the flour, baking soda, and

salt. In another bowl cream the butter and sugar until light and fluffy, using a whisk or hand mixer. Beat in the egg until well blended, then add the buttermilk (or yogurt), vanilla, and almond extracts. Beat until mixture is smooth. Stir in the flour mixture and, using a spoon, blend in well. Drop the batter by tablespoonfuls over the fruit, creating a cobbled effect. Bake in preheated oven for 35–40 minutes, or until a fork or toothpick comes out clean. Serve with whipped cream or ice cream.

Yield: 4–6 servings.

Variations:
Raspberry-Peach Cobbler: Add 2 cups fresh raspberries to the peaches.

Blackberry Cobbler: Use 6 cups fresh blackberries instead of the peaches.

SIMPLE HONEY CAKE

Another recipe from my first cookbook that I am including for use in the following trifle recipe. This is a good, plain cake that is moist (because of the honey) and delicious. It can be topped with your favourite frosting, or served with your favourite fruit and whipped cream.

½ cup butter
1 cup honey
4 egg yolks
2½ cups minus 3 tbsp. unbleached white flour
2 tbsp. cornstarch
2½ tsp. baking powder
½ tsp. salt
1 cup milk, at room temperature
1½ tsp. vanilla, or 1 tsp. vanilla and ½ tsp. almond extract
4 egg whites

Preheat oven to 350°F. Grease and flour a 9" x 13" baking pan. Set aside.

In a large mixing bowl, soften the butter and honey. They need to be very warm and soft—although not melted. Beat them together well, with a whisk or egg beater.

Add the egg yolks, one at a time, beating well after each addition.

In a separate bowl mix the flour, cornstarch, baking powder, and salt. Sift these ingredients into another bowl. Add the dry ingredients alternately with the milk to the butter mixture, blending gently but thoroughly after each addition. Add the vanilla (or vanilla and almond extract) and gently mix in.

Whip until stiff the 4 egg whites. Gently fold them into the cake batter. Spread batter evenly in prepared pan. Bake in preheated oven for 40–45 minutes, or until cake is lightly browned and a toothpick comes out clean. Let it cool.

Yield: 12 servings.

CHRISTMAS TRIFLE

This is a festive, delicious, beautiful dessert. The red of the berries makes it perfect to serve on Christmas—but don't limit it to that occasion. It is a perfect dessert for a crowd, which makes it good for any winter potluck. Make it the day before to allow the flavours to mellow. Any basic sheet cake is good, or use the *Simple Honey Cake* (above).

Custard:
1½ cups milk
1½ cups light cream
1 cup sugar
3 tbsp. cornstarch
¼ tsp. salt
6 egg yolks
3 tbsp. butter
2 tsp. vanilla

In a small saucepan heat milk and cream until just to the simmering point. Keep it warm.

In the top of a double boiler mix the sugar, cornstarch, and salt. Gradually stir in the milk mixture (a whisk works best). Cover and cook over boiling water for 10 minutes without stirring. Uncover and cook for another 10 minutes.

In a small bowl beat the egg yolks until they are light and creamy. Stir a bit of the hot cream mixture into the egg yolks and then slowly add these ingredients to the cooking mixture along with the butter. Cook an additional 3 minutes. The custard should be smooth, creamy, and quite thick. If it is not, cover again and cook, stirring every few minutes, until it is thick and creamy. (It will thicken more as it cools.)

When it is thickened, remove from heat, stir in the butter,

and cool, stirring occasionally to hasten cooling. When it is close to room temperature stir in vanilla, cover, and chill until needed.

Assembly:
1 sheet cake, your favourite recipe, or **Simple Honey Cake** (above)
1 recipe custard (above)
2 cups frozen strawberries, thawed
2 cups frozen raspberries, thawed
sherry, to taste
1 cup heavy cream, whipped (sweetened to taste and 1 tsp. vanilla added)

Use an attractive casserole that will hold all the layers. I use a 4 qt. oval baking dish 9½" x 12" x 3" deep. (You may use two smaller dishes or bowls—but they need flat bottoms.)

Cut the cake to fit the bottom of the dish. Split the cake in half and place the bottom layer in the dish. (I find it easier to first cut the cake in half and split one half at a time.) Sprinkle the bottom layer with sherry to taste. (If children are going to be eating the cake you will want to go easy on the sherry.) Cover the cake with the strawberries and all of the juice. Pour custard evenly over the strawberries. Place the top layer of cake (cut-side down) over the custard. Sprinkle this layer with sherry and cover with raspberries. At this point cover and chill until 1 hour before serving time.

One hour before serving time remove from fridge. Before serving, cover the trifle with the whipped cream and enjoy!

Yield: 12 or more servings.

CHOCOLATE-RASPBERRY TRIFLE

Your favourite chocolate pudding, or:
2 oz. unsweetened chocolate, coarsely chopped
⅔ cup sugar
pinch of salt
1¼ cups milk
3 tbsp. cornstarch
¼ cup milk
1 tsp. vanilla

In the top of a double boiler melt unsweetened chocolate. Add sugar and salt and mix well. Slowly pour in milk while stirring. Heat these ingredients to the boiling point, stirring often. In the meantime, dissolve the cornstarch in the ¼ cup milk.

Stir the cornstarch and milk mixture slowly into the hot milk mixture. Cook over boiling water for 10 minutes, stirring constantly. Cover and cook another 10–12 minutes. Remove from heat. Let cool, occasionally stirring gently. When cool, add vanilla.

To assemble:
rounds of yellow cake, pound cake, or sponge cake (or chocolate cake)
4–6 tbsp. sherry (or Amaretto)
2 cups frozen raspberries, thawed
1 cup heavy cream, whipped with 3 tbsp. sugar and 1 tsp. vanilla

In round casserole or bowl, place a layer of cake slices. Sprinkle with the sherry (or Amaretto). Distribute half the raspberries over the surface. Spread half the chocolate pudding over cake. Repeat layers.

Let the trifle set a few hours before serving. Serve with dollops of whipped cream on top.

Yield: 6–8 servings.

Variation:
Black Forest Trifle: Canned **Bing cherries** and their juice may be substituted for the raspberries.

FROZEN RASPBERRY MOUSSE WITH HOT FUDGE SAUCE

If you are lucky enough to have access to raspberries in the summer months, you probably know how well they freeze, mixed with a bit of sugar and put into plastic bags. Nothing could be simpler. And nothing could be better in midwinter than this delicious raspberry mousse, topped with homemade hot fudge sauce.

½ cup cold water
1 tbsp. unflavoured gelatin
2 cups frozen raspberries, thawed
½ cup white sugar, more or less to taste
2–3 tbsp. Amaretto (or ¼ tsp. almond extract plus 1 tsp. vanilla)
3 egg whites
1 cup whipping cream
1 tsp. vanilla
2 tbsp. sugar

Stir the gelatin into the cold water in a small bowl. Set aside to soften.

In a small saucepan, place the thawed raspberries with all their juice and the sugar. Cook a few minutes, stirring constantly over medium-high heat. Remove from heat. While raspberries are still hot, strain through a sieve into a large mixing bowl, forcing the pulp through the strainer with a spoon. Whisk the raspberry mixture with a whisk until it is smooth. Stir in the softened gelatin and set aside to cool for about one hour.

When the raspberry mixture is beginning to thicken stir in the Amaretto or almond and vanilla extract. Whip the egg whites until they are stiff and fold them into the raspberry mixture with a spatula. Whip the cream with the vanilla and 2 tbsp. white sugar until it holds a peak. Fold into the raspberry mixture.

Set the mixing bowl over cracked ice in your sink or in a larger bowl (or go out and set the bowl into a snowdrift, if possible). Keep folding, gently blending the mixture with the spatula until it begins to set. Pour into serving dish, cover with plastic wrap, and freeze until serving time. Serve with **Hot Fudge Sauce** (below).

Yield: 6–8 servings.

HOMEMADE HOT FUDGE SAUCE

Great on good vanilla ice cream—or try it over poached pears, topped with vanilla ice cream

1 tbsp. cocoa powder
¾ cup sugar
1 cup whipping cream
¼ cup corn syrup
4 oz. bittersweet or semi-sweet chocolate, chopped—the better quality the chocolate, the better the hot fudge sauce
1 tsp. vanilla
pinch salt

In a heavy medium saucepan whisk together the cocoa powder and sugar. Slowly add the whipping cream, then the corn syrup, and then stir in the chocolate with a large spoon. Over medium-low heat, then medium heat, slowly heat the mixture, stirring often, until chocolate is melted. Carefully bring sauce just to a boil and let it cook 3 minutes without stirring. Watch it carefully. Remove from heat and let it cool a bit; then stir in the vanilla and salt.

Optional Suggestion: 1 cup 2% milk and 2 tbsp. butter may be substituted for the whipping cream.

FROZEN MAPLE MOUSSE

This recipe is from my first cookbook and is a special treat during the maple sugar season. It is an exciting time of year, since it heralds the beginning of the spring. If you are lucky to be near a "sugar bush," it is worth the trip to drink some of the fresh sap, smell the syrup boiling off, and sample the results. In our "neck of the woods," it has become a tradition to partake of this goodness thanks to one friend who keeps a funky sugar shack working. We gather once or twice each season to share with each other the delights of "Maple Margaritas" and "RumDums," and have great times up there (needless to say)! This mousse evokes many fond memories, since it enhances the taste of real maple syrup with creamy whipped cream. A little of this goes a long way.

4 egg yolks
¾ cup pure maple syrup
1 tsp. vanilla
1 cup heavy whipping cream

In the top of a double boiler, combine the lightly beaten egg yolks with the pure maple syrup. Stir over (but not in) boiling water until the mixture thickens and coats the spoon. Remove from the heat and cool.

When cool, add the vanilla. Whip the cream until it holds soft peaks and gently fold into the maple mixture until it is well blended. Freeze until firm and serve.

LAST, BUT DEFINITELY NOT LEAST...

"CHOCOLATE-WAGNER-JACK DANIELS-YOUR-DIET-IS-ALL-DOWNHILL-FROM-HERE" CHEESECAKE

A wonderful creation indeed, compliments of Cheryl Wagner.

Crust:
1⅓ cup chocolate wafer crumbs
⅓ cup melted butter

Combine wafer crumbs and melted butter. Press evenly over bottom of 9" springform pan. Refrigerate while preparing the filling.

Filling:
2 large pkgs. (250 g/8 oz.) cream cheese, softened
1 cup granulated sugar
3 eggs
¼ cup Jack Daniels, or strong black coffee, or a combination of the two
8 oz. bittersweet chocolate, melted in the top of a double boiler
½ cup sour cream

Preheat oven to 350°F.

Beat cream cheese and sugar together until smooth. Beat in the eggs, one at a time. Beat in the Jack Daniels and/or coffee, the melted and cooled chocolate, and the sour cream, mixing until smooth.

Pour into prepared shell. Bake in preheated oven 40–50 minutes, or just until centre is barely set. Cool completely on wire rack, then refrigerate, preferably overnight. Just before serving remove from pan and glaze with the following:

Glaze:
4 oz. bittersweet chocolate
½ cup whipping cream
another ½ cup whipping cream

Heat ½ cup whipping cream slowly, bringing it almost to a simmer over low heat, stirring all the while. Add chocolate, stirring until melted and smooth. Spread over cake, letting glaze drizzle down sides.

Whip remaining ½ cup cream and pretend it's snow and dream of the next toboggan party or put a dollop on top of each slice of the "Chocolate-Wagner-Jack Daniels-Your-Diet-Is-All-Downhill-from-Here" Cheesecake!

Yield: 12 or more party servings.

NOTES